THE GOLDEN LAND

The Story of a Jewish Family's Journey from Ukraine to America in the Early 1900's

Ann Binder Anovitz
Keith Kramer

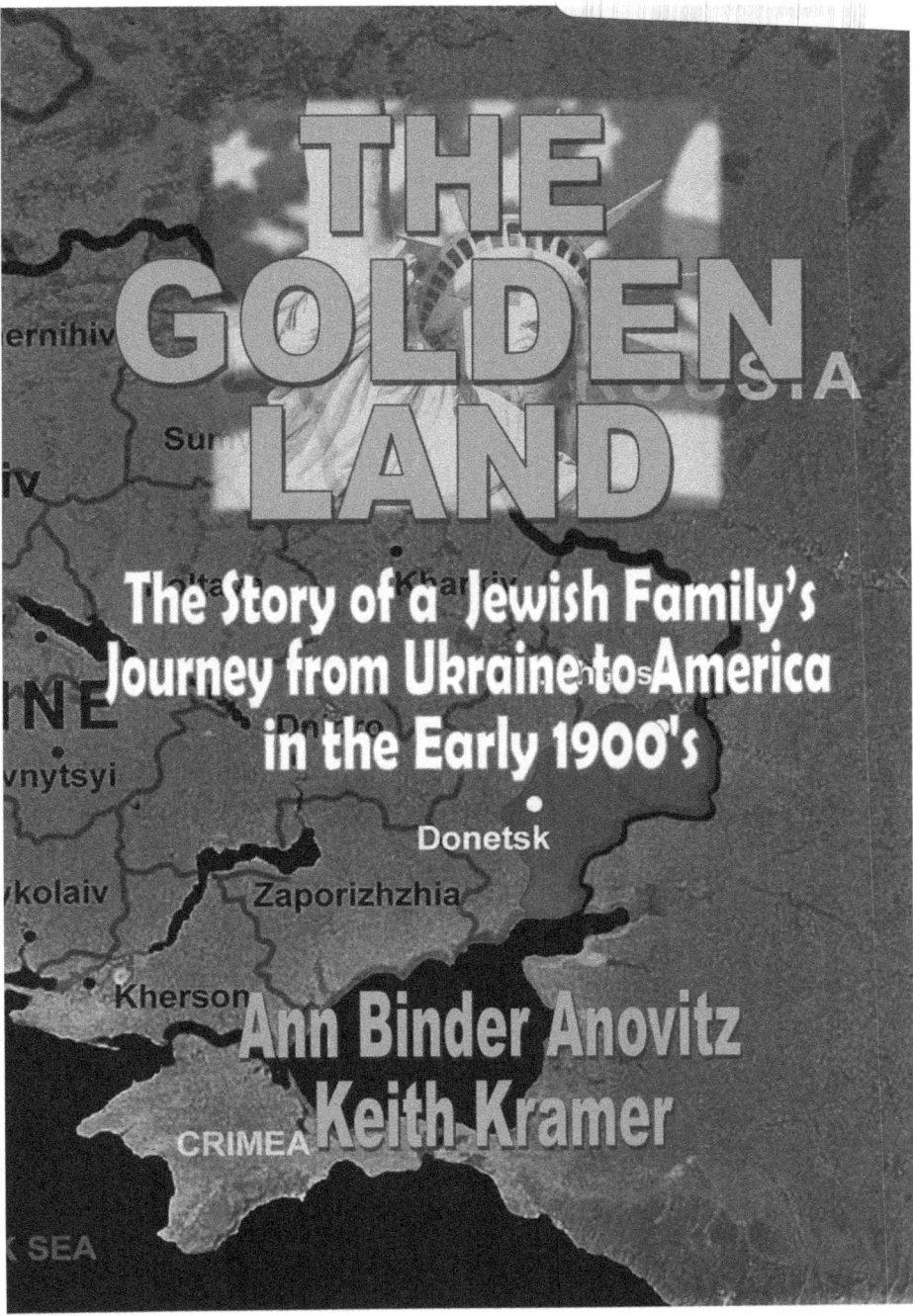

Published by RICHER Press
An Imprint of Richer Life, LLC
5710 Ogeechee Road, Suite 200-175
Savannah, Georgia 31405
www.richerlifellc.com

Cover Design: RICHER Media USA
Photographs: Courtesy of Binder-Anovitz Family

THE GOLDEN LAND
The Story of a Jewish Family's Journey
from Ukraine to America
in the Early 1900's

Ann Binder Anovitz and Keith Kramer

1. World History 2. Immigration 3. Memoirs
(pbk : alk. Paper)

Library of Congress Control Number: 2022938957

Paperback ISBN-13: 978-1-7335693-9-2
Kindle eBook ISBN-13: 979-8-9863598-0-9

PRINTED IN THE UNITED STATES OF AMERICA

DEDICATION

For The Children

CONTENTS

CONTENTS

INTRODUCTION

THE GOLDEN LAND is a memoir of my father's life, taken from the stories he told his grandchildren.

My father always was a storyteller. Before he passed, he sat with his family and we recorded some of his stories. Sometimes the stories were recounted in no particular order, and some of the tapes later proved difficult to hear. With the help of my son-in-law writer, what started as a simple task became a years-long research project and writing effort that resulted in this story of our family's journey to America.

This book is based on my father's memories. His stories, told from his viewpoint, might differ from stories recounted by others who survived similar journeys. But as a whole, these stories are America – the story of all the immigrants coming here from all the other countries of the world, looking for the freedom to live their own way and make something of themselves. This book could be the story of your family.

I have done my best, and I give you this book with all my love.

Ann Binder Anovitz

1935-2019

Questions. Always questions.
How bright he was, this
youngest grandchild.

PROLOGUE

Russia 1908

THE LITTLE HAND was warm in his. The three-year-old did not seem to feel the cold wind tousling his hair and burning his cheeks.

Questions. Always questions. How bright he was, this youngest grandchild. How to answer the questions. How to teach him of his great heritage, how to explain the hunger and death of war.

How to tell him of the visions.

Yankel Wolfe Aynbinder knew he shouldn't have a favorite grandchild. But this little one, Beryl, was such a little devil and so smart — only three and already starting school. And it wasn't likely there would be more grandchildren. The oldest, Morris, already was on his way to America, and Yankel Wolfe hoped his own son, Mordecai, would soon follow.

"We must get everyone out before the war," Yankel Wolfe muttered, clouds of steam puffing in front of his face as his breath met the frigid winter air. It was a thought that came to him many times each day, and it flashed through his mind now as he tightened his grip on Beryl's small hand and quickened his pace across the hardened snow.

The comforting rhythm of his heart, still beating strong after eighty-eight years, sent Yankel Wolfe's mind drifting into familiar thoughts as he led his youngest grandson through the darkness.

Ay, it will be good to leave this place. When Beryl was born, on Shavuos 1905, the pogroms were very bad. The Russians were revolting against the tsar again, like they did in the 1880s, but this time the rioting was everywhere. This tsar,

Nicholas II, is a weak man, so the people have won a little relief from the taxes and tricks of the government officials. Of course, the Jews got nothing. The government always tells the peasants, "It's the Jews' fault. The Jews collect your taxes. The Jews sell liquor to keep your men drunk." The Jews this, the Jews that… they blame the Jews for their own corruption.

And the peasants? Ach, what can you expect? They have nothing themselves and can't reach the government officials. But us they can reach, so they make us the scapegoat and have their pogroms. They kill our women and children. They burn our homes.

I remember the day so well, a Sunday with a cold, angry sky — January 22, 1905, less than five months before little Beryl was born. Bloody Sunday, they call it now.

Somehow, the workers of Saint Petersburg had decided they could talk to the tsar. They marched to the winter palace, so righteous, so brave — so foolish! What made them think the tsar would permit such a thing? Of course, he would not. He sent the government troops to meet them. Hundreds were killed, thousands wounded.

Then the peasants joined with the workers and students, and there were riots and strikes. For almost a year, the Cossacks were sent against the strikers, again and again, until finally, to gain a little peace, the tsar agreed to form an advisory board. The Duma, he called it. Of course, only aristocrats were chosen as deputies of the Duma, but at least this quieted the workers and students. And the peasants, they'd had their fill of murder for a while.

But the quiet is temporary — there is so much turmoil in the world. I feel it. I see it. In my dreams, the chariots of war fly across smoke-filled skies. The peasants are hungry these days, as always, but now there is talk that the intelligentsia, the university students, are marching with the peasants. Socialism, they say. Work for everyone… the aristocrats must change… the tsar must give his people more freedom.

Ah, but are they ready for such freedom? This they don't ask.

And with all this freedom, what will happen to the Jews? Will Jews be included, accepted as equals to the Russians? No. We will remain outcasts because we have no homeland. Since the destruction of the ancient temple, we are scattered to the winds. People without homes are unwanted and feared for their differences.

Just then the cheder, the school, appeared in the distance, windows bright with lamplight against the predawn horizon. The smell of damp coats and shoes mixed with burning wood and candles as Yankel Wolfe opened the door. He lingered for a few minutes in the warmth as the rebbe began teaching Beryl the Hebrew alphabet — with each letter his grandson correctly recited, Yankel Wolfe produced from his pocket a bite-sized morsel of honeycake and gently placed it in Beryl's delicate mouth. Soon the pocket contained only crumbs too small even for Beryl's tiny tastebuds, and Yankel Wolfe knew it was time for him to go.

"Teach him well, rebbe," Yankel Wolfe said. "Make his learning sweet, sweet as the honeycake. He will face hard times as he grows to become a man, and you and I won't be there to guide him." With that, he turned and headed for the door.

Trudging home under morning's first gray light, Yankel Wolfe found himself reflecting on how it came to be that bright little Beryl would spend his early years attending the tiny schoolhouse especially for Jews. Their little shtetl, or ghetto village, was in the town of Horchov, in the state of Volhynia, in the area of Russia known as the Ukraine. The

Russian government confined the Jews to this area of the country, which they called the Pale of Settlement — twenty-five provinces of the Russian empire near Poland that the government considered outside the main part of Russia.

"The Pale" had been established by Catherine II in 1791 and now, one-hundred-and-seventeen years later, remained mostly intact.

The government had moved all of Russia's Jews, sometimes entire towns, into this restricted area to keep them from competing with other Russians in trade or farming. To live outside the area, a Jew needed special permission from the authorities. Some skilled workers or professional men like doctors were given permission, but the rest of the Jews lived within the confines of the Pale.

Horchov was a town with some twenty-two-hundred people. The Jews lived in a ghetto surrounded by Christians. There were a few brick houses and a handful of apartment buildings, but most people lived in homes of wood and clay with straw roofs. The roofs lasted about ten years and the clay actually kept the houses warmer than brick.

Each house was heated by a big brick stove, and children slept on top of the stove to keep warm in the winter. Many houses were two stories. The first floor was a root cellar used for storage and farm animals. Extended families often lived together in the same house, adding a room for a newly married couple.

The Hebrew cheder was their school and the Jews made their own life with their synagogues, called shuls, and their writing, music, dancing and studying of the Torah. With what little they had, they helped each other.

Pulling his scarf up onto his face to soften the icy morning air, Yankel Wolfe's thoughts shifted from the past and present to the future.

Ach, things will never change for the better for Jews here in Russia. Ah, but America — the goldeneh medina, the golden land — they say things are different in America.

This I will not live to see. But this little Beryl… God willing, he will live to see it.

Yesterday in shul, again a dream – a vision. Men fighting in trenches, cold and hungry. Machines raining death from the sky. Skeleton horses falling in the white snow. Then deep-red blood clouds my vision, as men with frostbitten feet drag comrades with no legs.

We must get everyone out before the war.

***

America 1982

MY DEAR CHILDREN, this is your grandfather talking. I'm going to tell you the story of my life. Some people may think my life has been exciting — I don't know about that, but thank the Lord I made it until now.

To begin with, I was born in 1905, June the tenth, on Shavuos, the holiday commemorating the day on which Moses came down from Mount Sinai with the Ten Commandments for the Children of Israel.

My Zayde's name was Yankel Wolfe Aynbinder, and we lived with him in a little Russian shtetl town called Horchov. We had no liberty, no freedom to go anywhere we wanted, work where we wanted or go to the universities for an education. Nights, as far as radio and television, that was not even in existence in those days. We could not have an education, like you children are blessed to have an education here in America.

My Uncle Moishe, who was my father's youngest brother, and his wife, Brendel, lived with us in my Zayde's house. Tante Brendel was from a nearby town, and when it came time for her to marry, Brendel's mother went to a shadchen, a matchmaker, to find her a good husband. Once the parents had agreed to the marriage, a contract was drawn up describing Brendel's dowry and what was expected of Moishe and the in-laws.

After the wedding, it was customary for the couple to live with the bride's family for several years to get a start in life. But later, after my Bubbe died, Moishe and Brendel moved into my Zayde's house with their two boys and baby girl, and had another four children while they lived with us. My Tante Ruchel and Uncle Ule lived nearby with their sixteen children.

Now, my dear children, these days, as I sit in the sunshine in this wonderful country, it's usually the smell or feel of something that starts my memories rolling in. The smell of hot candle wax, the touch of a tallis cloth, and suddenly I'm a child again — and it's Russia, 1908 ...

PART I
PRELUDE TO WAR

CHAPTER 1

Russia 1908

When my mother picked me up from my warm spot on the brick stove, scrubbed my face, combed my hair and put clean clothes on me, I knew something special was about to happen. It was the day after Shabbes, and Zayde took me from Mama and wrapped me in a tallis, a prayer shawl. Suddenly, I remembered. He was taking me to cheder today. Even though I was only three, I would be a big boy now, like my brothers Jerry and Sam.

As we started our walk, Zayde held me close against his warm coat. His long, scratchy beard smelled of soap and chicken soup. Then he put me down and took my hand — it was cold and dark outside and the snow squeaked and crunched as we walked. I noticed a lot of people were already out, going to shul or work. They all walked fast with their hands deep in their pockets and their caps pulled down over their ears.

The rebbe welcomed us as we entered the warm cheder. The older boys were already reading in small groups as the rebbe began pointing to the letters of the alphabet, the aleph-bais. I repeated them carefully because I wanted Zayde to be proud of me. Zayde stayed for a while, and each time I said one of the letters correctly, he gave me a little

15

honeycake. The cake tasted good. The cake, the sing-song murmur of prayer, Zayde's praise — it all made me feel warm and good inside.

Soon Zayde left and I sat down on a bench near another boy and studied the letters. Then, before I knew it, Sam came to take me home. As we walked back through the deep snow, he told me Zayde would take me to cheder early each morning and he would come to get me each day at noon. It was all very exciting, and when I got home, I ran straight into the kitchen. "Mama, I learned my aleph-bais today. There are a lot of other children in the cheder and I made friends with one boy, and Sam says I'll be there until I'm a Bar Mitzva boy. I think I'm going to like it a lot!"

"Good, Beryl," my mother said with her gentle smile. "Come eat, and tell us all about your first day."

I was hungry and the cabbage soup tasted good. Everyone seemed to listen closely while I told them about the aleph-bais and the rebbe and the honeycake. Then Sam went off to work, Jerry went outside and my sister Rose began helping my aunt, Tante Brendel, with the baby. So, I decided to curl up on Zayde's comfortable lap, and he sang me a lullaby.

"Oyfn pripetchok brent a fayerl...

In the little stove a fire is burning, what a cozy place.

Rebbe teaching, children learning, to read the aleph-bais.

Look here, children, think hard, reading has its law.

Say it after me, and keep repeating it —

kometz, aleph, aw,

kometz, aleph, aw."

Soon I was busy with cheder and playing with my friends and helping my mother and Zayde. And like the child I was, I didn't think about time passing, the troubles around me or how quick I was growing up.

Shabbes, the Sabbath, began at sunset Friday and lasted until sunset Saturday. Shabbes was the most important day of the week and the most important Jewish holiday since it was given to us by God.

CHAPTER 2

Summer 1913

Every day except Shabbes I went to cheder, and in the afternoons I might fish at the river in back of our house, or help Zayde, or play with my friends or Jerry. And every Thursday morning I went with my mother to the market, so she could spend all day Friday preparing for the Sabbath.

Shabbes, the Sabbath, began at sunset Friday and lasted until sunset Saturday. Shabbes was the most important day of the week and the most important Jewish holiday since it was given to us by God.

Our market was held in an open square in the center of town, and each merchant sold his goods from a stall or right off his wagon. Farmers came from miles around on market day to sell their fresh produce and buy finished goods. The market was bright with flowers and fruit and dry goods. But what I remember most about the market is the noise and the smells.

On this particular day, Ma took a long time looking at the live chickens in their little cages, poking them and inspecting their feathers. The chicken area was always a madhouse, with wooden cages filled with screaming birds, feathers flying everywhere, women in their gay kerchiefs calling to one another. Finally, Ma called to the shochet, the butcher trained to perform the ritual slaughter.

"Mr. Miller, I've decided on this one."

"And a good choice it is, Mrs. Aynbinder. Nice and fat. It will make a good soup."

Mr. Miller continued to chat amiably as he took the hen from its cage, expertly slit its throat, let the blood drain over a large barrel and began to pluck its feathers. I knew it would not be kosher if he did not get all the blood out.

"Mrs. Aynbinder, good to see you today. And how is the family? Have you heard anything from Morris? How is he doing in America?"

"Well, you know, it took him so long just to get to the boat that we thought he might never get to America," Ma said. "But he finally made it. We got a letter from him last week. He is working for my oldest sister and her husband. They have their own grocery store, you know, and soon Morris will have a store of his own, then he'll be well-established."

"I'm tickled to hear such good news," Mr. Miller replied, dipping the bird in boiling water and opening it wide to clean it out. He inspected the inside of the bird to make sure there was no disease.

Mr. Miller played a very important role in our little town. He was a learned man who knew about various animal diseases and what to look for, inside and out, to ensure an animal was clean and healthy. My Zayde also knew these laws, and sometimes he would kill and kosher one of the chickens we raised in our back yard. But mostly we kept those chickens for eggs.

Mr. Miller wrapped the chicken in paper and handed it to my mother. "Here you are, Mrs. Aynbinder. Enjoy in good health."

"Thank you, Mr. Miller, and please say a Good Shabbes to your wife." With that, Ma turned and nudged me along toward the fish stand. There was always fresh fish at the market because the river ran right through our town, and my mother might buy some to add to the fish we caught ourselves.

The ground was always wet and muddy at the fish stand, and the smell hung heavy in the air. The fish were spread out on tables and piled in barrels. Mr. Ruben, the fish monger, wore a long leather apron like Mr. Miller and he had on big black rubber boots. I liked looking at the different fish, and if Mr. Ruben wasn't too busy, he would tell me what kind they were.

"Ah, Mrs. Aynbinder, what can I get you today? We have some nice pike, just came in. And how are you, Beryl?"

"Just fine, Mr. Ruben."

"Do you remember what kind of fish this is?" he asked, holding up a long, skinny one.

"Oh, yes, that's easy," I answered. "That's a herring."

"Good for you," he smiled, his hands already busy cleaning the pike Ma had chosen for us.

Mr. Ruben didn't ask about my oldest brother, who, as I had just learned, would soon have his own grocery store in America. But as Ma and Mr. Ruben chatted, I thought about Morris, and I found myself wondering what America was like. They said the streets were paved with gold. I would have to remember to ask Zayde about America.

But just then I saw a lady selling sweets across from the fish stand, and for the moment I forgot all about Morris and America. "Can we get some halava today, Ma?" I begged.

"No, Beryl, not today. We have only enough money left for a few fresh vegetables." I looked longingly at the sweets and reluctantly turned away. We continued our walk around, looking at all the good things on the tables and in the wagons. Some had food, some had clothes, there were hardgoods salesmen and tinkers who repaired things. I especially liked to dig through the wagon full of tools – harnesses, saws, hammers and various things that I couldn't even figure out a use for.

People wound around the carts and wagons and waved to each other. Everyone came out on market day, filling the town square. The Jewish men wore long aprons over black vests. Their tallises, or prayer shawls, and the accompanying stranded ends known as tzisis, extended below their jackets. Their long sidecurls hung down from beneath their black hats, entwining with their long beards. The women wore big, colored shawls wrapped around their shoulders, with bright kerchiefs that sometimes made it look like groups of flowers were wrapped around each stall.

"Hello, Mrs. Abraham," my mother said with a wave. "Good day to you. And how is the family?"

Mrs. Abraham said all was well and then smiled down at me. "Look at your Beryl!" she exclaimed. "He's growing so fast, kine-ahora."

"Kine-ahora," an expression all the ladies used, meant "may he avoid the evil eye," and it was almost always followed by a painful pinch on the cheek. Sure enough, Mrs. Abraham bent down and got her fingers around a little piece of my face before I could get away. How I hated that pinch!

Ma smiled. "Yes, eight years old already. Can you believe? Well, have a Good Shabbes, Mrs. Abraham... Ah, here we are, Beryl, look at the nice squash. Take these over to the scales while I get some onions and potatoes."

I piled all the packages of food into Zayde's little wagon and began pulling it along as we started our walk home.

"Channah!" my mother's friend Rivke Preipont called, running up with her arms full of packages. Her little girl toddled behind holding on to her skirt. "I've got a new job at the pottery factory. Would it be possible to leave my little Leah with you during the day?"

"Of course, Rivke," Ma answered without hesitation. "I'm sure Leah will be no trouble at all. Here, put your packages in our wagon."

Ma and Mrs. Preipont chatted all the way home about the pottery factory and other things. Mr. Preipont, I learned, had gone to America, and Mrs. Preipont needed to work at least until he could get established and send her some money.

Just as we got home, we saw Sam coming back from work, and he helped carry the packages into the house. Then, after bidding Mrs. Preipont a final "Good Shabbes," my mother turned her attention to us.

"Put everything in the root cellar, Sam, except the chicken," she instructed. "I want to clean it first and make some schmaltz."

"Oh, Ma, can I have some of the gribenes?" I cried.

"You'll have some for dinner, Beryl, but not before. It's got to cool, anyway. Meanwhile, you can help me. Here, cut up this onion and

23

put it in the pan on the stove while I singe the pinfeathers off the chicken."

I hated the smell of singeing pinfeathers, but it was the only way to finish cleaning the chicken. Meanwhile, I began cutting the onion. A minute or two later, my sister Rose came in and laughed at the tears streaming down my face.

"Beryl, it will help if you put the onion in water first," she said, still giggling.

"Now you tell me, when I'm almost finished."

By now, Ma had taken the fat out of the chicken and dropped it into the pan. Everything sizzled and smelled delicious as the fat became liquid except for the little pieces of onion and skin — this was the gribenes I loved.

"It's ready, Ma," I called out over the din of the kitchen. "Should I pour the schmaltz into the jar?"

"After it cools a little, Beryl," Ma replied. "Rose, set the table, please, and Beryl, you go find Jerry. It's almost time for dinner. Tomorrow will be a busy day, and I want to get an early start on the kitchen tonight."

On Fridays my mother, like all the other Jewish women in town, turned the house practically upside-down cleaning and getting ready for Shabbes.

Shabbes was the most important day of the week.

***

The next afternoon, I sat at the kitchen table reading my lessons and watching Ma work. Bent over the old tub, her body moved to the rhythm of the clothes rubbing on the washboard. The front of her old dress was wet from the sloshing water. Her sleeves were rolled up and sweat ran down her face. Strands of hair clung to her damp forehead.

Rose worked with the heavy iron she kept heated on the old stove. Her shirtwaist was wet with perspiration and she kept wiping her face with the back of her arm. From time to time, whenever Ma asked, she added steaming-hot water to the washtub.

I studied my lessons and listened as Ma and Rose talked and worked.

"Oy, it's so hot," Rose said. "I wish I could jump in the river and cool off like the boys."

"Just a few more shirts, Rose," Ma said. "Then we can go to the mikva and clean ourselves for Shabbes. Ah, the mikva, the bath house. We'll soak a little and talk a little with the other women. Such a mechaieh, such a blessing. I can almost feel the soothing water already."

"After Papa got home last night, he stayed up late talking to Zayde," Rose said. "What were they talking about, Ma?"

"The troubles in the world, Rose, and the chance of war. I hope the women at the mikva don't want to talk about war. I don't want to hear about it. I don't want to think about it."

"Ma, if a war comes and we're still here, what will happen to us?"

Ma turned to my sister and took a deep breath. "Well, the Russians will probably come and take Sam and Moishe to the army. God willing, they will survive, but in any case, they will be away a long time.

Beryl is only eight years old, kine-ahora, and Jerry, that rascal, I don't worry about him. He's too young for the army and can take care of himself — and Beryl sticks close to him. Always into something, those two. You Rose, you're a good girl — we'll have to find a good husband for you soon."

"Oh, Ma, not yet," Rose said, blushing.

"Well, thank God your brother Morris has made it to America. I don't know when your father will be able to leave, but God willing it will be soon. Ah, America — the goldeneh medina, the golden land. No more pogroms, plenty of food, work for everyone. A chance for you children to live."

"Ma," I asked, "if a war comes, will it be just like the pogroms?"

Ma stood up straight and stretched her back.

"War I don't know about. But from pogroms, I know. Before I was married, we certainly had our share of trouble in our little town of Restechka. I remember my mother pushing us under the bed when the Cossacks attacked. My sister Ida and I held our hands over our ears trying not to hear the screaming in the street. We were so afraid. And I will never forget the smell of burning – burning houses and burning people. So many were killed.

"And remember, Rose, how afraid we were the night Beryl was born? They said the worst was around Kyiv. But that night, right here, through the pain, with the midwife running back and forth worrying that her own house was on fire or her family was being beaten or killed.

"My screams mixed with the screams of terror outside in the street. It was very bad. Your Zayde did the right thing then, keeping us all in the cellar until it was quiet again and Beryl was born. Somehow, thank God, we remained safe."

Ma bent back to the washtub.

***

Ma and Rose worked quietly for a few more minutes before Rose started up the conversation again. "Ma, why were the men who came home with Zayde last Shabbes asking about passports?"

"Your Zayde was trying to help those men. He told them the story of how he came here from the town of Chitrisk with his brothers. Their name was Miller then, not Aynbinder, but they didn't have passports. And if you don't have a passport, you are not a registered subject. If you are caught without a passport, you are punished. They can send you to the coal mines in Siberia."

"Siberia might feel good right about now," Rose laughed.

"Maybe now, but not so much in the winter," Ma replied.

"You know, Rose, sometimes people try to bribe an official to get a passport, but that can be very dangerous. You never know what those paskudnyaks, those bastards, might do. So, it came about that if someone dies, someone else buys his passport from the family, and that was how your Zayde and his brothers got their passports. They left Chitrisk, where the pogroms were very bad at that time, and they came to Horchov."

I had heard this story about the night I was born, but the rest, about soldiers and war, was new to me. I put away my books and headed outside to cool off by the river and look for Jerry to talk about war. Maybe he would play soldiers with me. As I ran down the steps, it sounded as if Ma and Rose would soon be finished with the wash.

"Last shirt, Rose," Ma said. "Then I'll throw out the water, you'll put away the iron, and we can go to the mikva."

***

The river behind our house was a big part of our lives. We ate its fish, used its water for our garden and to wash our clothes and in the summer we bathed ourselves in it. It was part of a very big river called the Boog that ran from Austria to the Black Sea. The river was wide and deep, and when it froze over in the winter we used it for a road.

I found Jerry sitting under the drooping old willow tree with Sam, trying to keep cool and talking about little things as the lazy afternoon drifted by in tune with the sluggish water and droning bees. They were too hot and lazy to play, so I joined them under the tree. We talked a bit and then we heard Ma call.

"Sam, Jerry, Beryl, it's getting late. It will soon be Shabbes. Rose and I are going to the mikva. So, get in the river and wash yourselves."

Several neighbor families were already knee deep in the river washing themselves. The weather was hot and sticky, and the sun reflected off the river into our eyes in glaring splotches. The old willow drooped unmoving and uncaring in the still air, dragging its feathered switches in the tranquil water.

Sweat dripping, we could barely wait to cool ourselves. Jerry and I threw off our clothes and jumped in. Sam, who was older and acted more grown up, carefully folded his clothes and eased himself into the water. Cousin Tevia came strolling down from the house and joined us.

"Stop splashing, Beryl, you'll only make it muddy," Sam complained.

"Beryl's only having fun," Jerry answered, slapping the water and spraying it all over us. We laughed and scrunched down until the water came up to our chins.

I loved Sam and Jerry and Rose. Sam was quiet and comfortable and didn't talk much because he'd had a problem speaking right when he was little, but Jerry made up for him. Jerry and I always stuck together — as Ma used to say, we were always into something. And Rose had practically raised me when I was a baby because Ma had so much work to do. As for my brother Morris, I was very young when he left for America, so I didn't really know him.

After we finished our bath, we put on clean clothes and went to shul with Zayde, Papa, Uncle Moishe and Tevia. Everyone said the evening prayers, and after the rebbe's blessing, the men took a little drink of wine. Then we walked home for dinner.

When we got back to the house, Ma, Rose, Tante Brendel and Cousin Toby were waiting in their best dresses. In the dim lamplight, the house smelled good, all clean and scrubbed with a good dinner cooking in the oven. The table was set with a white cloth, the shining brass candlesticks waiting in the middle. Ma lit the Shabbes candles to welcome the Sabbath, and they flickered gently in the warm air.

Zayde had brought two sheltering men home from shul. Sheltering men were wandering rebbes or students or men too far from home to go back for Shabbes. They usually came to town on Friday afternoon and sat on a bench in the shul reserved for them, and some of the men preached on Shabbes.

People from the shul would take these men home for the weekend and give them food and shelter. Sometimes Zayde would bring home five or six men, but tonight there were only two. Zayde said he felt God would be angry with him if he did not bring home anyone who needed shelter. "Beryl," he would say to me, "angels watch over Shabbes dinner. Shabbes is the only holiday given to us directly by God. Shabbes is like a queen that we must especially honor."

On Shabbes day, all the men would get together and study and discuss the Torah. It was something they looked forward to all week. And after the sun went down and Shabbes was over, the men talked of what was happening elsewhere. In this way, news was passed from town to town and the Jews kept in touch with each other. And the next day, after Shabbes, everyone went back to work trying to earn a living.

When I was really little, Papa had contracted with a local farmer to run the man's farm. But then the Russian government banned contracts between Jews and gentiles. That made it much harder to make a living. Nowadays, Papa worked for farmers and ranchers as a foreman. He had to go much farther out of town and only came home every few months. While he was away, his father — my Zayde — took care of us.

But Papa was home tonight. He came in from washing, and Zayde said the blessing over the wine and the beautiful challa bread Ma had baked. "What are we having for dinner?" I asked Ma as we all sat down at the table.

"What God has provided," Ma answered, as she always did. Then she set a big, steaming bowl of chicken soup in front of me. After the soup, there was kasha and a little chicken, and the gribenes I loved to spread over it all.

Over dinner, I asked Zayde why he had told the gabbai of our shul to give each of the sheltering men a few pennies.

"These are wise, learned men, Beryl," my Zayde replied. "They go from town to town to teach us. We must take care of them, because according to our law we must do good deeds each day. The few pennies they earn from teaching they send home to their families. That's how they make a living."

"Oh, I understand," I said, even though I wasn't sure I did. "Should I make the tea now?"

It was my job to make tea in the big, shiny samovar. I poured in the water, enough for eighteen glasses. The coals I had lit before Shabbes were really hot by now, and I carefully set the brass teapot on top to brew. After a while, the tea was ready, and Jerry and I served it to the men.

Each man had a glass on a saucer. We poured the tea into their glasses and the men bit off a piece of sugar and held it in their teeth as they drank.

The tea was so hot that the men could not hold the glasses in their bare hands, so they wrapped the edge of their coats around the glasses while they drank. Sometimes people poured a little tea into their saucers to cool, but Zayde said the tea lost its taste that way. The two men Zayde had brought home tonight apparently agreed, because they drank the tea right from their glasses.

"Zayde, the tea is too hot to even hold. So how can you put it into your stomach?" I asked.

The men laughed. "Phew," Jerry teased, "you're really dumb, Beryl."

He acts like such a big shot sometimes, I thought. But then the men started talking and became very serious.

Everyone was afraid because of the priest. The priest had come to shul one day and told the men he would like to study Torah with them because he had been a Jew before converting to the Catholic religion.

Everyone was very upset. The community became angry when anyone converted, and the men didn't trust the priest. They thought he was a spy. The gabbai of our shul went to the police, who came and told the priest to go home and leave the Jews alone.

"Psst, Beryl," Jerry whispered, nudging me in the ribs. "I heard some of the older boys followed that old priest when he left the shul. They said they caught him and beat him up, and the priest complained to the police. But the boys said it was some Russians who beat him up because he is a convert. The Russians don't like converts either. They think converts are really still Jews."

"The police believe the priest," Zayde was saying. "They have levied a fine on the entire Jewish community. Tomorrow, after Shabbes, I will go to every shul and every family and collect money to pay the fine. It will be all right. But for now, no one must say anything about the priest or do anything to him. We must all stay together on this and tell everyone to keep away from him."

This was the first time I had heard about the Jewish priest being beaten. It seemed really weird. And I was worried because I knew some of the boys who were being accused were friends of Jerry's.

The men talked a few more minutes. Then Zayde announced, "Come, children, it's getting late, it's time to sleep. Jerry, show these good men to the loft, where they can rest for the night."

"I'll be there as soon as I check the seal on the oven," Ma called out to Pa. The Jewish laws didn't allow us to light the oven on Shabbes, so a stew called cholent was made up on Friday and sealed in the hot oven to bake until the next day.

Some of our neighbors would ask a Christian acquaintance to come and light a fire or the lamps for them on Shabbes, but Zayde didn't think that was right. Zayde was a dayan, a rabbinical judge — he was a very learned and respected man and was very strict about the Jewish laws. I was very proud of him because people from our town and for many miles around came to him when there was a quarrel, dispute or divorce. The Russian authorities usually let the Jewish people handle their own legal matters as long as it had nothing to do with the gentiles.

***

A few days after all the talk about the priest, I came home from cheder just as two men approached our house looking for Zayde. I found him studying Torah at the kitchen table. "Zayde, there are some men here to see you," I said.

33

"All right, Beryl, show them in. And be a good boy and make us some tea."

I was used to strangers coming to our house and asking for Zayde, and I pulled out a bench for them to sit on and brought some tea and sugar. Then I went outside again.

When the men left, I asked Zayde why they had come to see him.

"Beryl, I will tell you their problem, and then you tell me how you would solve it. One man sold the other a horse, and after only one month the horse died. The man who bought the horse accused the seller of giving him a sick horse and wanted his money back. The seller said the horse had been sound when he sold him. How would you judge such a problem?"

"Was the horse old?" I asked.

"No. The horse was only five years old."

"The man who bought the horse, did he know about horses or was he a city man?"

"The buyer was a farmer and knew about horses."

"Well," I said, "if the man knew about horses, I think he would have carefully looked over the horse before he bought him and would have known if he was sick. So, something must have happened after he took the horse home."

"Yes," Zayde said. "The seller said his son had seen the horse left outside at night in the bitter cold. The buyer said the seller coddled the horse by keeping him in the barn, and that's why the horse got sick when he was left outside."

"Zayde, I think the buyer knew the horse had been kept in a barn before. He is a man who does not take care of his animals and should not get his money back."

"Beryl, you will make a good dayan someday," Zayde replied, a satisfied smile creasing his wrinkled face. "That was exactly my judgment."

I was feeling pretty proud of myself, and I ran out to tell Jerry about what had just happened. But I immediately bumped into several of the older boys, who were huddled by our door talking in excited whispers.

"Beryl, where is the rebbe?" asked Mendel, the oldest of the group. "We have to talk to him."

Something was wrong. I led them upstairs to the kitchen.

Mendel approached Zayde, wringing his hands.

"What is the matter?" Zayde asked. "Come in, boys, come in."

"Rebbe," Mendel began nervously, "we just heard something terrible from Dr. Shanowitz. One of his gentile patients told him that the converted priest was found in the river, dead. His head was cut off. We're frightened, rebbe. We never touched him. We didn't kill him."

"None of us did anything wrong," one of the others chimed in.

No one said anything as Zayde looked down and stroked his beard. After a long time, he looked up again. "I will go to the officials and try to find out what happened. In the meantime, you boys, go on home. Continue just as before. Go to shul, study, do your work. We will see what happens."

The boys slowly and quietly filed out, each heading his own way home. Zayde sat for a while, then got up and also left the house. I don't think he even saw me standing there. All I could think of was a dead man with his head cut off.

When Zayde returned, I was sitting on the step waiting.

"Beryl, please go get Mendel and bring him to me," he said.

I ran all the way. "Mendel, Mendel," I called as I neared his house. He hurried out the door.

"Zayde wants you," I said between gasps. "He just got back from the police."

"How did he look?"

"I don't know. Sort of quiet."

We ran all the way back, and Mendel tapped softly on the door and went inside. "You, too, Beryl," Zayde said, as Mendel was about to leave me outside. "Come in and listen. God is with us today."

"The police know who killed the priest," Zayde began. "It was a gentile. Fortunately, there was an honest witness, so they are not coming after you boys. But they warned me that they can't control what the peasants will hear and what they might do. So, we are not out of this yet.

"Now you've seen what anger and fighting can cause. Not just trouble for you but the entire community. We must be very quiet and careful for a while, and I don't want any of you boys going into the gentile part of town. We don't want more riots with people killed and homes burned. Now go, and warn the others."

"Yes, rebbe," Mendel said, an expression of great relief washing over his face as he backed out of the room. "Yes, I will go tell the others." He turned and raced out the door to spread the word.

I thought about things for a while. If the police knew who had killed the priest, why would the peasants cause trouble for us? I still had not realized we could be the scapegoats for anything that went wrong in their lives.

Things quieted down for a while after that, and we went about our lives, studying at cheder, helping Ma around the house and playing with friends.

It was the last peaceful summer we would have for a long time.

On the way home we'd stop along
the riverbank to wash up. On this
particular day, it was obvious that
winter was on its way — we already
had to break through some ice at
the river's edge.

CHAPTER 3

1913-1914

Fall came. The leaves turned colors, the farmers brought in the grain and everyone laid in stores for the winter. My friend Louie Preipont and I began going down to the town pier to watch the boats arrive with their catch. If fishing had been good, the men might give us some fish if we helped fold the nets and wash down the boats.

On the way home we'd stop along the riverbank to wash up. On this particular day, it was obvious that winter was on its way — we already had to break through some ice at the river's edge.

By the time I came home, the sun was going down. But I was surprised to see so many lamps lit. I was certain Zayde was still at shul for evening prayers and I did not hear Ma and Tante Brendel talking.

I didn't hear anything. So, I walked into the house and there, lying on the kitchen table, was Uncle Moishe — in his funeral suit.

"Oh, my God!" I screamed.

Uncle Moishe jumped up — and I nearly fainted. "Beryl, why are you screaming?" he yelled.

"Uncle Moishe, I thought you were dead!" I yelled right back. "Why are you wearing your funeral suit?"

"Oh," he said, looking down and laughing, "I was just trying it on to see how it felt."

Ma and Tante Brendel came running from the bedroom. "What kind of mishegoss, what kind of nonsense is this?" Ma scolded. "Moishe, have you gone crazy? Look at you."

Tante Brendel shook her head. "Moishe, dear God! In the middle of everything, you have to go try on that suit. Don't tempt fate. And look how you scared poor Beryl. You are crazy. Go change out of that suit this instant and come to dinner."

Then we all burst out laughing and Tante pushed Moishe out of the kitchen into their bedroom where he changed his clothes.

***

I pretty much forgot about the incident with Moishe and his funeral suit until a couple weeks later. I was watching Ma and Rose make gefilte fish when Tante Brendel came running in.

"Gottenyu, dear God!" Tante cried. "Channah, they're taking Moishe."

"What do you mean they're taking Moishe? I just saw him at the store."

"The soldiers came in and brought papers from the government. His army unit has been called back. Last time he went into the army was bad enough. Who knows what will happen to him this time? Now, with all the children, how will we live?"

"Stop crying, Brendel," my mother urged. "Beryl, go make us some tea. Come, Brendel, sit. We'll talk, we'll make plans. You'll see, it will be all right."

They sat down at the kitchen table. Rose kept on making the gefilte fish with one eye on the two women. *Uncle Moishe in the army!* As I lit the samovar, I thought about all the talk I had heard about the army from the grownups.

No one wanted to go into the army. Everyone was afraid. The officers were strict and mean. If you didn't do what you were told, you were beaten. And even if they just didn't like you, you could be beaten — or even killed. The food was not kosher so the Jewish men had little to eat, and you had to stay in the army at least four years. After that, they kept you in the reserve until you were an old man of forty-five, and they could call you back any time there was trouble. My Uncle Moishe was being called back now.

"You know, Channah, Mr. Kravitz from the butcher shop was in the store when the soldiers came," Tante Brendel told Ma after calming down a bit. "He told Moishe about the terrible things some men do to themselves so they don't have to go into the army. Even the Christians do these things, he says."

"I know, Brendel. Sometimes they cut off a finger or shoot themselves in the foot. Oy, I don't think I could stand to see Moishe do something like that. It isn't right to do such a thing."

Ma was calm. "We all knew this was going to happen, Brendel."

"Yes, I know, but not so soon after the baby. I'm just not ready."

"I've done a little thinking," Ma told Tante. "You and Tevia will keep working in the store. Jerry and Beryl will help you after cheder, and I'll take care of the other children."

"But Channah, you have so much to do already."

41

"Don't worry," Ma said. "Rose will help me. I'm already watching Rivke's little girl since she had to go to work in the pottery factory. A few more under my feet won't make any difference."

"Oh, Channah, do you really think so?"

At last Ma seemed to be making some headway, and by the time Rose and I served the tea, Tante Brendel's thoughts had already turned to what she should pack for Moishe. "Plenty of oiled cloths for his feet and an extra set of winter underwear," Ma suggested.

As Rose began to chop the fish again, she added that she wanted Uncle Moishe to have the sweater she had just finished knitting. As I helped Rose knead the fish into balls and we listened to Ma and Tante talking, I thought some more about Uncle Moishe's predicament. I wondered if he should consider cutting off a finger. Hey, maybe he would let me help him!

Zayde says we are going to have a war. If we have a war, Uncle Moishe will have to kill people! Otherwise, the officers will beat him. What would it be like to kill someone? God said not to kill. Did he mean even in a war when someone was shooting at you?

What exactly is war?

I would have to remember to ask Zayde about it soon.

***

The following Monday, the whole family accompanied Uncle Moishe through town to the train station.

Jews hardly ever went into the gentile part of town. We had our own stores and tradesmen, and although everyone got together on market day, Ma was always telling us to keep away from the gentiles.

Anything could happen. Why just the other day, Mr. Ruben the fish monger told Ma that he'd seen the Cossacks beat an entire Jewish family who happened to be walking in the wrong part of town. So, it was kind of scary just being there.

But then I saw the station — and the trains! I had never been this close to the trains and I couldn't get over them. I was so busy looking around at everything I almost forgot Uncle Moishe was leaving.

Soldiers lined up in front of officers who shouted instructions over the hissing roar of the huge steam engines. There were lots of people saying goodbyes and lots of people crying. We didn't have much time — Uncle Moishe and the other soldiers were hurried into the cars and the train began pulling away. We couldn't see Uncle Moishe inside but we all waved anyway, hoping he could see us.

Then the train was gone and we began our walk home. Tevia was very sad. "Tevia, you can have my new fishhook if you want," I said, putting my arm around his shoulder.

Besides being a cousin, Tevia was probably my best friend except for my brother Jerry. And while Jerry was older, Tevia was my age. We'd hang around together and Ma would yell things like, "What have you two gonifs gotten into now?"

"Gonifs" means rascals, and the term sure fit us — we did get into all kinds of mischief together. And it didn't take us long to get over Tevia's father going off to the army.

First there was the incident with the rebbe and the egg.

The rebbe who taught us at cheder was an old, pious man with a long gray beard. He liked to arrive at cheder hours before the sun came up to study and pray. The first students arriving would often find him asleep, face down on his book, and he would stay that way until just before our lessons were to begin.

One morning as the rebbe snored away, Tevia looked over at me. "Hey, Beryl," he whispered, with a mischievous grin. "What do you suppose would happen if the rebbe couldn't pick up his head?"

"Now just how would that happen?" I asked with interest.

"Oh, I don't know. Maybe if his beard still had egg on it from breakfast, it would stick to the book or something."

"Not a bad idea, not bad at all," I whispered back with a wink. "I'll tell you what, meet me in back of the outhouse tomorrow morning, while it's still good and dark, and we'll see what we can do about this idea of yours."

It was pitch black when I slipped out of the house the next day. I tiptoed carefully into the chicken coop so as not to disturb the hens and get them all excited. I put my hand under the first one, took an egg, then ran out of the coop and around behind the outhouse to meet Tevia.

He was already there, hugging himself and jumping up and down to keep warm. "Where have you been?" he complained. "I'm freezing to death."

I pulled the egg from my pocket, just enough to show a little bit. Then I held onto it as we ran all the way to cheder, hoping to be the first to arrive.

Sure enough, we made it before the others, and the familiar snoring told us our timing was perfect. I took the egg from my pocket and looked at Tevia. He nodded and I tapped the egg gently on a table until it cracked. Then I opened it and spilled some out over the book and the rebbe's beard. He snorted and grumbled a bit but didn't wake up. I threw the rest of the egg out the door and we quickly sat down and studiously focused on our books as the other students drifted in.

A few minutes before our lesson, the rebbe woke up and attempted to lift his head. He tried for a second time, then a third! Pretty soon the entire room was in an uproar, but Tevia and I pretended to be as baffled as everyone else. A couple of the older students tried to help, but the rebbe waved them off and scurried out of the room holding his book and his beard. When he finally came back, he didn't say a word about it — he just started the lesson as if nothing had happened.

That afternoon Tevia and I howled with laughter as we reminded each other of the baffled look on the rebbe's face and the concern of the older students. We were pretty sure no one would figure out who was behind the incident of the rebbe and the egg. But that night at dinner, as Jerry told the family what had happened, Zayde looked pretty hard at Tevia and me.

We knew Zayde's stern look was a warning, so Tevia and I tried mightily to stay out of trouble for a while. But we were young, with too much energy to sit and study all day. So later that fall, we managed to get in trouble but good.

One Shabbes day, as we started out for shul, I had a great idea. "Tevia, it's a great day and the river is frozen over," I said excitedly. "Let's go skating."

"You know we're not supposed to skate on Shabbes."

"Oh, come on, we'll say we were sick or had to help at home. No one will miss us. The river is finally frozen and we haven't skated since last year."

It didn't take long to persuade Tevia, and before I knew it we were running down to the river. We found some wood to tie onto the bottoms of our shoes and off we went.

On this beautiful, crisp autumn morning, the river was frosty blue, glinting darkly where the trees hung over and sparkling where the sun reflected off the ice. Some older boys and girls were having a party, holding hands and skating to music from a concertina. The girls clapped in time to the music while some of the boys tried to do a kazatska on their skates. They tumbled about the ice laughing so hard they fell over one another.

Two girls went flying by with fur hats and muffs to keep their hands warm, laughing and waving at the dancers as they passed. We watched the dancers but stayed away — they were gentiles, and you could never tell what gentiles might do to a couple of Jews just to show off.

My hands were cold so I stuck them in my pockets. Then we took off, up and down the river, in and out between other skaters and horse-drawn sleighs, unable to resist the fun even though we knew we should be in shul. If we stayed in one place too long our skates stuck to the ice, so we kept moving. We'd skated in one direction for maybe half a mile or so when we suddenly spotted Zayde along the riverbank, still well off in the distance but undoubtedly looking for something — probably us.

As we turned around to head back, I remembered they had been cutting ice from certain parts of the river's edge to store in cellars for the following summer, and the ice was thin in those areas. I looked up just in time to see Tevia headed that way.

"Tevia, we'd better go around," I shouted.

Too late. "Beryl, help, it's cracking," Tevia hollered as one foot and then the other broke through.

I dashed over, only to fall right in with him. Fortunately, we weren't far from the riverbank, and the two of us struggled through the icy water and onto dry land. "It's a good thing we weren't farther out," I said with relief.

But Tevia was shivering. "I'm freezing," he stammered through chattering teeth. "What are we going to do?"

"Come on, we'll go up to the little shul where Zayde teaches the men. The stove is always warm there."

We got rid of the pieces of wood we'd been using as skates, ran all the way to the shul, crept inside and slid behind the old brick stove. It was nice and warm. We sat behind the stove giggling and peeking out from time to time. Then, after a while, when our clothes dried, we came out and sat down near Mr. Abraham, one of the students. They were all so busy studying that they didn't even know we were there. Then Zayde came through the doorway.

I could tell he was happy to see us. But as he got closer and peered down at us through his big bushy eyebrows and long white beard, his look changed to thunder.

"Nu? Where have you two been all day?"

47

"Why, Zayde," I replied without even blinking, "we've been sitting right here next to Mr. Abraham."

Zayde gave us quite a talking to and told us we would have to clean up the entire shul before next Shabbes. And of course, when we got home, he immediately told Ma what we had been up to.

"Channah, do you know what these two gonifs got into today?" Zayde asked. Before Ma could answer, Zayde told her all about the day's events, with plenty of emphasis on the part about me telling a lie.

Even before Zayde finished my mother was glaring at us, lips pinched together, hands on her hips. "No wonder I smelled fish when you came in," she said sternly when Zayde was done. "Now you get out of those clothes and wash them good. And from now on, listen to your Zayde and behave yourselves. But first, come over to the sink so I can wash those lies out of your mouths."

After we left the room, I heard Ma laughing with Zayde, so I knew they weren't really too angry. But I still muttered to Tevia something about maybe trying to not get into any more trouble for a while, and Tevia muttered back something about how he agreed with me. But then, as we took off our clothes and began filling the wash bowl, we caught each other's eye, and that was all it took — we laughed so hard tears rolled down our faces and we could hardly breathe.

"Skating was great, wasn't it?" Tevia sputtered, trying to catch his breath.

"Yes, we'll have to try doing the kazatska next time," I gasped, doubled over with laughter.

We hung our clothes on the line and came back into the kitchen, trying to swallow our giggles. Ma gave us a hard stare and we gulped hard trying to stop our laughter.

"If you think I'm done with you, think again," she scolded, shaking her finger at us. "Tevia, your mother will take care of you. As for you, Beryl, your Zayde brought home a lamb today that Dr. Shanowitz gave him for teaching David his Bar Mitzva. Tomorrow, you will come straight home from cheder and help him butcher it."

"Oh, Ma, do I have to?"

"Yes, you do."

With Uncle Moishe in the army and Papa away at work for months at a time, my brothers Jerry and Sam, my sister Rose, and Ma and Tante Brendel — with Tevia and Brendel's six other children — lived together in Zayde's house. Zayde was the only man and he was very old, but he did what he could. In between his studying and rabbinical duties, he guided us kids, helped us with our lessons and worked plenty around the house.

I really didn't mind helping Zayde, and lately I had even been thinking of talking to him about becoming a butcher when I got older. He always explained what he was doing and why, and I learned a lot from him that way. But I couldn't let Ma know her punishment wasn't really a punishment.

The next afternoon after cheder, Zayde and I went to the back of the house where he had already spent the morning sharpening his knife.

For the lamb to be kosher, Zayde would have to kill it by slashing its throat with a single stroke. Then we had to drain all of the blood. After it was killed and cut up, we picked up the pieces, washed them in a big pot of water and carried them down to the cellar. There I packed the meat with lots of salt in the barrel so it would keep through the winter.

As we cleaned ourselves up in the river, I asked Zayde if we would have enough food for the winter.

"Well, let me see," he said, rubbing his hands together. "We have two barrels of sauerkraut and another with the meat your Papa brought from the ranch. There's the lamb, some kasha groats and plenty of potatoes and onions. So far, so good, don't you think? Of course, we still need to buy flour and sugar or we'll have no bread."

We stored as much food as we could in the cellar because in the winter it was difficult to go out and buy anything. The snow would be five or six feet high — you could barely see the houses over the drifts. Although some people had sleds that were pulled by horses, the horses could only go out when the snow got very hard; otherwise, they would sink too far down and flounder and it would be almost impossible to get them out.

Most people did the same thing we were doing, smoking or pickling food and storing it in their cellars, or digging a big hole in the snow to keep the food cold. They also brought their animals into the cellar in the winter if they didn't have a barn.

But this year, it seemed to me we were storing more than in the past — I wasn't sure if we really were, or if I was just paying more attention now that I was older. But before I could ask Zayde about it, he reminded me there was something else I had to do.

"Beryl, I think Jerry should be back from Brendel's store by now, and you can go with him to the Young Pioneers meeting. Isn't that tonight?"

I'd almost forgotten about the Young Pioneers meeting. I ran inside.

"Beryl, I was just coming to get you," Jerry said. "Let's get to the meeting. Tevia and Sam are waiting outside."

"Isn't Rose coming?" I asked.

My sister usually came with us to these meetings, but she wasn't going tonight. "She's helping Tante Brendel with the kids," Jerry said.

There were usually fifteen to twenty boys and girls from as young as seven or eight to as old as eighteen or twenty at the Young Pioneers meetings, but Jerry thought there would be an especially large turnout tonight because we were going to hear about someone living in Palestine.

"Tonight, Zvi Eisenberg is going to tell us about his brother, who's with a pioneer group on a kibbutz," Jerry said as we made our way toward the old shul where the meetings were held. "Zvi gets letters telling him all about what it's like there."

The thought of working and living as a farmer in the Land of Israel excited me, and I could hardly wait to hear all about it. When we arrived at the meeting hall, I saw Jerry had been right — most of the chairs were already taken. "Let's have some quiet," an older boy named Dov shouted above the noise. "Zvi has some very interesting information for us tonight."

We quickly found some seats and Zvi started telling everyone about his brother's life in Palestine.

"My brother and the rest of his group of pioneers arrived in Palestine two years ago and settled on a piece of land along the Mediterranean coast that the Jewish Committee bought from the Turks," Zvi began. "The land isn't very good, mostly sand and rock. It's desert land, not fertile like we have here in the Ukraine. So, the first thing they had to do was dig a deep well and build a cistern to collect and store any rain that might fall during the rainy season.

"At first they lived in tents and found work wherever they could. They picked oranges, built roads and did any work they could find to make a living. Their wages were very low. They didn't have much to eat besides oranges and dates and a chicken once in a while that a farmer gave them. They used most of their money to buy tools, fertilizer and animals for their farm, and from time to time the Jewish Committee sent clothes and medicine.

"Medical supplies are very hard to get and they really suffer from the poor food and working in the hot sun ten hours a day. And then, when they're done with their day jobs, they still have work to do on their own settlement. Remember, most of them never farmed before because here we aren't allowed to own farms. So, they had to learn, and they made a lot of mistakes," Zvi explained with a shrug.

But then, with his chin jutting out, Zvi proudly declared, "But this year they've planted their first vegetable garden and bought some chickens, a few goats and some bees. They're going to sell some of the honey and use the rest at the kibbutz. Also, they've now built a kitchen, laundry and carpentry shop. While they still live in tents, they've just finished building a communal shower and a big dining room that they can also use for meetings and classes.

"My brother says it's very important for the kibbutz to be self-reliant. Next year they might even start a fishing business since they're next to the sea.

"In his last letter, though, he was very upset because two of his friends were killed by the Arabs while working in the garden. After that, the group decided to always be on watch, and everyone takes a turn on duty in the watchtower. They all had to learn to use the two rifles the kibbutz owns, even the women.

"The British mandate officials won't protect them and in fact they are not even supposed to have guns, so they have to hide them. If the Brits find out they'll confiscate the weapons. And, of course, they don't have much ammunition, so they have to be very careful about shooting at anything.

"Anyway, my brother asked me to tell everyone that they desperately need medicine and money to buy animals and seed for next year. And by the way, they are still recruiting — they are definitely looking for more people to join the group. Even though it is a very difficult life, my brother says he feels he's 'home'. He can really mean it when he says, 'Next year in Jerusalem' like we do at the end of a Seder. He's never felt so good about anything because the land belongs to them. So, if you have anything to give, please help, and ask at home and at each of your shuls."

With that, Zvi turned to step down from the podium — then he stopped and turned toward the audience again. "Oh, I almost forgot," he quickly added. "If anyone would like more information about joining the group, come and see me later."

Then he returned to his seat as everyone applauded. To think that these people were living and working on their own land in the ancient homeland of the Jews.

Someday I'll go there too, I thought.

But my thoughts were interrupted by Dov, who shouted, "Let's have some singing and dancing! How about a Hora?"

We all jumped up, pushed chairs aside and leaped into the dance circle with Zvi wildly playing his clarinet. Even our shy Sam loved to dance, and you should have seen Jerry. "Davi, melach yisrael, hai, hai, vicayom!" we sang. Arms linked together, we danced and sang and danced some more.

All that evening, on and off in the back of my mind, I kept thinking about Palestine. But we weren't going to Palestine. We were going to America.

CHAPTER 4

Winter/Spring 1914

I t had been very cold, snowy and gray that winter, so one bright morning in January, I was really anxious and restless. I felt like I was sitting on pins and needles. All through cheder I kept peeking out the window when the rebbe wasn't looking. It was cold and crisp outside. The snow sparkled brilliantly in the bright sunlight. What a perfect day for ice fishing!

I knew the older fishermen were already out and the river would be dotted with their fishing holes and makeshift protection.

"Come on, rebbe, come on," I muttered to myself. "Let's go, already."

Finally, it was time. I grabbed my books and ran out the door, down the streets and into the house. "Beryl, what's the matter?" Ma called. "Where are you off to in such a hurry?"

"Ma, it's a perfect day for fishing. I'll bring you home a nice pike for dinner."

"All right," my mother responded. "Your Papa came home today, and a fish will be a good change for him from what he eats at the ranch. But be careful."

"Oh, Ma, you're always saying that. I'll be careful, I promise."

I grabbed my line, my hooks and a knish off the table before Ma could catch me — and scurried out the back door. I pulled out Zayde's little wagon, threw in some straw and a couple of old boards, and dragged it all down to the river.

I was right. There were already lots of other fishermen there. Some sat huddled in blankets, others had put up boards to protect themselves from the wind. I wasn't cold now but knew I would be after sitting awhile, so I started pushing snow around to make a wind break, then put the boards down with the straw on top to make a good place to sit. By the time I was done chopping a hole, I was sweating in the warm sun. I baited my hook with a little bit of knish and was ready to fish.

We always caught fish in the river, summer and winter, and I loved to fish. I settled down quietly and waited, sheltered from the wind and cold. It was quiet between my snowy walls, with the sunlight pushing through the top and the jumping shadows keeping time with my heart. The sky above looked blue and deep.

I waited. I thought about having a taste of knish, then decided against it since I might need it for bait. So, I closed my eyes and thought about how good the fish would taste. Would Ma make a fish soup, or would she bake it with some potatoes? I drifted off toward sleep.

Then, a bite! Suddenly I was wide awake.

Oy, he's big. Don't hurry, keep him on the hook, let him run a bit. All right, gently now, start pulling him in, gently, gently — there, I can see him. Oh, he's big. Oy, I can't get him out! He's too big!

I leaned back against the snowy wall, braced my feet and pulled. But the fish couldn't come through the hole.

Keep calm, I told myself. "Fish, if you think I'm going to let you go, you're mistaken. I want baked fish tonight."

I held the string with one hand, reached into the hole with my other, took hold of the fish's gills and tried again to pull him up. I still couldn't get him through the ice.

Oh, no. I'm stuck!

The fish and my hand were beginning to freeze together in the small hole in the ice. The fish looked me in the eye and I looked back at him. "I've got you, and I'm not going to let you go," I told him.

But no matter how I tried, the fish would not fit through the hole.

I started to feel a little panicked. "Gevalt! Somebody, help!" I finally hollered.

"Who's that hollering in there?" It was Jerry. And I knew I was saved.

"Jerry, I've caught a fish but I can't get him out."

Jerry poked his head over the wall. "I think the fish caught you," he laughed. "Just a minute, Yankel and I will help."

Jerry and his friend Yankel climbed in, chopped away some of the ice and pulled me out — with the fish practically frozen to my hand.

"A thirty-pound pike, at least," Jerry roared, "with a hundred-pound boy attached!"

We carried the fish up to the house, Jerry and Yankel laughing and teasing the whole way. That night, over dinner, Jerry had the whole family howling as he told the story of how the big fish had caught the little kid. Zayde laughed so hard tears ran down his cheeks.

By the time dinner was over, I was really tired. It had been a long day, so I turned in early and fell right to sleep. But later, in what seemed like the middle of the night, I found myself wide awake. It was very dark and I was nice and warm, snuggled atop the big, old oven with the other kids. So why did I wake up?

I realized Ma and Papa were talking in the kitchen below the oven.

Why were they up so late?

"Channah, you know a war is coming," my father was saying.

"Yes, Mordecai, I know. Your father sees things — he knows. He's been storing food in the cellar, pickling cabbage and salting meat."

"Channah, while I'm home for a few days we have to make plans. Morris is settled in America now, in Washington where the government is."

"Yes, I know," Ma said. "Thank God, he doesn't have to sleep on the counter in my sister's store anymore. Now he has a room of his own behind the little store he bought. We have enough for you to go now too, but will there be enough time to get us all there before the war? What will happen to us if you go but we are caught here?"

Pa sighed deeply. "I don't know," he finally said. "But I must go or we'll never get the family out. You know that. My father will take care of you and the children."

"But for how much longer, Mordecai? He's a very old man."

"Channah, I must go."

"I know. And I have been getting things ready for you. The trunk is already packed with warm clothes, a blanket and everything you will need. I have been putting aside little by little, and Rose just finished a new shirt for you yesterday."

"I'll go see Mendel the tailor tomorrow to get measured for a new coat. The jacket I wear at the ranch won't do."

"When will you go?"

"In the spring."

Papa was leaving, going to America like my oldest brother Morris. I wriggled in my warm cocoon atop the oven, hugging myself with excitement. If Papa was going, how much longer before we would go? *Wait till I tell Jerry and Tevia,* I thought. Then, as I thought some more, I decided not to say anything. This would be my own little secret. It took a long time for me to fall back to sleep and after that night, America was almost always on my mind. I forgot about Palestine.

***

Later that winter, our town had a visitor. A man from the Jewish Committee came all the way from England to bring news and talk to the Jewish community. Everyone came together at a meeting in the big red shul to hear him. He was a fine-looking, tall man with black hair and a black beard. He wore a beautiful dark suit with a tie and a white shirt.

The chief rebbe shook hands with the man and introduced him to the congregation.

"My friends," he began, "when Germany invaded French Morocco back in 1911, Russia, France and England got together and made a pact to help each other if Germany ever tried to expand again.

Now Germany wants colonies. Some countries think the only way they can grow and be more powerful is to have colonies all over the world so they can have more raw materials and people to buy their products. Germany thinks it has the right to expand, that it is surrounded by enemies, and in a sense that is true, because no country wants Germany to take over its land.

"Meanwhile, France wants revenge against Germany for attacking Morocco, and the Balkan countries want independence from Germany's ally, Austria-Hungary. Russia signed a pact to help the Serbs in the Balkans, and Germany seems to be pushing Austria toward a war with the Serbs.

"The German kaiser thinks England won't go to war to help the Serbs and Russia. But he is mistaken. England will honor her pledge."

The man paused, looked over the hushed audience, then continued.

"Right now, the world is like a tinderbox that could catch fire at any time. And as always, the ordinary people and the Jews are caught in the middle. Please, you must make plans to emigrate as soon as possible. I have literature here about Palestine for you to look at, and also America. I will be here for another day if you wish to speak with me. The Jewish Committee can help you arrange transportation and there are landsmen to help you when you arrive in your new country.

"Russia has nothing for you. Leave while you can."

At first there was no sound at all when he finished speaking. Then everyone started talking all at once, asking questions and making plans.

I tried to listen, but it was very warm in the shul with all those people and I was tired. Before I knew it, Jerry was nudging me to wake up because it was time to leave.

As we walked home, I heard Papa, Ma and Zayde making more plans for our family. It was February 1914 — Papa would leave for America in April and we would stay home with Zayde until Papa could send boat tickets and money for traveling. I didn't like that at all, especially after listening to the tall, black-haired man. *Why couldn't we just all leave now? If a war started before we could leave, what would happen to us?*

Ever since Uncle Moishe had gone into the army, it had been on my mind to find out more about war. My friends and I talked about it but they didn't know any more than I did, and the older boys pretended they knew everything but couldn't be bothered to tell us little kids. Maybe if I asked Zayde, he would tell me exactly what people meant when they talked about war.

That spring, just before Papa was to leave, I was walking home from Tante Brendel's store when I heard something strange. I looked up and saw something high above in the sky. It wasn't a bird. It was too big and it made a lot of noise. I ran the rest of the way home and found Zayde standing outside, looking up at the strange thing in the sky with that dreamy look he sometimes had. The sky was blue and the sun was shining, but for some reason the pit of my stomach felt cold and hollow.

"Zayde, what are those things flying around up there?"

"Machines, Beryl. Air machines. Can you see them? Like small crosses they fly across the sky. One after the other, raining death on the earth. Armageddon. The time is near."

61

"What are you saying, Zayde? I don't understand. What is Armageddon? And what exactly is war?"

Zayde looked down at me, shook his head, and ran his hand across his eyes as if waking from a dream. "Ach, Beryl, I know you don't understand," he said at last. "Come inside. I will show you in the book."

Zayde was shaking his head and muttering as we entered the house. "Ach, Beryl, there is nothing new under the sun," I heard him say.

Zayde had lots of books, and some he kept in a locked cabinet. Undoing the lock, he carefully removed one large book and then put on his tallis before opening it. I knew the tallis meant he considered this book holy.

After reading a bit to himself, he called me over and pointed to three paragraphs. "Beryl, can you read what the book says?"

Before I could answer, Zayde continued. "It says war will come and then it will end, but there will be another war and many, many people will die.

"This second war will not really end. When you think it has ended, it will actually have just spread out in small pieces all around the world. Eventually, Beryl, mankind will destroy itself in a third world war. This is Armageddon — the destruction of the world."

"But Zayde, why? Why does this have to be?"

Zayde looked at me. He looked sadder and older than I'd ever seen him look.

"Beryl, it is because men live like animals, cheating, raping and killing, and not acting as we were commanded to do by God.

"God told us that everything in the world is part of Him and is therefore holy. We must treat every living thing as if it were holy. But men do not understand. Too many are greedy. Too many want power."

He closed the book and put it back in the cabinet. Then he got up and walked very slowly toward his bedroom.

I stood there thinking, the hollow feeling still in my stomach. I wasn't sure if I had found out about war, but I felt I had learned something very important.

I found out about war when it came.

During fall 1914, the Austrians and Russians traded victories and losses in Galicia in the south of Poland, with Austria finally retreating to regroup.

PART II
OCCUPATION AND EXILE

A FTER RUSSIA WAS defeated in the 1904-1905 Russo-Japanese War, it found an outlet for its expansionist desires through Pan-Slavism. Russia deemed itself protector of all Slavic peoples, including the nations of the Balkans such as Bulgaria, Serbia and Bosnia — a policy that ran head-on against that of the old Austro-Hungarian Empire.

Industrial growth in Germany also spurred expansionist ideas. Seeing France and Great Britain expand through colonization led German leaders to conclude that their country could benefit from additional territory.

Germany encouraged Austria to pressure the Balkan governments for better trade terms and improved treatment of Germans living in those nations. This pressure increased local animosity in the Balkans between the Serbs, Croats, Austrians and Germans, resulting in small but savage wars that kept the threat of larger-scale conflict looming over the entire region.

Russia had a pact to protect the Serbs, and Germany had a pact to protect Austria. These protection agreements between the larger countries and their smaller satellites put the world on a course that inevitably led to World War I.

Germany, however, wasn't particularly concerned about other world powers intervening. It felt certain Great Britain would stay out of any conflict since it was busy on other fronts, and the United States was deemed too distant to warrant serious consideration.

The shooting of Austria's Archduke Ferdinand while on a state visit to Sarajevo was the spark that ignited the world. Austria declared war on Serbia. Russia's pact to aid the Serbs led Russia to declare war on Austria and immediately call up its army reserves.

During fall 1914, the Austrians and Russians traded victories and losses in Galicia in the south of Poland, with Austria finally retreating to regroup.

When German leaders saw Austria retreating, they sent troops to southwest Poland to bolster the Austrian army. At the same time, Russia was taking a beating from the Germans in East Prussia to the north.

Russia was also plagued by supply and communications problems. It urgently pushed its industrial base to produce supplies that never reached the military while suffering acute food shortages due to decreased manpower on the farms.

By late-September 1914 the Germans were advancing toward Warsaw, eventually meeting the Russian army in a battle near Lodz, Poland.

Russia was ill-prepared, having no trained replacements and no supplies. Russia lost more than one million men, and by Christmas 1914 most of Poland was in German hands.

In January 1915, the kaiser agreed to a joint campaign in the Carpathian Mountains in southern Galicia between his German army, headed by Field Marshal von Hindenburg, and the Austrian army, headed by Field Marshal Conrad.

Meanwhile, the Russian army regrouped and on January 31, 1915, attacked in the north, in East Prussia. But the Russians were caught in a trap near Warsaw when the Germans turned on them from the south. As a ferocious blizzard blanketed the region, the Germans advanced over frozen lakes and badly beat the unsuspecting Russian army. The Russians retreated and began to establish a new line of defense inside Mother Russia, just east of the Boog River.

I could hear Jerry getting washed and dressed, but I didn't want to open my eyes.

CHAPTER 5

Spring 1914

I t was morning already and I'd been dreading today. Papa was leaving.

I could hear Jerry getting washed and dressed, but I didn't want to open my eyes.

For the past few weeks, I'd tried to stay busy so I wouldn't have to think about Papa. But then last night, with all the friends and relatives stopping in to say goodbye and wish Papa luck, it suddenly became real.

I had watched the faces and listened to the voices. With a shaking, spotted, old hand, Mr. Rabinowitz held a piece of paper out to my father. "Mordecai, here, I've written down my son Judah's address in New York City. Please stop by and see him and tell him we are well." He paused and looked down at the floor.

"Tell him maybe a letter once in a while, a picture of the children," Mrs. R. pleaded. Her voice trailed off sadly, and Mr. Rabinowitz just stood there holding her arm, his worn old eyes looking up into my father's.

"Of course, of course," Papa replied. "My Morris will help me find him. I'm sure Judah is fine, probably working hard so he can save enough money to send you the boat tickets."

"Thank you, Mordecai, and may God go with you," Mr. Rabinowitz said. The two old people turned away, their slow, shuffling steps taking them out the door. My father and mother watched them go, then looked at each other for a long time without saying anything.

I knew Ma was worried about what would happen to us after my father left. Maybe we wouldn't hear from him either and we would be left here to die.

I turned to watch my little cousins, laughing and playing around the oven and the table. The smallest ones were crawling between the table legs and around everybody's feet. Aunts and uncles talked, Tante Brendel fed her baby, Uncle Ule drank tea with Zayde by the fire, Jerry and Sam smoked cigarettes and talked with Cousin Joe.

People came and went. Mr. Schwartz, the tailor, came in with Papa's new coat and everyone gathered around to admire it. "Ooh, Mr. Schwartz, what a beautiful coat," Tante Ruchel said, running her hand up and down the fine material. "You have goldeneh hands." Turning to my father, she added, "Mordecai, this certainly should keep you nice and warm in America."

Mr. Miller the butcher arrived with his wife. The rebbe from our shul came and so did Dr. Shanowitz. It was very late by the time everyone left and we went to sleep.

***

"Beryl, time to get up." Jerry was calling me.

Maybe if I pretend I'm still asleep they'll go without me.

Next thing I knew, Jerry was poking and pushing at me. "Come on Beryl, I know you're awake. Ma's got some hot kasha for breakfast before we take Papa to the train." He yanked off the covers.

I rubbed my eyes and pulled on my pants, my sleepy head filled with angry questions. *Why does Papa have to go and leave us here? Why can't he wait until we have enough money for all of us to go?*

I poured water into the wash basin, splashed some on my face, then headed into the kitchen for breakfast. Papa was away working at the ranch most of the time and everyone usually came and went from the kitchen at different times of the morning, but today everyone was there at once. The room was crowded and smoky, and everyone seemed excited. *Why can't I be excited too?* I stared into my bowl.

"Come on, Beryl, hurry up and eat," Rose said, nudging me with her elbow as she started to clear the dishes. I gulped down the hot kasha while Ma and cousin Toby helped Rose. Everyone got their coats and hats.

It was spring, but it was still plenty cold. The snow was melting slowly and the streets were one big ooze of thick mud. We piled into a wagon Zayde had borrowed, and the horse began plodding down the street. I watched people in heavy coats and fur hats playing leapfrog between the piles of snow and the deep, muddy ruts, trying to avoid the worst of the muck.

When we got to the station, Jerry and Sam carried Papa's trunk and I needed both hands to carry his heavy satchel. The station was very busy with people coming and going. Some were laughing, some were crying.

Soldiers with rifles slung over their shoulders or cradled in their arms milled about, while over to one side two officers talked and lazily smoked cigarettes.

Papa looked very nice standing there on the platform in his new coat, his beard combed and his new black hat firmly on his head. We all hugged him and then Ma handed Pa a package of food for the trip and he got on the train. I tried to see him through the windows, but there were too many people and the windows were too high up for me.

"All aboard," the conductor called out, and the train began to move.

And then, before I knew it, we were in the wagon again heading home. It had turned colder and a little snow fell from a gray sky. We were all very quiet, even Jerry — the only voice was Zayde's, urging on the horse. I had that funny, hollow feeling in my stomach again, the same feeling I'd had when I asked Zayde about the machines flying around in the sky.

Everyone was still pretty quiet that evening, and after a little supper I went straight to bed. But as the house fell silent, I could hear Zayde and Ma talking quietly at the table over their tea.

"Nu, Channah, the first step to America," Zayde said. "I pray you can all go before the war starts."

"What do you see, Pa? Is the war coming soon?"

"Yes, very soon."

"But now," Zayde continued, "Pesach is coming and we have work to do. Tomorrow I will prepare the barrel for the pickled beets."

"Oy, Passover already," Ma said. "And we haven't done a thing yet. Tomorrow we start a good housecleaning. Everything to do. All the Pesach pots and dishes have to be gotten out and washed, and everything taken out of the house so we can clean ..."

"Don't worry," Zayde interrupted. "Everyone will help. You will see. We will have a good Pesach."

So, there we were. Papa had just left and we were already busy with Passover. The next day, Jerry and I helped Zayde with the beet barrel. We filled it halfway with clean water and then brought in big stones, washed them and heated them in the oven. When they were hot, Jerry and I removed them with big wooden paddles and dropped them in the barrel to get the water to boil. After the barrel was clean, we poured in a little fresh water and vinegar. Then Rose and Toby added the cut-up beets and Zayde covered the barrel and set it aside to sour.

Meanwhile, Ma and Tante Brendel were tearing apart the house, starting with the bedding. The straw bed mats and feather pillows were dragged outside, beaten and left to air. Tante and Rose took all the linens down to the river and washed everything. Tevia, Jerry and I carried the straw floor mats outside and hung them over ropes we strung between the trees. Then we beat them good with brooms and big sticks.

"Gotcha!" Jerry yelled, swatting me with his broom. Then, laughing, he dashed behind a mat. I ducked under after him and chased him around the yard swinging my broom at him.

"Gotcha!" I said, bringing my broom down on his head. By this time, the chickens were running around making a ruckus.

Not to be outdone, Tevia gave a poke with his stick from the other side. Jerry and I both ran back around and attacked him.

Around we went, beating mats and heads and bottoms, laughing so hard we finally fell to the ground gasping for breath. "Enough already, you gonifs," Ma yelled. "The mats are clean enough."

Meanwhile, Rose, who'd been washing the linens with Tante, came up with a bucket of dirty water in her hand. She pretended she was going to throw the water all over us as she walked down to the river, but we ducked out of the way and Jerry chased after her with his broom. She ran, laughing and screaming, as Tante hollered at him to stop.

Then we all tumbled into the kitchen, hot and sweaty and laughing, looking for a cool drink of water from the big jug. The delicious smell in the kitchen reminded us that in between all the housecleaning, the women had also been busy cooking cholent, dumplings for the soup, tsimmes — all the special things for the holiday week!

"Here, Beryl, if you're through with the running around, cut up some of this yarn for the candle wicks," Toby instructed. "Jerry and Tevia, come here and hold the wicks up for me while I pour the wax into the molds."

"Where's Ma and Tante?" Jerry asked.

"They went to the baker's to pick up the Passover Matzo, but they'll be back soon, so don't run off," Toby warned. "There's plenty more to do yet."

"What else?" Tevia groaned as we flopped down onto the dirt floor and drank our cool water. And Toby began ticking off a whole list of things that included cleaning the cellar and dragging the bedding back inside. Sam got home and offered to help, so we trudged back outside, rolled up the mattresses, carried them back into the house and unrolled them on the newly swept floor.

By the time we finished that, more good smells were coming from the kitchen. Ma was baking honeycakes and Tante was preparing a big goose for the oven. "Here, Tante," Rose offered. "I'll tie the legs while you hold."

Ma told me to take Tevia and finish cleaning the cellar, but I begged to stay and watch her make the honeycakes. "All right, I know you, you gonif, you just want to lick the bowl," Ma laughed. "One lick, then it's the cellar. Your Zayde will be home soon and ready with the goose feather."

Just before supper, Zayde returned from shul. "Is there any chumetz left in this home?" he called out from the door, meaning any tiny crumbs of leavened bread that might have somehow escaped our exhaustive Passover cleaning.

"No, Zayde," we all called back.

"All right, good. Where is my feather?"

Ma brought Zayde a big goose feather, and Zayde began walking from room to room with everyone following, even the littlest cousin crawling after us. He swept the feather over the furniture, the shelves of the larder, everywhere to make sure not even one crumb of chumetz was left in the house. Any crumbs he found he brushed into his hand. When we were done, he took the crumbs outside, put them on a little piece of paper and burned them.

"Everything is good," he pronounced. "Now we are ready for Pesach."

The next evening was beautiful. The table was set with a white cloth, candles gleamed in their brass holders, the Seder plate held all the ceremonial items — the lamb shank bone, the mix of apples and nuts called charoset, the baked egg and salt water, and the bitter herbs. The sweet red wine sparkled in the glasses. "Tante Ruchel and Uncle Ule are here," I called, taking a large bowl from Tante Ruchel as their whole family arrived.

"Hi, Joe. Hi, everybody. Boy, Tante Ruchel, this smells good. What is it?"

"Tsimmes, Beryl. Take it into your Mama like a good boy." Tante Ruchel took off her coat and followed me to the kitchen.

"Yom tov, happy holiday, everyone," Tante Brendel called out, taking the bowl from me. "What a pretty dress, Ruchel."

"Oh, it's nothing, Brendel. I just put some new lace on that dress Mrs. Schwartz made me a few years ago."

"Well, it certainly looks beautiful that way," Ma said. "The lace adds a nice bit of color."

"Why, thank you, Channah," Tante Ruchel replied. "Now, what can I do to help?"

"Nothing really, Ruchel," Ma said. "Just start taking the matzo and fish to the table."

Just then Mrs. Preipont and her kids came in, her hands full of sweetcakes.

"Yom tov, everyone!"

"Rivke, I'm so glad you're here," Ma said from her post at the stove. "You know my sister-in-law, Ruchel?"

"Of course. Yom tov, Ruchel."

"How are you, Rivke? I hear you are working at the pottery factory these days. Have you heard from your husband since he left?"

"Yes, he's doing just fine. He has a job in the garment district in New York City. Oh, Ruchel, I see you made your wonderful tsimmes. You'll have to give me the recipe."

"Really, Rivke, there's nothing to it. Just some sweet potatoes, a cup of brown sugar, a little salt, about a pound of prunes and a little lemon or orange juice. Whatever I have, in the pot with a little water. Then I add a couple of carrots, a piece of flanken beef, and let it cook for a couple of hours."

"But Ruchel, your tsimmes tastes so different."

"Well, maybe it's the little bit of sweet wine I put in," Tante Ruchel admitted.

"Aha! That's what makes it so good," Mrs. Preipont said, putting her cakes down on the kitchen table.

"Oh, but Rivke," Tante Ruchel said sadly. "I won't be able to eat any of your delicious sweetcakes. I'm afraid I'm allergic to them."

Ma turned to Tante Ruchel with a puzzled look. "Allergic?"

"Yes," Tante Ruchel said. "They make my tuchas grow bigger."

"You're right," Ma laughed. "I must be allergic too!"

They all laughed as Tante Ruchel and Mrs. Preipont carried plates to the table and came back for more. Ma stirred the pots on the stove.

On Shabbes and holidays, everything was always special, but for Passover this particular year the women had outdone themselves. We had cold gefilte fish with onions and carrots cooked in broth, pickled beets, borscht, hot chicken soup with matzo ball dumplings, a big goose, pot roast with potatoes, garlic and horseradish, Tante Ruchel's famous tsimmes, and all kinds of sweetcakes and honeycakes, made with matzo meal instead of flour.

"Ma, Zayde says it's time to start the Seder," Jerry said, poking his head in from Zayde's bedroom.

Ma removed her apron. "Come, ladies," she said. "Let's go to the table."

We settled into our seats. Zayde entered from his room, the white robe he wore on festive occasions covering his clothes, a white yarmulke on his head. We had padded his chair with pillows because you are supposed to recline while you eat during the Seder. The table stretched all the way across the kitchen and into the bedrooms, with the babies in their mother's laps and the older children sitting together at one end.

Everyone became quiet. Ma lit the candles and Zayde said the blessing over the matzo and the wine. And so once again we began telling the old story of the Jews' exodus from Egypt. It would be our last Passover together in our old home.

BULLETIN: June 28, 1914

AUSTRIAN ARCHDUKE KILLED

SARAJEVO — Austrian Archduke Ferdinand and his wife, the Duchess of Hohenberg, were killed shortly before noon today. The couple was motoring through the city, celebrating their fourteenth wedding anniversary while on a state visit, when two shots were fired at point-blank range ...

CHAPTER 6

Summer 1914

T he news spread fast, from the one side of town to the other, from shul to shul, family to family.

It was June 29, 1914, and I was standing outside our shul with some friends when suddenly we heard shouting from down the street. Mr. Pinkus, the tin man, was madly driving his rickety wagon and cracking his whip over his poor old horse.

"News!" he yelled as he reached the shul in a cloud of dust. He jumped down and ran inside. We ran after him.

"News!" he shouted again, rushing up to the rebbe and gabbai. The sing-song praying stopped abruptly. Everyone crowded around.

"The Serbs have killed Austria's archduke. The Russians are calling up the reserves and soldiers have already been seen moving west. The burgomeister says they'll probably come through Horchov," he panted.

Everybody began talking and shouting. "What does it mean, rebbe?" someone asked above the din.

"It means no good," the rebbe responded. "It means we will soon be at war, because Russia has a pact to defend the Serbs."

The gabbai could only shake his head and mutter, "Ai-yi-yi, what will happen to us now?"

And things began to happen quickly after that. It wasn't that we hadn't expected war — it had been coming for a long time. But no one is ever really prepared, especially children.

By July, the armies were on the move.

"Beryl," Jerry called, running into the kitchen. "You want to go see the soldiers? Yankel's father just saw them — they're marching right past his tailor shop."

I grabbed my cap and we ran out of the house, just in time to see Tevia coming down the street. "Tevia, come on, we're going to see the soldiers!" I shouted. We ran all the way to the main street, and there they were — Russian army units heading west.

Row after row of soldiers marched down the street. And wagons. Lots of wagons, pulled by big farm horses. Fancy horses, carrying officers, trotted back and forth between the columns of men and wagons. The choking dust made it hard to breathe.

And the noise. Clumping feet, clanking equipment, shouts from the wagon masters, officers barking orders — it all made such a tumult. I looked around. Yeshiva students, in a group on the other side of the street, talked excitedly among themselves, long sidecurls bobbing in rhythm with their nodding heads and gesturing hands. Some of our friends from cheder ran up to join us, everyone talking and pointing.

I felt strange. I wanted to keep watching, but I also wanted to turn away, run home and pretend it wasn't real.

"My father says the government has called for full mobilization, and these troops are moving to meet the Austrians someplace southwest of here," Yankel said importantly. Jerry just looked at him and sniffed.

Then, over the rumble of the wagons, we heard a lot of jangling.

"Hey, it's the cavalry!" Jerry shouted. "Boy, just look at them. Everything's so polished and shiny. Look at their swords, and the fine horses they ride. If I have to go into the army, I want to be in the cavalry."

"You can't," Yankel promptly informed my brother. "They're all officers, and a Jew can't be an officer."

"Oh, well, I'll just take care of the horses then," Jerry replied without missing a beat.

The cavalry kept coming, line after line. We watched as they rode past, sitting on their horses so proudly, looking straight ahead. The horses pranced and snorted nervously, distracted by the strange smells and all the people standing at the edge of the street.

"Here come the cannons!" Louie yelled. Horses pulling caissons with big-barreled cannons were coming up from the river and moving down the road. We spent the rest of the afternoon watching, discussing the merits of the different kinds of horses and how far a cannon could shoot.

Finally, it was getting late. The crowd began to break up. A child cried. A mother picked him up, took another child by the hand and turned toward home. An old man, back bent, head bowed, walked away slowly, leaning heavily on his cane. The group of Yeshiva students began breaking up into twos and threes, still discussing the pros and cons of the political situation, their hands flying about to emphasize their thoughts.

There was less excitement now, and we walked home slowly, talking quietly. But as we neared the house, Jerry and I ran ahead, eager to tell Zayde about the big event. He was at the kitchen table, reading.

We babbled non-stop for a few minutes about the soldiers and horses and cannons, but for some reason Zayde didn't seem impressed. When we were finally quiet for a moment, he looked up, very slowly, from his book.

"So, it begins," was all he said.

Then he looked down again and went back to his reading.

We were surprised that Zayde had thrown cold water on our excitement, but we didn't have time to ask why he was so troubled because just then Ma called us over.

"Jerry, Beryl, here," she said, handing something to Jerry. "I've put the brass candlesticks and the little silver salt dish in this bag. You know the old sunken rowboat under the willow tree? Put the bag down in the boat. Tie it down good, and put some rocks and tree branches around so no one will notice."

"Why, Ma?" I asked.

"Soldiers take."

That's all she said.

It was getting dark as Jerry and I climbed down to the old boat, and the water felt cold around our ankles as we waded in. Jerry spent a long time carefully tying down the bag, and I brought over some rocks and branches to cover everything. We didn't have much of material value in our lives, but the candlesticks and salt dish were important to our little family. They had been wedding gifts from Ma's family.

"Ma and Zayde are worried, aren't they?" I asked Jerry.

"Yes," Jerry answered quietly. "I guess we're in for it now."

He was right, because then it really started.

BULLETIN: August 1, 1914

GERMANY ENTERS WAR

BULLETIN: August 25, 1914

GREAT RUSSIAN VICTORY AT GILA LIPA

BULLETIN: September 3, 1914

STAVKA REPORTS ROUT: AUSTRIAN ARMY RETREATS FROM GALICIA

"Does the newspaper say anything about the war?" I asked.

CHAPTER 7

Fall/Winter 1914-1915

By the middle of August 1914, we were anxiously looking for any news we could find. We were still able to get an occasional newspaper and hear things from travelers. Every evening we would gather around the kitchen table and exchange the latest bits of information each of us had picked up during the day. For the past month, there had been rumors of big battles.

One day Jerry and I came back from helping Tante Brendel in the store to find Zayde and Sam sitting at the table. Zayde was reading the monthly *Jewish Star*.

"Does the newspaper say anything about the war?" I asked.

"Come and sit, boys," Zayde said. "I was just about to read the latest reports to your mother and Sam."

Ma turned from the sink, where she had been cutting potatoes, wiped her hands on her apron and came over to the table. We all sat and Zayde started to tell us what was being reported.

"The government has called for full mobilization, and Russian troops are moving west into the eastern provinces of Poland," Zayde began. "The Austrian army is moving northeast, toward the Russians, and there has been a big battle near Krasnik ..."

"Why that's only about ninety miles southwest of here," Jerry interrupted.

"Yes, you're right, Jerry. According to the paper, the Austrians and the Russians fought for three days somewhere between the Vistula River and the Wieprz River. First the Austrians pushed the Russian division back many miles, but then the Russians replaced General Salza with General Ewerth and brought in General Plehve to help him, and they won the next battle.

"And at the same time they were fighting that battle, a couple of other army groups smashed into each other near Komarow, just east of the battle going on at Krasnik. After four days of terrible fighting, Austria drove back both Russian units."

Zayde paused and the look on his face told us the worst news was yet to come.

"Five-hundred-thousand men have been killed, and almost as many have been wounded," he said softly.

Everyone was quiet.

"Ach, such a waste," Ma finally said. "So many killed."

"Yes," said Zayde. "And before this is over, many more will die."

"What happened then, Zayde?" I asked. "I mean after the battle."

"Well, now it seems that for some reason the Austrians have pulled back. And the Russians are regrouping, getting ready for the next battle."

"Boy, Zayde, it sure is confusing. What do they do with all the dead men?" I asked.

"Bury them right there where they died, Beryl."

I had seen the columns of Russian soldiers marching down our main street only a couple of months earlier, looking so proud, equipment so shiny. I still couldn't quite imagine how all that changed once they met up with soldiers from another country.

But apparently, I would soon find out.

"The wounded will be coming now," Zayde said. "And refugees, peasants and workers from the towns near the fighting. And our people too will be running from the war. I must talk to the shuls. We must be ready to help where we can."

Jerry turned to Sam. "If they're calling up everybody, will you have to go soon?"

Sam nodded. "Yes," he said softly. "I'll be nineteen this winter and I'll get my orders to go."

Ma just shook her head, got up and went back to cutting the potatoes. Rose came in holding Tante Brendel's baby. I headed out to find Yankel and Tevia. We left Zayde sitting alone at the table staring at the newspaper.

***

By October 1914, we were beginning to feel the changes. Very few trains were coming through and food became in short supply.

Jerry and I were still going to cheder and helping Tante Brendel and Tevia in the store in the afternoon. One morning, just as we were about to leave, Ma asked Jerry to ask Tante if she could spare a little sugar from the store.

"I don't think she has any," Jerry replied. "Not much is coming in. The men at the market say all the trains are being used by the army, and they've taken most of the heavy wagon teams too."

"Well, bring some if she has," Ma instructed.

"Channah," Zayde said, looking up from his book. "Why not let the boys go out to the farmers and help with the harvest. The men have all gone to the army, and the women will need help and may give them some food."

"You're right, Pa," my mother said. "I heard Farmer Ponskia went into the army with his two sons. Now listen, Jerry and Beryl, your Zayde is right. Go over to the Ponskia farm this afternoon and see if you can help. I'll tell Brendel you won't be coming into the store today."

"She doesn't need us right now anyway, Ma," Jerry said. "There isn't much there to sell these days."

"All right, then," Ma said, waving us on our way. "Go on to cheder and bring home what you can from the farmer."

As we gathered up our things, we could hear Zayde and Ma continuing to discuss the food situation.

"There will be less and less," Zayde said. "We must be very careful using what we've stored and make it last as long as possible."

"What about money, Pa?"

"A little left yet, but it won't last long."

"Ma, Mr. Schwartz may need help at the tailor shop since Mottle left for the army," Rose volunteered. "Maybe he'll give me some work."

"That would be good, Rose," Ma said. "Mrs. Schwartz remarked only last week how nicely you sew. But you must be home before dark."

"I will come for you after evening services and we will walk home together," Zayde told my sister. "That will be better, eh Channah?"

"Yes, Pa, that will be better," Ma agreed.

Rose went off to help Tante Brendel, and Jerry and I heard Ma sigh as we headed out the door.

"Just a minute, Jerry," I called, "I forgot my cap." I ran back inside just in time to hear Ma and Zayde.

"We must watch the children carefully, especially Rose," Ma was saying. "The women were talking about some girls in Kovno who were taken by the soldiers. Who will marry them now? How will they live? What a burden for their families — everything is going to change now isn't it, Pa? We have to be prepared. The children must understand what can happen. We must be strong and keep going until Mordecai can send the boat tickets."

"You are strong, Channah," Zayde said. "And you will be strong."

***

That afternoon Jerry and I trudged along the road to the Ponskia farm, kicking stones ahead of us as we went. Dust flew up from the dry roadbed and hung in the still October air. The trees shone golden in the bright light, matching the sunbaked crops in the fields ready for harvest.

Everything seemed so peaceful.

"Look, Beryl," Jerry said, pointing. "They're all over there in that far field. Let's cross over." We climbed the low post fence and headed down the rows toward the little group bent to its work.

"Mrs. P.," Jerry called as we neared. "My mother thought you might be able to use some help with the harvest."

Mrs. Ponskia stood — a big, heavy woman with a kerchief tied around her head, a sack half-filled with potatoes hanging across her ample bosom, sweat dripping from her red face in the unseasonably warm weather. "Yes, we could use help," she said. "But I have no money to pay."

"That's all right," Jerry said. "Maybe you could give us some of the potatoes."

"Yes, why not," Mrs. P. shrugged. "Either we get them in or they rot. Take a sack over there and start at the end of that row." Then she looked down at me. "You too, Yisroel?" she asked with a laugh. "You think you're strong enough to carry such a heavy bag?"

"Oh, yes, Mrs. P.," I said seriously. "Besides, I love potato kugel!"

At that, everyone laughed and went back to their work. Friends and people in the family still called me Beryl, but outsiders called me by my given name, Yisroel.

It was back-breaking work digging potatoes, and because I really was too little, Jerry had the extra burden of shlepping both our sacks to the barn. The army had taken all the horses and wagons, so everything was carried on the backs of the workers.

That evening we came home hot, dirty and tired. "Potatoes, Ma," Jerry announced wearily but triumphantly, thumping down a sack on the kitchen table.

"And Mrs. P. said she could use us two more days, and she gave us a little milk too," I said, handing over a pail of creamy, white milk from the farm's goat.

"Good," Ma said. "Now go wash up, then we'll have some supper. Your Zayde is still at shul but he'll be home as soon as he picks up Rose at the tailor shop. Beryl, set the table and call Brendel and the children."

We were already eating soup when Zayde, Sam and Rose came in. "Any war news at shul today, Zayde?" Jerry asked.

"Yes, and it's not so good, I'm afraid. Some of the men heard there is heavy fighting near Warsaw. Wagons with wounded soldiers have started coming this way. The very bad ones they are leaving here in the hospital; the others they are trying to get to Kyiv."

"They don't have enough doctors," Sam added, "so the authorities have even asked Dr. Shanowitz to help in the Christian hospital. He says the Germans are throwing gas shells at the Russians, and the wounds are so bad because they're using exploding bullets."

I looked at Sam with surprise. This was quite a lot for him to say all at one time.

"The road from the west was full of people today," I piped up.

"Yes," Jerry said, picking up where I'd left off. "We could see them from the farm, carrying everything on their backs or pulling carts loaded with everything they own. They looked terrible."

"Yes, I know," Zayde said. "The gabbai has put several families in the cheder. Boys, I'm afraid there will be no school for a while. But, Beryl, I will expect you to keep up your Bar Mitzva studies here at home with me."

Tante Brendel came in looking tired, carrying the baby on her hip.

"Nu, Brendel?" Ma said. "Sit. I'll get you a plate of soup."

"How are the food shipments, Brendel?" Zayde asked.

"Not good, Pa. The market is getting only a little here, a little there, what with the army using all the horses and trains."

Something Brendel said seemed to give Ma an idea.

"Boys," she said, looking at Jerry and me, "on your way home from the farm tomorrow, go by the train yard and see if you can find a little coal or wood they dropped."

"But be careful," she quickly added. "Don't get caught by the Cossacks." Jerry and I exchanged knowing glances — Ma thought all policemen were Cossacks.

Meanwhile, Ma continued with her instructions. "Sam, you go by the forest up-river and chop some wood. Take Zayde's little wagon with you. I'm afraid it's going to be a hard winter, children, and we'd better be careful with what we have. Look for anything you can find to eat or burn, and try to catch a few more fish. We'll salt them down and store them in the cellar with everything else. Do we have enough room in the cellar, Pa?"

"Plenty of room yet," Zayde said. "Get as much as you can, boys."

The next day, after digging potatoes, Jerry and I took a couple of extra sacks and stopped by the train yard on the outskirts of town. Some other boys, and a few old men and women, were already there.

Jerry quickly sized up the situation. "It's no use looking here, Beryl. Everybody has the same idea. Let's walk down to the water tank at the first bend. I bet we'll find something there."

Jerry was right. The old steam engines would stop to fill up with water from the big tank at the bend and the firemen would stoke their engines, so that's where we found some dry wood and a few nice pieces of coal before it got too dark to see.

"Come on," Jerry said. "If we take the side spur through the woods, we'll get home faster than if we go all the way back through the train yard."

"I don't know, Jerry. It looks awfully dark in there."

"Oh, come on, don't be silly."

I shook my head but reluctantly followed. Somehow I just knew Jerry was going to get us in trouble.

The old spur connected with the main track again down by the river near our house — but first we would have to go through a patch of dense forest. The air among the trees felt cool and refreshing after the hot, dusty day. But with the sun setting, it was so dark we had to walk right on the tracks so we could find our way. Not even a firefly broke the blackness. A shiver ran down my spine.

Suddenly there was a strange, eerie sound above the deep quiet of the woods, and ahead, I could just barely make out a dark shape. "Jerry, what's that?" I whispered.

"I'm not sure, but I think it's a train car. Come on, maybe there's something in there we can use."

Jerry crept forward and I followed, right on his heels. "Be careful," he turned and whispered back. "There may be some of Ma's Cossacks around."

Something didn't seem right as we drew closer, and suddenly I realized what it was. "Ugh," I said. "What's that smell?" And before Jerry could answer, I heard soft crying and the murmur of talk mixed with the chanting of prayers.

We stopped and looked at each other through the darkness, then tiptoed closer. No one seemed to be around. We were now close enough to see the train cars plainly, and we saw a small window high up on the front car. Jerry cupped his hands around his mouth and called up toward the opening. "Hello," he called softly. "Is anyone in there?"

Nothing. Then a white hand. I shivered. The hand retreated and a pale face appeared.

"Who are you?" Jerry hissed. "And what are you doing here?"

"Jews from Lodz," the face answered. "We've been sitting here since yesterday. Where are we? And who are you?"

"You're in Horchov," Jerry answered, "near the Boog River. They must have needed your engine and just left you here. We're Jews too."

"Thank God," the face replied. "They called us spies and said we couldn't stay near the fighting. They shipped us out — to where we don't know. But now we're stuck here. We haven't had food or water for days.

The children and the old people are very bad — two have died, I think. Can you help us?"

Jerry turned to me. "Beryl, I think we'd better get some help." I nodded. "Mister, we're going for help," I called up to the face. "We'll be back as soon as we can."

Childish fear of the dark woods gone, we ran down the tracks as fast as we could, bundles of potatoes, wood and coal flopping against our backs.

We were gasping for breath by the time we came into the clear near the river, but the easier going gave us a second wind and we sprinted the rest of the way.

We came bursting into the kitchen, startling everybody. "Boys, what's the matter?" Ma said, jumping up so fast her knitting fell to the floor.

"Is someone after you?" Rose asked fearfully.

"No," Jerry panted.

"Boys, come and sit," Zayde said. "Catch your breath and tell us what has happened."

When we finished our story, Zayde stood. "I'm going to see the gabbai," he announced. "Channah, see if you can put together a little food between you and the other women. If we're going to help them, it will be a busy night. Jerry and Sam, come with me. Beryl, you go for Dr. Shanowitz and then help your mother and Rose. It's a good thing the weather is still warm."

We rushed out into the night to spread the word. Everyone we talked to was shocked, and even though they had very little themselves

95

they all gave something. Soon we had food, water and clothes accumulating at the big red shul. Jerry told me later that when they got back to the train, they had to break the locks on the doors and move the people out of the area very quietly so as not to alert the police or soldiers.

Then there was the problem of how to get the sick ones back to town without any wagons. But slowly, in the dark — without torches, for fear of being seen — everyone was led down the tracks toward the river. The able men helped the sick, and the women carried the children. At the river they were met by more people and taken to the shul, where we were all waiting to help.

By dawn, everyone had been fed, given what clothes they needed and assigned to go to someone's home temporarily so the authorities would not find them. We went home with the little family assigned to us and I fell asleep the instant I laid down.

After that, the shuls got together and set up a store of food and clothes for the refugees passing through town. The stream of refugees — gentiles, Jews, peasants, and townspeople — kept coming and coming. Wagons brought the wounded and the dead, and a pitiful line of broken people walked through from the west, going, they thought, to the safety of the cities in the east. Every public building in our town filled up with the sick and the wounded.

Then the weather turned cold.

BULLETIN: November 5, 1914

**GERMAN TROOPS ATTACK, RENNENKAMPF
FIGHTS BACK AT WARSAW**

BULLETIN: November 25, 1914

**ARMY HALTS GERMANS AT BITTER-COLD LODZ;
1 MILLION DEAD**

***

The fighting continued all winter around Warsaw, with first one side winning a little and then the other. The stream of refugees became a flood. Food, clothes and other necessities became impossible to get.

BULLETIN: January 31, 1915

**FOREIGN GOVERNMENTS ACKNOWLEDGE GERMANY USING
CHLORINE GAS IN WARSAW CAMPAIGN**

BULLETIN: February 14, 1915

**RUSSIAN ARMY TRAPPED IN AUGUSTOW FOREST
100,000 KILLED; 100,000 CAPTURED**

BULLETIN: February 15, 1915

ARMY FORMING NEW LINE INSIDE MOTHER RUSSIA

***

By early 1915 we heard that the workers in the big cities had gone on strike after being forced to work extra-long hours for very little money in the wartime production push.

The Russian government was completely disorganized. Supplies were hoarded or sent to wrong destinations. Guns and ammunition failed to get through to the soldiers, while the aristocracy commandeered trains to move their personal belongings and treasures. Entire towns in the path of the war were being deported to the east. The people were hungry and angry.

Ma built a fire in the oven only once a week now for Shabbes, and we cooked whatever we had all at once, then kept the food in the cellar or outside in the snow so it wouldn't go bad. The oven stayed warm for a couple of days and we huddled close by it.

One evening, Ma said softly, "Children, Sam got his papers today." She didn't even look up as she spoke, just continued to darn by the light of a little piece of candle — we couldn't get any more kerosene for the lamps.

No one knew what to say.

"Sam, I have an extra pair of stockings for you," Zayde finally offered. He got up, went to his room, returned with the stockings and handed them to Sam. "Is there anything else we can put together for you?"

"Thank you, Zayde, but the army will give me a uniform and a great coat."

"Well, we'll try to put together a little extra food for you to take along on the way to camp," Ma said. "Jerry and Beryl, see if you can get through the ice and find a fish or two. Anything left from the store, Brendel?"

"I put aside a bar of soap, a little salt and some tea for you to take, Sam."

"Thank you, Tante. I'll be all right."

We sat there, all of us sad and quiet in the cold darkness.

"Sam, eat whatever they give you," Zayde said. "You'll need your strength and God will forgive you for not eating kosher. Also, the officers are less likely to find insult and give you trouble. Do you understand what I am saying?"

"Yes, Zayde. I'll eat everything and I promise to do whatever they say. Don't worry, I'll be all right."

"Mr. Pinkus came back today from the Russian lines," I said, changing the subject. "I saw him drive by the mill. He thought he might be able to sell some pots to the soldiers. Anyway, he says the Germans have joined the Austrians and they're pushing the Russians back east, a little at a time. The Russian soldiers are trying to make their own tools and bullets and wanted all the metal he had."

"I went to the butcher shop today," Ma said. "I was hoping they might have a little something to buy, but they haven't had anything come through for a couple weeks. The meat from Poland can't get through because the Germans have pushed the Russians back out of Lodz and taken the trains for themselves."

"So, they're in Lodz already," Zayde said. "With the Germans coming into the southern front, it won't be long before they're here. When do you leave, Sam?"

"This Sunday, right after Shabbes, Zayde."

"Ach, you don't have much time. The food your Mama packs up for you, keep it with you in your pack. Don't leave it lying around where someone might take it."

"And remember to keep your feet warm and dry," Rose added.

"Are they going to give you a gun, Sam?" I asked. "Will you have to shoot people?"

"Only if they are shooting at me, little brother," Sam said with a soft laugh. "But I think if I don't fight, the officers will shoot me."

"Zayde, do you really think the Germans will come near Horchov?" Jerry asked.

"I think by spring or early summer, they will be here, Jerry. I hope they go to the north or south of us, because if they come through here, it will be very hard on everyone — but I think this is where they will come. This is a good place to cross the river, and a good position to fight from."

**

Ma held back her tears when Sam left that Sunday, and things settled down for a while. It was February 1915, and although we missed Sam, we were kept plenty busy looking for food and supplies, trying to keep warm and working here and there for a few pennies.

Everything was hard to come by, and people began to barter with one another. If one had fuel and another had food, they traded. Many of the skilled people had been taken into the army or put to work in factories making things for the soldiers. So even if someone had a little money, there was nothing to buy.

But we had managed to store quite a bit of food in our cellar, and that got us through the winter. And life went on. We studied with Zayde for part of each day and we still had Shabbes. And even though there was very little to eat, Zayde still brought home as many men as he could for Shabbes dinner.

News was very scarce, so we lived on rumors. What real news we got was bits and pieces from refugees coming through town and the wounded coming from the front lines. One evening, as we were crowded around the big oven eating a watery potato soup, Jerry came in late.

"Jerry, where have you been?" Ma scolded. "These days it's not safe to be out after dark."

"Sorry, Ma. I was helping Dr. Shanowitz bring some wounded soldiers into one of the empty factory buildings by the river, and I got so interested in their stories I forgot what time it was."

As Ma got Jerry some soup, Zayde asked him what news he'd picked up.

"That German general, Mackensen, is really on the march now," Jerry said. "The main part of the Russian army is retreating and heading this way. The doctors are trying to evacuate as many of the wounded as they can, so it looks like you were right, Zayde. They'll be coming through here pretty soon."

Ma waited until Jerry started eating, then turned to Zayde with a worried look. "Pa, do you think it's all right for the boys to be so close to the soldiers?"

"Let them be, Channah," Zayde replied. "They might pick up some food or other things we can use."

"Yes, Channah, let them help," added Tante Brendel. "Maybe they can get some food from the soldiers. God knows there doesn't seem to be anything else coming in."

"Mr. Schwartz says the iron workers are on strike now," Jerry said between spoonfuls of soup. "And the factories making ammunition tried to go on strike too, but the government called out the militia and a lot of people were killed."

"This is only the beginning," warned Zayde. "Come, children, finish up. We must get our rest. Tomorrow is another day, and we have a job to do."

"What job is that, Zayde?" I asked.

"To stay alive."

***

The next Shabbes evening after services, we talked with some of the Jewish families coming through town on their way to Kyiv. "Yes, the fighting is terrible," one old man said. "But even worse, the peasants are very angry right now. They are blaming the Jews for their shortages because one of the few jobs we can get is working for the landlords. And we hear that even though our men are fighting in the army, they are shot by the officers for the least little thing. And you know, Jewish soldiers don't get furloughs like the gentiles do."

"As for us, we were made to leave our home because the authorities said they didn't want any spies near the fighting. Us, spies? How could we be spies? So we decided it would be safer if we left with some of our neighbors. We were hoping things would be better as we came east, but the people in the cities are in a panic."

Another man sitting across from us interrupted. "There is no food or fuel in the cities. The Russians are burning everything as they retreat, warehouses, silos, barns, and everyone is running from the army. We don't know where we are going, but we'll keep running too — until we fall down dead."

"The cities won't be able to handle so many refugees," Zayde told us. "It will only make things worse."

Zayde was right. Things got worse, much worse. But little by little it got to be the spring of 1915, and I was almost ten years old.

BULLETIN: February 28, 1915

GERMANS STOPPED AT BOOG RIVER: BOTH ARMIES DIG IN FOR REST OF WINTER

CHAPTER 8

Spring/Summer 1915

Panic. It spread from the big cities, where the workers were rioting and the people were starving. They fled to the countryside in search of food, but there was no food, the farmers were in the army. The retreating Russian soldiers were taking any food that had been stored and burning the barns and fields behind them so the advancing Germans would find nothing to eat.

There was word of mass desertion by the peasants in the Russian army. Thousands of refugees turned to millions. People ran east to escape the war and west to escape the cities. And we were right in the middle.

The roads were clogged with carts laden with belongings and wagons with wounded dripping blood that mixed with puddles of water and dirty snow. People begged for food. Dead bodies littered the landscape.

It was one horrible, stinking, mired mess.

Jerry and I often stopped to help push carts and wagons along and bring wounded into hospitals that were being set up in any building that had room.

The Germans trickled in slowly at first. But then the main units arrived and, suddenly, soldiers were digging up the entire riverbank, even right behind our house.

I knew soldiers rode horses and fired guns, but I couldn't imagine why they would dig giant holes next to the river. So I asked Zayde.

"They are digging trenches," Zayde explained. "When they are done digging, they will stay down in there to protect themselves from shells and bullets. The Russian soldiers are doing the same thing on the other side of the river. You can see them in some places, even from here."

Zayde was very old but he didn't need glasses, and if he said the Russians were doing the same thing across the river I knew it must be so. Sure enough, when I looked hard, I saw sun glinting off their rifles and smoke rising from their fires.

"Will we dig trenches to stay in, Zayde?"

"No, Beryl. We will go to the shelters in the basements of the apartment buildings."

***

We had no food, no wood, no coal. Jerry and I went to the soldiers' kitchen and, like everyone else, waited in line every day for a piece or two of bread. After a couple weeks of that, they began giving out what they called conserves, which were little cans of food the soldiers ate in the field.

I was beginning to understand some German now, since it was very close to Yiddish, and I was able to tell from the writing on the cans that some were milk, some had fruit preserves or jam, and some contained a kind of meat.

Then, one day, Zayde took his little wagon to the mess hall and got two loaves of bread, some flour, six cans of beans, six cans of milk and a little fat. They told us we had to make the food last a long time. And that's how we lived.

***

"Eat slowly, children, this is all you'll get today," Ma said, serving up a piece of bread and jam and a cold potato to each of us.

"Zayde, why aren't you eating?" I asked, wiping my mouth with the back of my hand.

"I'll eat tomorrow. I'm an old man. I don't need so much food."

"Pa, you have to eat something," Ma protested.

"No, Channah. I've decided to fast on Mondays and Wednesdays so the children can have a little more."

"Pa, you can't do that. You have to eat — we're all eating so little as it is."

But Zayde's mind was made up. "Let the children have," he said. "I'll take a little jam tomorrow with a potato. That will be enough. Give the children my share today."

Ma shook her head but didn't say anything more as she divided Zayde's food between us.

"More wounded came in today, Zayde," Jerry said as we finished eating. "They're putting them in all the churches and apartment buildings."

"Yes, I know, Jerry. They're using the shuls, too."

"A sergeant asked me to help carry some of the wounded today," Jerry continued. "The men were lying all over the place — and they smelled just awful. The sergeant gave me a can of milk when we finished and asked me to come back tomorrow."

"I'll go with you, Jerry," I said. "Maybe they'll give us some more food."

"What do you think, Pa?" Ma asked. "Maybe they shouldn't be so close to those men."

"Let them go, Channah," Zayde said. "It will be good if they can get a little more food." Then, turning to us, Zayde said, "Children, take the little ones in to Brendel. I want to talk to your mother alone."

Jerry picked up the baby, and Rose and I led the other young ones to Tante's bedroom. But I hung back in the doorway to listen to what Zayde had to say to Ma.

"What's the matter that you couldn't talk in front of the children, Pa?"

Zayde didn't answer for a moment. Then he said, "It's going to get even worse, Channah."

"I know, Pa. But we will keep the family together and we will get by."

"It will get bad, Channah, very bad. You are a good woman, a strong woman. Prepare yourself and the children for what is to come."

Ma didn't say anything and Zayde continued.

"Yesterday in shul, a mist came before my eyes and I was very cold. I saw you and the children in a dark place, nearly frozen. You were crowded between a lot of people. The children could barely breathe. Then you came to a dark house, no fire, the wind blowing through. You were all huddled together trying to keep warm. There was no family with you and the children, only strangers."

"Pa, you were just dreaming. The Germans have been good to us so far, and the peasants around here haven't bothered us."

There was silence before Zayde spoke again.

"Take care, Channah. Take care. I wasn't with you in the darkness."

***

The next day, Jerry and I headed toward the mess kitchen.

"There's the sergeant from yesterday, Beryl," he said, nudging me in the ribs.

"Do you need any help today, sergeant?" my brother called out.

The sergeant approached us, his arms full of bloody clothes. A single boot hung limply from the pile. "Yes, son," he said with a nod toward a nearby wagon. "Go help them unload those men over there."

Jerry went to the wagon and I wandered around staring at the men. Some sat on the ground just outside the kitchen, eating wearily. Some lay sleeping right on the road, their rifles or crutches next to them. Their clothes were filthy and many wore bloody bandages.

Two soldiers came walking down the street and went into a building with a big red cross. I walked over and followed them inside. It was hot and smelled terrible. Wounded men were everywhere.

A soldier on the floor near the door held a bloody hand out to me. "Water," he begged. "Please, some water."

I looked around, found a water bucket and brought some to the man. Then I gave some water to a few others nearby. An orderly ran up and handed me a roll of bandages. "Here, boy," he said. "If you want to help a little, please, change the bandage on this man."

The soldier he pointed to was feverish and talking to himself, his head rolling back and forth. I unwound the bloody bandage from the stump that had once been his left leg. The wound was ugly and smelled bad, but I poured some water on it and wrapped on the clean bandage.

Suddenly the soldier opened his eyes and looked at me. He was clutching his boots to his chest — he didn't seem much older than me. "Would you like some water?" I asked, and without waiting for an answer I lifted his head and held the cup to his lips. He sipped a little and fell back to the damp mat on the dirty floor.

I spent all afternoon helping, giving the men water, changing their bandages and feeding the ones that needed help. Jerry went back and forth carrying bloody men in and out on litters. Finally, he came over to me and said, "Come on, Beryl, it's getting late. We'd better get home. Here, one of the men gave me some conserves. Take a couple."

We washed ourselves at one of the wash buckets and made our way home. The next day when I went to help again, I looked for the young soldier with the stump. "He's gone, kid," another badly injured man said. "Here, take his boots. He won't need them anymore and neither will I."

***

By August, the two armies were well entrenched and shelling each other in earnest. We lived with the constant deep growl and boom of the German cannon and the shrill scream of incoming shells. The noise seemed to pound at the insides of our heads, and we could barely breathe through the acrid smoke and dust. Bullets were flying, so we only went outside when we really had to.

We lived on and forgot how things used to be.

When the shelling was especially bad, everyone went to the cellar of the nearest apartment building to wait it out.

It was damp and dark in the cellar except for the little pieces of candle people brought. At first, everyone sat quietly with their own family up against one of the walls. Later, when we were used to the dust falling every time a shell hit nearby, we talked to one another and ate a little food.

One day, we had twelve or fifteen families in the basement with us. We children played our children's games and fought our children's fights.

Some of the men studied with Zayde in one corner. And some older boys and some of the men played cards to pass the time.

Tevia and I had been collecting bullet casings, and we sat and sorted the good ones from the crushed ones. Jerry was near the stairs playing cards at an old wooden table. Smoke from a cigarette dangling from the corner of his mouth curled in front of his eyes, making him squint at his cards. He leaned to one side in his chair, his left elbow propped on the table revealing a hole in the arm of his shirt, as he considered his chances of winning.

A couple of little ones were under the table — one little girl clung to her father's trouser leg and sucked her thumb.

"Nu, Jerry, so when are you going to decide?" Mr. Abraham shouted, trying to be heard over the screaming shells. We'd all pretty much gotten used to the noise, but now the thumping from the cannon started coming faster and the screaming shells got louder and closer. The talking stopped, and everyone looked up as a shell whistled overhead and exploded near the apartment building.

"That was close," I said to Tevia, spitting dust out of my mouth.

"It sure was," he replied, a quiver in his voice. "The floor shook."

Suddenly, an even louder shell screamed overhead. We sat helplessly, looking up, trying to see right through the ceiling. Where would it hit this time?

Silence.

Then an explosion.

Everything crashed down on us. Fire, dust, light. Dirt and pieces of building fell through the ceiling. Screaming, shouting. Men and women desperately trying to douse the fire with blankets and pots of water. Blood everywhere. Jerry's face was burned, his hair in front and his eyebrows seared off. He just sat there with his mouth open. The card table was gone, a big hole in the ground where it had stood. And, oh my God, the children underneath were gone.

I saw a little leg. A little boy's head all smashed in.

A little hand still clinging to a piece of trouser.

A mother screamed and ran toward the hole. Another woman tried to hold her back. We were all in shock. Men began to gather up the broken children in a blanket, others tried to fashion makeshift bandages for the wounded. Ma smeared something on Jerry's face, as Tevia and I coughed and coughed from the choking dust.

I looked up, rubbing the dust from my eyes, and saw men pulling parts of the building away from the hole. They reached down to us and started taking out the wounded. Finally, it was my turn, and a soldier hoisted me up over his shoulders, up into the dusty twilight. The shells still screamed overhead, but the explosions were farther away.

Out in the street we stood, looking back at the building. It was only a shell now, with men sifting through the rubble to make sure no one was left inside. We made our way home. When we got there, Zayde gathered us together for a prayer to thank God that none of us had been killed.

We hadn't been sleeping well for a while, but that night was especially hard. Jerry was in pain from his burns and Rose cried softly. I couldn't stop thinking about the children who had been under the table, and the little hand.

This is war, I thought. *Dead children.*

***

We finally fell asleep, and Jerry and I didn't get up until late the next morning.

"Zayde's gone with some of the men to the cemetery," Ma told us when we made our way into the kitchen. "It's quiet right now and the Germans are letting us bury the dead — the soldiers are helping to dig the graves. How are you feeling, Jerry?"

"OK, Ma. It's not bad."

"Let me see," Ma said, taking hold of Jerry's chin and closely inspecting his face. He looked funny with no eyebrows or eyelashes. And the right side of his face was red like he had been sunburned. "All right," Ma said after a moment, "put a little more schmaltz on those burns."

Ma offered us hot tea but said we had no food this morning. "Keep the tea, Ma," Jerry said, rubbing the schmaltz on his face. "We'll get some food at the mess kitchen."

"Be careful, and watch out for Beryl."

"We'll be fine, Ma," I said, "and we'll try to bring something back."

"All right, but be home before dark and stay out of the main streets, where all the shooting is."

"We will, Ma," Jerry and I called out together as we headed for the door.

By the time we got over to the mess kitchen, there was a long line of people. "I'll get something to eat later, Beryl," Jerry said. "I'm going over to the surgery tent. They need help moving those men."

"I'm going to the red cross building over there to see if I can help," I called to Jerry as he hurried away. "I'll see you later."

I walked into the building, picked up the water bucket and ladle, and started going up and down the rows of men lying on the floor.

After a while, a doctor who was checking on some of the men looked up at me as he finished changing a bandage. His white coat was full of blood and dirt, and he looked very tired. "Leave the water a minute and come with me, boy," he said. "What's your name?"

"Yisroel."

"Jewish, huh? Well, Yisroel," he said, putting his hand on my shoulder as we walked toward the back of the big hall, "I'm going to give you some medicine to keep you from getting sick."

He picked up a needle and filled it with some clear fluid from a small bottle. "You're not afraid of a needle, are you?" he asked, smiling down at me. I shook my head no but kept staring at the needle as he brought it toward me. At the last minute I shut my eyes and was surprised when he said he was finished.

"This will keep you from getting sick with typhus," he said. "All right now, go ahead and give the men some water."

I looked at my arm but didn't see anything different. When I turned to thank him, he was already busy with the next man they were carrying in. I went on my way.

After a while, I went back to the kitchen and the sergeant gave me some bread and a few cans of conserves. Jerry wasn't around so I headed for home and caught up with Zayde, who was pulling his wagon with more conserves and a jug of water.

For some reason, Zayde seemed tickled.

"Beryl, look what a soldier gave me. Boots. Almost new."

"It's a good thing, Zayde," I said. "Your old ones wouldn't have stayed tied together much longer. Your feet were sticking out the front."

"Yes, you are right, Beryl. And look how strong these boots are, with nails in the soles for the snow this winter. Come, put your things in the wagon and we'll take them home. Give a push."

That evening in the building we were now using as a shelter, Ma opened two cans. Zayde would eat only some fruit preserve on a piece of bread. The rest of us shared the meat and the rest of the bread.

Zayde, Ma and Tante Brendel talked quietly while we ate.

"Surah's two little ones, killed, gone just like that," Ma said, shaking her head. "How could it happen? Why should it happen? It's so hard on the children with all this death. What can I say to them when they have to go look for more food? Brendel, at least your little ones are too young to understand what is happening."

"Thank God the Germans have been good enough to give the children some of their food," Tante said. "But what are we going to do about clothes? If they haven't grown out of their clothes, they're worn out from washing. And how are we going to keep warm this winter?"

Zayde licked a little fruit preserve from his mustache.

"I know it's bad, children. And it will get still worse. The money is almost gone and there are only a couple-dozen potatoes left in the basement. Yes, it's good the Germans let the children eat from their kitchen. They're better to us than the Russians."

"But you have to eat more, Pa," Tante said.

"Me, what do I need with food? I'm an old man. Give my share to the children. I only pray God will let me live long enough to see the family through this."

"Last night was horrible," Ma said. "Only the good Lord saved Jerry. Look at him this morning, already over it and gone with Beryl to help with the wounded."

"Children shouldn't have to see such things," Zayde said. Then he sighed and told Ma something I didn't quite understand.

"I can't see very far ahead these days, Channah, only today and maybe tomorrow. I think my time on this Earth is very short now."

***

During periods of shelling, we continued going down into cellars of the remaining apartment buildings. We couldn't be out much, especially after dark. The soldiers were very nervous and shot at anything that moved. And it got harder and harder to get food and supplies.

But in the middle of everything, or "in miton derinnen," as Tante Brendel would say, I got home late one afternoon to find the rebbe from our shul sitting with Zayde and drinking tea. They were deep in conversation and the rebbe seemed very pleased.

"Come have some tea, Beryl," Ma said, turning to the samovar. She also seemed a little happier than we'd seen her lately.

"Good day, rebbe," Jerry said. "What's new?"

"Ah, I have some very good news for a change," the rebbe said, leaning forward in his chair. "The Americans have been pressuring our government to do away with the Pale of Settlement and open the borders to the Jews, in return for all the money Russia wants to borrow from America. And today word came from the Grosse Rebbe in Kyiv that the Duma has indeed abolished this terrible ghetto."

The rebbe sat back and smiled in satisfaction. None of us said anything for a while as we considered this unexpected development.

"So, rebbe," Ma finally said. "Exactly what good will that do us right now?"

"Well, it will make it easier to leave, to go to America or Palestine, anywhere a Jew might be accepted. And for those who stay here after the war, it may make it a little easier to get an education or a job."

"But what about now? How can we do anything in the middle of a war, with no money, no food, no trains or even horses?"

"Channah," the rebbe said. "God willing, this war will be over one of these days. And then we will have more freedom, even here in Russia."

"I think not, Reuben," Zayde said.

Zayde apparently had decided that the government's decision to abolish the ghetto would mean little.

"This war will change many things, but once the war is over and the government doesn't need the Americans anymore, things will be pretty much as before," Zayde said. "The Jews will never be free here."

The rebbe didn't say much more, and I could tell he was disappointed in our lack of enthusiasm. But after shul that Shabbes, there was much heated discussion and arguing back and forth. It had been generations since Jews were free to move about Russia as they pleased, or to come and go across the borders as they wished. If and when the war finally ended, no one really knew how the new laws would affect us — assuming any of us were still alive.

CHAPTER 9

Fall/Winter 1915-1916

I came out of the dark building, away from the awful smell of the wounded, into a crisp, sunny September afternoon. The sky was bright blue, but the air was already cold for so early in the fall. The blinding sunlight bounced between big, fluffy clouds that looked like they would snow if they could just get together. High in the sky, tiny airplanes buzzed like bees.

We'd already had our first snow of the year, but the sun had melted most of it, coating the streets here and there with thin sheets of ice. The booming roar of the cannon hadn't stopped for more than five minutes since dawn and there was an occasional crackle of rifle fire as I walked between the old buildings filled with wounded men.

Suddenly I saw Tante Brendel running up the street, carrying her littlest one under her arm like a bundle of old clothes. "Tante, what's the matter?" I called out, running toward her.

"Oy, Beryl, thank God I found you," she gasped, grabbing my arm. "Where is Jerry? Zayde fell. He's lying in the street. I think he's broken his leg. I just left Tevia with him."

I felt a sharp stabbing pain in my chest. "Wait here," I managed to stammer. "I'll get Jerry."

I ran to the operating tent and found Jerry helping some men wash down litters. "Jerry, come quick. Zayde's fallen. Tante says he's lying in the street."

Jerry turned and grabbed one of the litters. "Let's go," he said. We started to run, found Tante and kept on running. Two blocks away, by the big red shul, there was Zayde.

Tevia, tears streaming down his face, was on his knees, holding Zayde's head in his lap. A few other people had gathered around and one man was covering Zayde with his coat as we ran up.

Zayde's leg was twisted under him in a funny way and he looked like he was in a lot of pain. Jerry bent down. "Zayde, we have to get you home. We're going to lift you onto this litter and carry you, but it's going to hurt."

"Ah, boys," Zayde said through clenched teeth. "Don't worry about hurting. Just take me home."

We slid our arms under him and gently lifted while a couple of other men pushed the litter underneath.

"Isn't there a wagon?" Tante cried.

The men who had helped with the litter shook their heads. "The soldiers have taken everything that can move," one of them said.

We began carrying Zayde toward the house. "Beryl," Jerry said. "Let someone else carry. You go see if you can find a doctor."

One of the other men took my place and I dashed back toward the makeshift hospital.

I ran around the buildings like a meshuggener and finally saw the doctor who had given me the typhus shot. He was very busy with the soldiers, but he told me to wait and he would come soon.

I sat in a corner and followed him with my eyes all afternoon. Just when I thought my heart would explode from waiting, he looked up and saw me.

"Sergeant, wake Dr. S. and tell him I'm going to go look at a civilian and then I'm going to get some sleep. Tell him to take over for a while."

The doctor approached me. "Come, boy — Yisroel, isn't it? Just let me wash up and get my bag."

"I'll carry the bag, doctor. Our house isn't far, just down by the river."

The doctor dried his hands, threw his coat over his shoulders and we hurried toward the river in the deepening shadows. *Zayde, don't die, don't die — I need you.* That thought just kept pounding through my head with the pounding of the cannon and the popping of the rifles as I led the doctor through the streets.

When we entered the house, Zayde was lying on his bed with the whole family standing around. As the doctor approached, Ma and Tante Brendel stayed by Zayde, but Ma shooed everyone else from the room and closed the door.

It was a long time until the door opened again, and everyone waiting in the kitchen looked up anxiously, trying to read the faces of those who'd been in the room.

"Unfortunately," the doctor was saying, "this is the way it is with old people. As I said, I could put him in a cast and we could try to keep him moving, but you heard him — he just kept telling me to go help the young people. He doesn't want me to waste my time trying to help an old man."

The doctor continued talking to Ma as he headed for the front door. "Once this sort of thing happens to old people, it's usually not long before they're gone. You must prepare yourselves. I've given him something to ease the pain, and I've set the hip joint so he'll be more comfortable. Keep him warm and try to get him to eat. I understand from the boy that he's been fasting. Make him eat."

Standing at the door, the doctor scrawled something on a piece of paper and handed it to Ma. "Take this note to the mess kitchen and they'll give you a little extra," he said. "The problem is, if he gets too weak he may get pneumonia and then it will be all over."

It hurt my heart to listen. I looked at Jerry, Rose, Tevia, my aunts and uncles who had run to the house — tears were running down their faces, and I realized I was crying too. Ma's lips were pursed and Tante just kept wringing her apron between her hands.

The house was quiet after the doctor left. Zayde slept, and we gathered around the kitchen table.

No one said much at first. Tante Brendel sat with her head in her hands, elbows propped up on the table. Tanta Ruchel rocked back and forth crying, Jerry smoked a cigarette, Tevia fiddled with a bullet casing and Ma tried to make soup for everybody with a couple of potatoes and a big pot of water.

"What happened?" Jerry finally asked.

Tante looked up, eyes red and swollen. "One of the men there said he slipped. The nails on the bottom of his new boots slipped on the ice."

"He was so proud of those boots," I sighed.

Just then the cannon started up again, and everybody jumped.

"I'll go to the mess tomorrow and see if I can get the extra food," Jerry finally said.

"You boys will have to help us move him before you go off in the morning and when you get home, so we can keep him clean," Ma said.

Jerry nodded. I just stood there staring into space, feeling like I wanted to cry more. But I had run out of tears.

***

The next morning Zayde seemed a little better, but when we moved him, we could tell he was in pain.

"I'll bring the doctor back tonight, Zayde," I told him. "He'll give you something for the pain."

"No, Beryl, let it be, don't bother him. The doctor has more important work to do. I'm an old man. He doesn't need to waste his time on me."

It was no use arguing with Zayde, so Jerry and I didn't say anything more about the doctor.

"Zayde, is there anything you need before we go?" Jerry asked.

"A little water, Jerry, that's all. And my Siddur, please, Beryl. I'll study a little."

We brought Zayde water and his prayer book and left him lying there.

***

BULLETIN: September 15, 1915

RUSSIAN GRAND DUKE DISMISSED AS COMMANDER-IN-CHIEF, TSAR TAKES COMMAND AT STAFKA HEADQUARTERS

The weather got colder. Frost covered the windows, making the house dim and gray. It started to snow. We put on every layer of clothing we had and wrapped ourselves with blankets and rags. There was no fuel, no oil for the lamps. What we ate, we ate cold. My stomach hurt from hunger and I felt tired all the time.

Zayde didn't get out of bed at all now. Ma kept him covered with the goose-down quilt.

Whenever we managed to find a few splinters of wood, Ma made Zayde some hot tea with a little piece of bread and jam we would bring from the soldiers.

Then, in the middle of the winter, an order came. All young families were to be shipped out, away from the fighting.

"What do you mean we have to leave?" Rose cried. "Where are we going? What will they do with us?"

We were standing in the kitchen, talking to a man who was going door-to-door spreading word of the order from the burgomeister. "Shah, Rose," Ma said softly. My sister quieted down and Ma turned her attention to our visitor.

"Do you know where they are sending us?" Ma asked, her breath coming in white clouds in the cold air. "My father-in-law is very sick and can't be moved."

"Mrs., I don't know where they'll send you. Somewhere west, in Poland I would think. Is the old man dying? If so, the Mrs. with the little ones can stay until the last transport," the man said with a nod toward Tante Brendel. "But then they will move her out too and take the old man to one of the hospital wards."

Tante Brendel collapsed onto a chair, put her face in her hands and sobbed. "Quietly, Brendel," Ma said, laying a hand on her shoulder. "Be strong. We'll make do."

"Mister, what can we take with us?" Ma asked.

"There won't be much room and you might be traveling a long time. Take warm things. Wear as much as you can and take any food you have. Be at the old depot at the edge of town tomorrow morning, six o'clock sharp."

"Oy, so soon," Tante Brendel cried. "There's no time to prepare, no time to say goodbye to anyone."

"If you are not there, the soldiers will come for you," the man said. "Anyway, I think you'll be better off out of here, away from the shelling. Goodbye and good luck."

The man left and for a few minutes, we just stood there in the cold kitchen, looking at one another.

We didn't sleep that night. We put on whatever clothes we had. Ma tied up some potatoes in a couple of blankets and rags and left the rest for Tante Brendel and her family.

Then we went in to say goodbye to Zayde. The candle Ma carried flickered as we entered his cold, dark room.

"Come closer, children, so I can see you," Zayde said.

We gathered close around the bed and he raised his hands to bless us.

"May God protect you, keep you and give you peace," Zayde prayed. "Take care of each other and keep the family together."

We lined up one by one to kiss the dear old face, then turned to leave, holding back our tears.

In the dark, we said goodbye to Tante, Tevia and the other children. We said goodbye to our home.

I didn't know what to think. It felt like God had abandoned us.

***

Jerry carried the blankets with the potatoes. Ma took Rose and me by the arm.

We walked along in blackness pierced only by the beam of a searchlight dancing overhead. All around us, neighbors dragged themselves through four-foot snowdrifts. Sighing breath misted in still air, silence broken only by feet crunching on icy snow. A baby whimpered.

Arriving at the depot, we saw a train waiting on the tracks, steam puffing from the old locomotive, cars being loaded one by one. "Oh, God, they're freight cars," Jerry said. "And just look at how they're stuffing everyone in."

We stood stomping our feet to keep warm and looking around to see if we knew anyone.

A soldier called out names and assigned families to the cars. "Aynbinder, car number six," he finally hollered. We went over to the train and some men lifted us into the car. It was already packed full of people, but more were being pushed in behind us.

Ma quickly looked around. "Keep together, children," she said. "Follow me and stay close. Come now, over here."

She elbowed her way over to a spot directly below a high window.

"Stay right here, close together," Ma whispered. "It will be warmer if we stay close. Don't let anyone push us away from the window or we won't be able to get air."

All the while, more people were packed into the car. You couldn't sit down or hardly even move. With all the tall grownups around me, I felt like I was in a hole and couldn't breathe.

They closed the doors. I couldn't see.

The train began to move, rocking back and forth.

It was dark. People cried. Someone moaned.

"Get away from her, give her room," a woman screamed. Another complained, "Oh, God, I can't feel my legs."

Little kids cried, "I'm hungry, Ma. I'm cold. I have to go."

The smell was awful.

Ma kept us in a tight little circle. We rubbed our hands together underneath our clothes and stomped our feet. The clickety-click rhythm of the train made me tired, but Ma wouldn't let us fall asleep.

The train crept along. So slow, so cold.

I lost all track of time. It seemed like we were in that frozen boxcar forever.

***

The train rattled to a stop and the doors opened. I blinked and shielded my eyes from the blinding sun glinting off the snow.

Everyone rushed toward the door at once, climbing over still bodies lying on the floor. We were so stiff and frozen we could hardly move. I jumped from the boxcar, pain shooting up through my legs as I landed.

I realized it was morning. We'd been riding all day and all night.

Sleds waited by the tracks, with horses stomping and wheezing. A man helped Ma and Rose down. "Come along with me, please, Mrs.," the man said to Ma. "My name is Leiben."

"Where are we?" Jerry asked. "And where are you taking us?"

"You're in Lublin, Poland, about sixty miles from Warsaw," Mr. Leiben said. "I'm going to take you to our shul for a few days. Then the authorities will find you a place in one of the villages."

It hurt to even move, but we followed Mr. Leiben to his sled and climbed up. We looked back. Some people were being carried off the train. They weren't moving.

"Dead," Ma said.

Mr. Leiben clucked to his horse and we started out across the snow. Soon we arrived at a big shul where we came among many other families.

They gave us hot tea and a little food. Then we found some room in a corner and settled down together.

"So where are you from, Mrs., if I might ask?" a woman next to us asked Ma. "Is this your whole family? Where is your husband?"

"We're from Horchov. Some of our family is still there. But my husband is in America."

"Oh, you are lucky. God willing, you will live through all this and see him yet in the goldeneh medina, the golden land."

Ma and the other woman kept talking. I wished Zayde was with us. I never had gotten around to asking him why people called America "the golden land."

But I was too tired to wonder about America for very long. After I warmed up a bit, I put my head down in Ma's lap and slept for the first time in a long while.

***

The people from the shul gave out food, medicine and a few pieces of heavy clothing. They did their best to help, just as we had helped the refugees back in Horchov.

We were the refugees now.

We stayed at the shul four days while the government figured out what to do with us and all the other refugees who filled the shuls, churches and apartment buildings. Finally, on the fifth morning, the mayor and several groups of peasants arrived with sleds to take us to little houses in their villages.

We were told that many of the houses belonged to Russian peasants who had run away from Poland and returned to Russia when the war started. They had been afraid that the Germans would kill them when they came through Poland.

Late that evening, we came to the little village we'd been assigned to. The house they took us to was one room with a big brick oven against one wall. There was a table in the middle, but no chairs to sit on or benches to sleep on. There was no glass in the windows and no coal or wood to burn. We had no food or water, and we couldn't even make water from the snow because we had no pots.

We huddled together in a corner of the dark room and covered ourselves with every blanket and rag we had.

This also is war, I thought. *Cold and hunger and darkness.*

Ma prayed.

"Oh Lord, God, help us," she said. "Thank you for the roof over our heads. If it be thy will, please give us the strength to survive this new test in this strange place.

"Amen."

She sighed, exhausted. Then she pulled the old rags closer around us and softly sang 'Rozhinkes mit Mandlen, Raisins and Almonds,' the lullaby she had sung to us when we were babies.

"In dem beis ha-mik-dosh, in a vinkel heder...
In a dark little corner of the ancient temple,
the daughter of Zion sits widowed, alone.
Her child, one and only, she rocks in his cradle,
and sings him a lullaby in tenderest tone."

"Unter yidele's vigeleh...
Under my little one's cradle,
stands a kid, small and fair.
Far and wide it must wander,
raisins and almonds his wares."

"Like him you'll roam hither and yonder,
now you must sleep without cares.
Sleep, my little one, sleep,
sleep, oh sleep without cares."

***

We shivered and clung to one another all night. Snow swirled through the gaping windows.

It was cold. But God was good. Somehow, we made it through.

In the morning, we awoke to knocking. A neighbor was at the door, with wood for a fire, candles and a couple of pots. Some other good people brought a little milk and bread, an egg, some kasha and beans, and some tea.

Ma was so happy she cried. "Thank the Lord we have come among people who have mercy. They have almost nothing themselves, yet they share with us."

We were very careful with the supplies the neighbors brought, keeping the fire small and eating only a little at a time. We lived that way for about a week. Then one morning, more knocking.

Standing there in the doorway in his big fur hat, with a big grin on his face and a pile of wood in his arms, was Uncle Ule Katz.

"Well, thank God I found you," boomed the familiar voice. "Come on boys, help me unload the sled. I've brought you some food and wood."

"Ule!" Ma cried. "Where did you come from, and how in the world did you find us?"

"We were taken to another town about ten miles from here. And you know Ruchel, she wouldn't let me have a moment's rest until I found you. She said to be sure to tell you that we are all together and doing fine. As for finding you, the Germans actually are very organized. The officials have a list of where they put everyone."

"Oh, Uncle, I'm so glad to see you," Rose cried, hugging him.

"Come now, everyone, and meet my good neighbor, Mr. K.," Uncle Ule said, putting his arm around Rose. "He brought me in his sled."

"Thank you, Mr. K.," Ma called as we carried in the bundles of supplies. "Everyone has been so good to us, Ule. If it hadn't been for the good people around here, we would already be dead."

"With us too, Channah," Uncle Ule said. "And take heart. I hear that soon the government will be coming by to board up the windows and make sure the oven is working. And the burgomeister told me they will be giving each family a pension of thirty marks so we will have something to live on."

"Alevai, it should only be so," Ma said. "Come in, both of you. Take some hot tea before you start home. Such a long trip, and it's so cold."

"Tea would taste very good right now," my uncle replied. Mr. K. got down from his sled, stomping snow off his boots and blowing on his hands. We drank hot tea and had a good talk.

"I brought you some flour, beans and a few potatoes and onions," Uncle Ule told us. "I'll try to come back again, Channah, but I don't know how long it will be. Stay together and try to make do until spring."

Then, before we knew it, Uncle Ule and Mr. K. were heading out so they could get back before dark.

"Say hello to Cousin Joe," I called as the sled began to pull away.

Uncle Ule just waved.

We felt a lot better after Uncle Ule's visit and settled in, determined to get through the winter. We got acquainted with our neighbors and asked to work for food, but there wasn't any work to do in the winter. Everyone said they could use us in the spring and would try to help us get by until then.

After a few more days, the soldiers came around to board up the windows and give us the pension Uncle Ule had mentioned.

"Mrs., our commissary is open for all refugees to go in and buy what they need," the lieutenant told my mother, handing her the thirty marks.

"Thank you, lieutenant," Ma replied, tucking the money in her bosom. "I know you mean well, but we don't know where the commissary is or how we could get there."

"It's about five miles straight west of here," he said as his men put their tools back on the wagon. "Ask the people as you go, they'll point the way."

When the soldiers had gone, Rose asked Ma if we could go to the commissary soon.

"Rose, five miles is a long way to walk this time of year, especially if you don't know exactly how to get there. If we were to get caught in a storm before we found the place, we would all surely die. We'll have to be patient and get by with what we have and with what our good neighbors can help us with."

So the commissary was useless to us, and soon we forgot it even existed. We ate very little and sat huddled around the stove most of the time. With the windows boarded up and the snow piled high on the roof, a small fire kept us from freezing — when we could find something to burn. Our neighbors did help with a little food and wood, and we tried to get along until spring.

Meanwhile, from the little bits of news we got here and there from the neighbors, we learned that the fighting was getting worse.

The next morning, I woke up to find Ma feeling Jerry's head again. "Gottenyu! He's burning up."

CHAPTER 10

Spring/Summer 1916

Jerry came in with a few sticks and some straw to start a fire. Then he dropped his load and collapsed to the floor, his back up against the stove.

"I don't feel so good, Ma," he said.

"What's the matter with you?"

"I don't know exactly. I feel sick to my stomach and I'm dizzy."

Ma felt my brother's head. "Oy, Jerry, you've got a fever. Rose, bring me a blanket. Here, keep this on, Jerry. I'll make you a little hot soup."

"No, I don't want anything, Ma. Just let me sleep awhile."

Ma turned to us with a worried look but didn't say anything. Jerry had a bad night, thrashing around and moaning. None of us slept very well.

The next morning, I woke up to find Ma feeling Jerry's head again. "Gottenyu! He's burning up."

"What's the matter with him, Ma? What are we going to do?" Rose asked.

"Go get some water, Rose. I'll make a little broth. Maybe he'll eat something."

I spent that whole day gathering wood so we could keep the fire burning. Ma sat by Jerry the entire time, every few minutes trying to get him to eat. But he was shaking and feverish and wouldn't touch a bite.

This really worried me because Jerry could always eat.

By evening, when he was no better, Ma sent me over to a neighbor to see if they knew where we could find a doctor.

After the neighbors heard Jerry was sick, they were afraid to come near us. And it turned out that the nearest doctor was in the town of Krasnitcha, many miles away.

We were very worried. The next day, Rose and Ma took turns wiping Jerry's face and I kept the fire going, but Jerry just kept shaking and sweating. Then, that evening, I heard a shout from outside.

"Yisroel, come outside!"

I opened the door. One of our neighbors, was standing in front of his sled, a good distance from the house, pointing a shotgun at the man in the seat next to him.

The second man got off the sled with a little nudge from the butt of the gun and walked toward me. Our neighbor stayed in his sled.

"I am a doctor," the man called out. "What is this your neighbor tells me, that someone is very sick here?"

"Oh, yes, sir, my brother Jerry has had a fever for two days. He won't eat anything and just keeps getting worse. Please come in."

The doctor followed me into the house and we got out of his way as he bent to examine Jerry. "You know," he said, "I was very busy with my patients when your neighbor walked in with his gun and insisted I come all the way out here. It's a good thing too. Typhus is spreading with all the new people in the area."

None of us said anything.

"Typhus, just as I thought," the doctor announced, standing up. "It's not good. We have to cool him down, that's his only chance. Have any of you had typhus shots?"

"I have," I answered. "The army doctor in our town gave me a shot when I was helping with the wounded soldiers."

"Well, boy, you'll have to listen to my instructions carefully, because I want your mother and sister to stay away from your brother. Get snow from outside and pack it all around him. Keep it packed on him day and night until he gets better or dies. That is his only chance.

"Now, Mrs., you and your daughter stay away. Keep everyone else away too. And I know it's hard, but make certain you boil all your water, even the water you get from the snow. We think the typhus comes from dirty water."

Ma nodded her head and walked the doctor to the door. "How much do I owe you, doctor?" she asked. "We have very little."

"Nothing, Mrs.," he replied. "Put your money away. You'll need it."

"Thank you, doctor," she said. "Thank you for coming."

"Well, that's some neighbor you have there, Mrs. He made certain I would come. Now start right away with the snow, and good luck."

As the doctor walked back to the sled, I ran outside and called a thank-you to our neighbor. He waved and drove off with the doctor.

Then I took a pot, gathered up the snow and packed it all around Jerry. I barely slept for the next two nights so I could keep fresh snow packed around him the whole time. I couldn't stand the thought of losing my brother. Even though he sometimes teased me, he was my best friend. I loved him.

On the third day, as I nodded off in a corner, I heard a faint but familiar voice.

"Can I have some water?"

Ma jumped up and held a cup to Jerry's lips. As he sipped, she felt his head.

"Danken Got, thank God. He is cool."

"I'll go get some more snow," I said, heading for the door.

"Oh, no you don't," Jerry said with a little grin. "I've had enough snow for a lifetime. Can I have some hot soup, Ma?"

We all laughed. But the scare with Jerry had taught us a lesson. From then on, Ma made sure we boiled all our drinking water and washed everything with boiling water.

***

The weather finally let up a bit and a neighbor took us to the nearest little town, where we bought a few supplies with our pension money.

And time went by. It was still snowy, but it was March. The drifts stopped piling up and the sun came out every once in a while.

After the longest winter of our lives, there was a hint of spring in the air.

***

As happy as we were to see winter fade away, spring brought its own troubles. As the snow melted, there was mud everywhere! Roads and paths were a mess. We rolled up our pant legs and Ma and Rose tied up their skirts. We kept a pail of water by the door so we could wash the mud off our feet.

Fortunately, the little hut we lived in had been built on a low hillock and water didn't seep in to make our dirt floor muddy.

Also, and more troubling, with the warm weather came more typhus in the area. Word had gotten around that I'd had a shot and would not get sick, so I was called on to help many neighbor families. I was glad to help. Everyone had been so kind to us. I was kept very busy most of the spring.

Little by little, our neighbors began to work in their gardens and fields. Ma and Rose helped the wives with their chickens and their gardens, or helped them make pillows and comforters. Jerry was big enough to work in the fields. They thought I was too small for field work, but one farmer gave me a job watching his cows.

I liked that. Every day I got to the farm by dawn and herded the cows out to one of the far fields. Then I sat in the sun most of the day, keeping an eye out for any wild animals and making sure the cows didn't wander off. It was easy work, but one time I did see a wolf. He wasn't really close, but I threw a couple of stones at him anyway.

At noon, the farmer's wife would bring me something to eat with a little pail of cool milk. "Yisroel," she called out one day, walking toward me across the green field. "I fixed up a pair of my son's old pants for you. I'm sure they'll fit. They're made from good, strong cloth that will last awhile — if you don't grow out of them first."

"Oh, thank you, Mrs. C.," I said, taking the pants and holding them up to me. "With everything that has happened to us, I'd barely noticed how bad my clothes had gotten. I can really use these."

That evening when I got home, Ma was pleased. "These are truly good people," she said. "Now if we could only find you some shoes, Beryl, you would be all dressed up."

She was right about the shoes. The boots I had gotten from the young German soldier had fallen apart. I had kept them tied together until spring but then I gave up. Now I went barefoot like Jerry and Rose.

One morning early that summer, Ma called us together. "Children, tell the farmers that you won't be working for a few days. I think it's time we tried to get to the commissary to buy a few things and get our lives a little bit back to normal."

"How are we going to get there, Ma?" Rose asked.

"The weather is good and God gave us two strong legs. We should be able to walk five miles. We'll start out early tomorrow, and God willing, we'll be back by Thursday evening."

***

We left early in the morning, headed in the direction where people said we would find the commissary. It was a beautiful summer day. With the sun shining down on us and the air smelling so sweet, we almost forgot about the war.

For the first time in a long time, we felt better.

Along the way, Ma stopped from time to time to ask people on the road if we were headed in the right direction. As the day wore on, we began to tire. The commissary, a man along the road informed us, was more like ten miles from our little village, not five miles like the German lieutenant had told us over the winter. But finally, from a hillside late in the afternoon, we saw a long, low building at the edge of a town. That was the commissary.

We went to the door and showed a soldier our papers, and he let us in. We mostly got basic things like beans, kasha, salt and flour. But Ma looked through the used clothes piles and found me a shirt, a pair of pants for Jerry and a skirt for Rose. We didn't find any decent shoes or boots, so we were still barefoot.

It was getting dark by the time we left the commissary. Lugging our packages, we climbed the hillside, curled up under a tree and spent the night. The next morning, we packed up everything onto our backs and began our walk home.

It was slow going with all the extra weight, but it was another warm, sunny day and our hearts were light.

"Children," Ma said determinedly as we started out, "first we are going to stop in Krasnitcha and give the rebbe a few pennies to thank God for his help. Then tomorrow, we are going to clean the house and make a real Shabbes again."

Jerry threw his cap in the air and shouted with joy, then began talking excitedly about how he would chop some extra wood. Rose added that although she never thought she would hear herself say it, she could hardly wait to clean the house.

I tried to think of something I could do. "I'll make the gribenes," I finally volunteered. And everybody had a good laugh.

The following night, we had a wonderful Shabbes. We didn't have a lot to eat, but Jerry said the blessing and the candles sparkled off the clean walls.

We felt like a real family again.

***

That Saturday, the farmer I worked for walked by our house. "What's this, Yisroel?" he called. "No work today?"

"Ah, Farmer C., good day to you," Ma said, wiping her hands on her ragged apron as she came out the door. "Today is our Sabbath and we don't work."

"But you worked every day this spring."

"Yes, that is true, we worked every day all spring. But now that we have body and soul together a little bit again, we will honor the Sabbath. God will forgive us for not doing so before."

Our neighbors were surprised that we didn't work for one entire day each week, but they were very respectful and understanding. So, from then on, we worked hard all week and kept the Sabbath on the seventh day.

We didn't get much news of the war, living way out in the country like we did, and Ma mentioned a couple of times that she was worried about Sam. We didn't get any mail so we didn't hear anything from Papa, and we assumed he had no idea what had happened to us. And Uncle Ule hadn't been back to see us.

But our summer in Poland passed, and it was hard but bearable because of the good people we lived among.

I missed working outside with the cows but I was glad to have work inside during the cold weather.

CHAPTER 11

Winter/Spring 1916-1617

Fall brought harvest time, and then we had plenty of work. The farmers were generous and gave us a goodly amount of food from the harvest in payment for the work we had done all spring and summer.

As it got colder, the cows began staying closer to the barn and I had to find different work. Ma found me a job helping in a shop.

Mr. and Mrs. Z., the man and woman who owned the shop, showed me what to do and gave me a new shirt to wear.

I missed working outside with the cows but I was glad to have work inside during the cold weather.

In the middle of the winter, Mr. and Mrs. Z. came to our house to visit. As we sat on the benches Jerry had made and sipped our tea, Mr. Z. told Ma he had something important he wanted to discuss.

"Mrs. Aynbinder," he said, "as you know, we have no children. Your Yisroel is a fine boy and we would like very much to adopt him."

Nobody said anything.

"We know you would not usually think of such a thing," Mr. Z. continued. "But you can barely feed yourself and the children. We are all facing a very hard winter, and who knows how long this war will last. We can give Yisroel a good life with us."

Ma was quiet. I was very surprised and worried. I knew how hard it was for my mother to take care of us.

I felt sick to my stomach. I liked Mr. and Mrs. Z, but I didn't want to be their son. I had a family.

"Mr. and Mrs. Z, you are fine people," Ma finally said. "And you are right, we are living from hand to mouth. But someday this war will be over and we will go home. And I could never live with myself if I left my Beryl here. No matter what happens, we will stay together."

I sat there listening, looking at Jerry and Rose. I was so glad Ma wasn't going to let Mr. and Mrs. Z. adopt me. Back home, such adoptions were not uncommon, when one couple had no children and another family had too many mouths to feed.

Mrs. Z. took my mother's hand in hers. "Mrs. Aynbinder, we could only hope to have such children as yours. Unfortunately, we were never blessed with children. We understand your feelings. Perhaps I may make another suggestion. Yisroel is working in the store all day long and it is dark and cold when he has to come home, with the snow piled up so high. Maybe you will let him live with us awhile, until you can go home?"

Ma was quiet again.

"I promise you, we will be good to him," Mrs. Z. continued. "He will have enough to eat and a warm place to sleep."

There was more silence, giving me plenty of time to think. Mr. and Mrs. Z. were good people. They weren't my family, but maybe staying with them awhile wouldn't be so bad. I would get more to eat.

"Yisroel," Ma finally said, turning to me. It sounded strange to hear Ma call me by my given name. She took a deep breath before she continued.

"Yisroel, I would be very thankful to have you in a good, warm place this winter where you will have enough to eat. I think for the time being, you should go live with these kind people. Things are only getting worse. We won't have enough to feed all of us through the winter. Stay with them. Come back to us when the weather is good, and we will visit as often as we can. What do you think?"

I was so relieved I wasn't going to be adopted that staying over the winter with the Zs sounded just fine to me. "Sure, Ma. It's just for the winter and I can come for Shabbes when the weather is good."

"I'll come visit every day, Beryl," Jerry said.

Rose was quietly crying. "Don't cry, Rose," Ma said. "This is a very good chance for your brother and will help us all. There is a war going on, and we have to do everything we can to survive."

Ma turned to Mr. and Mrs. Z. "Thank you, both. I am truly grateful for your help. Just last week I had a chance to ask the burgomeister how long he thought we would have to stay here and he didn't know. He said he would try to find out, but that he thought things in Russia were getting even worse. There has been rioting in the streets, and soldiers are deserting the army and roaming the countryside making trouble."

Ma turned to me again. "Beryl, you will stay with these good people starting tomorrow. Be good and do everything you are asked, with a good will."

Ma looked like she was about to cry. I got up and walked over to her. "Don't worry, Ma," I said. "It's all right. I like working in the store. I promise I'll work hard and be good."

Ma reached out and hugged me. Mr. and Mrs. Z. got up to leave and Ma thanked them again as they went out the door.

For the rest of the winter, I stayed with Mr. and Mrs. Z., working in the store all day and staying in their home in back of the store at night. I missed my family, even though Jerry stopped in to visit every few days between snowstorms.

And it was a good thing I stayed with them, because it was a very bad winter. Snow piled up to the tops of the houses and food was very scarce for everybody. But Mr. and Mrs. Z. treated me kindly and while I didn't have a lot to eat, at least I had enough. And I was warm.

***

We finally got through the winter. And in spring 1917, we heard about a revolution in Russia.

I was back at our little house for Shabbes when Jerry came bursting in. "Hi, Beryl," he said. "Boy, did I ever just hear some news."

"Not now, Jerry," Ma interrupted. "It's late. First we make Shabbes, then you can tell us your news." She turned to the table to light the Sabbath candles.

Jerry seemed so excited that I could hardly wait to hear what was so important. But first he made the blessing over the bread. Then, while we ate our soup dinner, Jerry told us what he had heard.

"I was in town, taking Mr. C's horse to the blacksmith. A bunch of people were in front of the burgomeister's office, and I went over to see what all the fuss was about. There was a notice posted on the door telling about a revolution in Russia."

"So, what's new about a revolution in Russia?" Ma said. "There are always revolutions in Russia. It has never meant any good for us."

"But I think this one is different, Ma. The whole country is completely in revolt. Oh, and by the way, there's no more tsar."

"What do you mean, no more tsar? Impossible! Who is the government?"

"I'm not sure, Ma. All the soldiers are running away from the army, and the different political parties are fighting over who is going to run the country."

Ma didn't know what to say. This was all very hard for her to imagine.

"Jerry, are the Russians still fighting the Germans?" I asked.

"I don't know, Beryl. Some of the men standing around the burgomeister's office said Russian soldiers were still fighting. But one man said he had heard the Russian soldiers were killing their officers and going to help the Bolsheviks take over the government."

"What's a Bolshevik?" Rose asked.

"I don't know exactly," Jerry answered, "but it seems like they want a different kind of government."

Ma decided she would try to find out how this news affected us. "Next week," she said, "I will go to the burgomeister and ask if he knows how much longer we will have to stay here."

"Oh, I hope we can go home soon," I said. "I know Zayde needs us."

Ma and Jerry looked at me. Rose started to say something, but Ma shook her head. They went back to eating their soup.

Later that evening, as Rose finished cleaning up and Jerry tended the fire, Ma called me over. I sat next to her on one of the benches. She put her arm around me and looked down into my face.

"Beryl," she said, "you're big enough to understand now. You know your Zayde was very sick when we had to leave home. And he was very old, ninety-six, to be exact. You must understand that he may be gone by now."

It was true that I was going to be twelve years old pretty soon and had thought I was starting to understand more about the world. But I was not prepared for this.

A lump swelled in my throat. My eyes burned.

"No, Ma," I said, my voice cracking as the first tear rolled down my cheek. "Zayde wasn't so old. He had all his teeth and didn't even need glasses."

"I know, Beryl. But just the same, it's hard enough on the young to get through this war. Zayde was happy God let him be with us for so long."

"But he'll be there when we get home, Ma. I know he will."

"Maybe so, Beryl. But if God has taken him, you must remember the happy times and be thankful you had such a Zayde."

I tried hard not to cry, but it was no use. Ma pulled me closer and I buried my wet face in her shoulder. Of all the bad things that had happened to us, thinking of Zayde not being there when we got home was the hardest.

I curled up near the stove next to Jerry and tried to sleep, but I just kept thinking about Zayde and home.

***

I went back to Mr. and Mrs. Z.'s, and early the next week, Jerry stopped in at the store. He said Ma had gone to see the burgomeister, who told her he hadn't heard anything yet about the refugees going home. But he promised Ma he would try to find out more.

Meanwhile, we started to hear more news. In May we heard that the tsar had abdicated in March and gone to live with his family at the palace at Tsarskoye Selo. In June we heard the Russians were still fighting the Germans but were losing.

And then one day later that summer, Jerry came running into the shop. "Beryl!" he shouted as he came through the door. I was on a little ladder arranging items on a shelf. As soon as I turned around and saw him, I knew he had good news.

"Beryl, we're going home! Ma just got word from the burgomeister. Everybody is going home!"

I hopped off the ladder and grabbed Jerry. I was so excited I was jumping up and down. "When, Jerry? When are we going!"

"Tomorrow or the next day," Jerry said, jumping with me. "The Germans are going to pick us up in a wagon and take us to the train."

That stopped my jumping. I remembered the train we had come on.

"A train? You mean a train like the one we took here?"

"I don't know, Beryl, but who cares? We'll be going home. Come on, say goodbye to everyone. Ma wants you back at the house."

Mr. and Mrs. Z had been listening with smiles on their faces but sadness in their eyes.

I turned and hugged them both and thanked them for being so good to me.

"You've been such a good boy, Yisroel," Mrs. Z. said. "You've been like my own child. I'm going to miss you." She hugged me again.

I went into the kitchen at the back of the store to gather up my few things. I heard Mrs. Z. softly crying as she quickly packed a little food for our journey.

Jerry was waiting outside when I left the shop and we ran all the way back to our little house.

Two days later, a wagon pulled up. It was already almost filled with another family, but we took our few things and piled in anyway, talking and laughing.

It took almost all day to get to the train station. When we got there, we came among many other families who had been staying in other little towns in the area.

This time it was a train with a few benches to sit on and windows. We all climbed aboard, friendly and happy. Even though we were all crowded together and had to take turns sitting, it was nothing like our last train ride.

We were going home.

PART III
ANARCHY AND EMIGRATION

T HE FRENCH REVOLUTION of 1789 precipitated the brave new social thinking that influenced Karl Marx and Friedrich Engels. In 1847, they conceived and published the "Communist Manifesto," which offered a plan of action to forcibly overthrow the old social order. The State would seize all land, introduce a confiscatory income tax and abolish the right of inheritance. The State would also seize control of banks, transport and factories, and provide free public education for all. This philosophy greatly influenced Lenin and the Russian Revolution of 1917.

At the beginning of the twentieth century, Russia was ripe for revolution. The Russo-Japanese War had served to undermine tsarist authority. And what started out on January 22, 1905, as a peaceful march by Saint Petersburg workers, to petition the tsar for an eight-hour workday and minimum wage, became a bloody slaughter by the tsar's troops. That ignited the revolution of 1905.

By New Year's Day 1906 the revolution of the previous year had been quashed, but between then and 1917, various political factions in Russia continued to feud. The Mensheviks were opposed to terrorism and wanted a legal, broad-based government.

Lenin, greatly influenced by Marx's writing, led the Bolsheviks and maintained that there would have to be a violent takeover of the government.

The losses and hardships of the Russo-Japanese War were soon followed by World War I in 1914. Placing even more stress on the backward nation of Russia, it again enhanced conditions for revolution — war, high-pressure speedup of industry, food shortages, high prices and the loss of loved ones.

By the end of 1916, the demoralized Russian army was disintegrating. As disaster overtook the army, the liberal members of the Duma blamed the tsarist bureaucracy. The evil influence of the monk Rasputin over the weak Tsar Nicholas II, and desperate shortages and panic in the country, led the Duma to consider either a separate peace with Germany or removal of the tsar. But they feared a mass revolution should they topple the tsar.

On December 29, 1916, a group of nobles, fearing impending revolt, killed Rasputin. This seemed to clear the way for some sort of reform. But nothing changed.

Then "the February Revolution" exploded in the streets of Petrograd, formerly Saint Petersburg. This five-day struggle did eventually lead to the downfall of the tsar.

The first impetus for revolt came with the recovery of Rasputin's body from the River Neva on New Year's Day, 1917. Food was already in short supply when bread rationing was introduced in Petrograd on March 1. Long lines of women waited in icy weather for a few ounces of bread. The misery of the people reached a new high.

On March 8, International Woman's Day, ninety-thousand women from the textile factories and as many men from the huge Putilov metalworks marched down the streets. The next day, the number of people in the streets doubled. At least half the industrial workers of Petrograd were on strike.

To quell the mob, the government turned to the Cossacks, that privileged tribe of warrior horsemen Russian rulers had depended on for centuries. This time, however, the Cossacks refused to intervene.

On March 10, the strike spread throughout the city. Students and businessmen joined 240,000 workers. The police went into hiding. The Cossacks still did not interfere. Then the government called upon the army regiments stationed in the city. The soldiers refused to shoot their own people but they were not yet ready to join the revolt.

By this time the revolutionary leaders, living in exile, realized what was happening and rushed to assume leadership. They called for a three-day general strike. By the morning of March 11, police stations were being wrecked and guns and ammunition were being handed out to the people.

Army officers again ordered their men to shoot, while the strikers continued to prevail upon the soldiers to join them in revolt. On March 12, the Petrograd regiments joined the mob. Officers who weren't killed fled into hiding. The great fortress of Peter and Paul was stormed and taken, and all of Petrograd was in the hands of the people. Then revolutionary regiments marched on the Duma at the Tauride Palace.

While the Duma was setting up a committee to sort out events in one wing of the palace, a council, or "soviet," was being established in another wing. By the evening of March 12, the diverse members of the soviet had approved fusing the proletariat of the capital with revolutionary forces of the army, creating an organization called the Soviet of Workers and Soldiers Deputies.

Faced with the new power of the Soviet, Duma members decided to send a delegation to the tsar with instructions to obtain his abdication. The night of March 15, 1917, Nicholas II abdicated and went to join his family at Tsarskoye Selo.

On March 16, things quieted. The Romanov dynasty was gone and a red flag flew over the tsar's winter palace.

A Provisional Government was formed by the aristocrat Cadets and the Soviet of Workers and Soldiers Deputies. These groups, however, had conflicting aims. The Cadets wanted to continue the war against Germany and get things quickly back to the way they'd been under the tsar. The Menshevik faction of the

Soviet believed they needed to side with the Cadets for a time to create order. The Bolshevik faction of the Soviet wanted an immediate end to the war and no interim social compromise.

Meanwhile, revolution spread all across Russia.

Into the leadership void came Lenin. Arriving on April 16, 1917, from exile in Switzerland, he came to wild acclaim from the Petrograd masses and immediately called for international social revolution. By the end of April there was a Provisional Government with no real power, a Soviet with almost no direction, and Lenin and his Bolsheviks.

The following period of Russian history illustrates the ebb and flow of popular political opinion and is divided into four periods known as "the April Days," "the June Demonstration," "the July Days" and "the Counterrevolution."

The first crisis at the end of April was caused by the Provisional Government's foreign minister sending a note to the Allied governments promising Russia would continue to fight Germany. When the note was published, the people spontaneously took to the streets and again marched on the Tauride Palace. The protesters forced a new Provisional Government to be formed, which included six socialists.

But the new Provisional Government proved no better than the last and under pressure from the Allies decided to send troops on the offensive against Germany. Angry soldiers began listening to the Bolsheviks, who seemed to be the only party wanting to end the war.

At the end of June, the Provisional Government called for a demonstration. The thinking was that the people would back their conservative views. More than 400,000 workers marched, however most carried banners backing the Bolsheviks. "The June Demonstration" was clearly a Bolshevik victory.

At this point the Russian army, which had been ordered to go on the offensive, was defeated in a major battle. The Cadet ministers resigned, leaving the socialist ministers to take the blame. This set off the public outburst known as "the July Days."

On July 16, the Bolsheviks sent delegates to the local regiments and factories asking soldiers and workers to join in forcing their demands on the Provisional Government. Tens of thousands took to the streets.

Disorder spread.

On July 17, sailors from the naval base at Kronstadt seized the Peter and Paul fortress. For two days and nights the crowd, in an ugly mood, tried to force the Soviet leadership of the Provisional Government to take power. The Soviet leaders refused, believing they were not yet ready to rule. "The July Days" came to an end.

It was apparent, however, that the masses would listen only to the Bolsheviks. The revolution was not over.

But the Provisional Government decided to take drastic action against the Bolsheviks and announced it had evidence that Lenin and the other leaders were paid agents of Germany. The effect was stunning. Workers, soldiers and peasants alike felt betrayed. The Bolshevik leaders escaped from Petrograd with the mob at their heels. Who would lead now? The forces of "the Counterrevolution" were ready to step in.

Former government officials, large landowners and industrialists, the rightists and army officers believed their time had come to again take command. But the people were not deceived. They understood this group was only trying to restore the old order. "The Counterrevolution" was defeated.

By the end of September, the Bolsheviks were again strong enough to demand new elections to the Presidium, the governing board of the Soviet, and won control of the governing body of the revolution. Trotsky was elected chairman. All over Russia, the Bolsheviks came into power in local soviets.

The Presidium immediately passed resolutions withdrawing support for the Kerensky government and demanding land redistribution and an end to the war.

Now came "the Bolshevik Revolution." On September 25, 1917, Lenin wrote a letter from exile declaring that the Bolsheviks must organize an armed insurrection to seize power. Still, the Central Committee was afraid to pick up the reins.

Lenin knew they couldn't afford to wait. The time was ripe. The power was already in their hands. Lenin knew he must strike before the land was redistributed to the peasants. He knew that once redistribution occurred, the peasants would lose interest and the revolution would fail.

Kerensky in the meantime had organized a "Pre-Parliament" to rule until the Constitutional Assembly convened on November 2. The Bolsheviks sent a delegation to the opening of the Pre-Parliament and condemned the Kerensky government. Trotsky called for an armed insurrection and the Bolshevik delegation walked out.

The Bolsheviks then set up a Military Revolutionary Committee with Trotsky as chairman and Lenin in overall authority. Meanwhile, in September and October the German army continued to advance, taking Riga and Reval and heading toward Petrograd.

On the night of October 23, 1917, Lenin returned to Petrograd in disguise. He met with the Central Committee and a resolution was passed calling for an armed uprising.

Now the real organization came to the fore. Hundreds of party rank and file, together with the factory workers and army regiments, took over the arsenals, armed the people, got out information pamphlets and organized the regiments. In effect, the Bolsheviks were already ruling Russia.

Mass meetings were held throughout the city on Sunday, November 4. The ecstatic masses poured out by the hundreds of thousands to hear speakers in factories and meeting halls. After a lifetime of poverty and bitterness, they felt certain they were on the road to a brighter future.

Kerensky left the city and headed for the front, hoping to return with new army detachments. His government holed up in the winter palace. On the night of November 16, 1917, organized squads of workers, soldiers and peasants went about taking control of the government. There was no resistance. At 10 a.m. November 17, Trotsky issued a proclamation declaring that the Provisional Government had fallen.

Meanwhile, the Congress of Soviets continued in session amid the uproar. The Mensheviks, Social Revolutionaries and Independents denounced the Bolsheviks, but Trotsky replied: "No compromise, you are pitiful, isolated individuals. Your role is played out. Go where you belong from now on, into the rubbish can of history."

BULLETIN: September 13, 1917

RUSSIANS ARREST GEN. KORNILOV
REDS GROW STRONGER

"So, who are these Bolsheviks?" Ma asked. "And what good are they to us?"

CHAPTER 12

1917-1919

The day was sunny and unusually warm for September. But even if it had been cold and gray, we would have been happy.

This time it didn't matter how long the ride would take, because we knew we were going home.

As we boarded the train, a soldier told us we would be left at a town about fifteen miles from Horchov. "I'll walk all the way home from there, Ma," Rose said. "I won't mind walking one little bit."

Jerry and I laughed. Before the war Rose had liked nice shoes but hadn't liked to walk a lot because the shoes pinched her toes. But that didn't matter now. None of us had any shoes.

As we traveled, everyone shared bits of news they had heard over the past few months.

"Yes, it's true, the tsar abdicated," an old man across the aisle said. "A group of soldiers and peasants are holding him and his family at the Tsarskoye Selo palace until they decide what to do with him."

"They'll probably send them to Germany, to the tsarina's family," another man suggested. "Or maybe to England, to his cousin."

"So, who's in charge now?" I asked no one in particular.

"Ah," a young man who had been helping his wife with their children answered knowingly. "We heard from one of the officers that

Kerensky is still prime minister, but the Bolsheviks are growing stronger. There's going to be a Constitutional Assembly in November."

"So, who are these Bolsheviks?" Ma asked. "And what good are they to us?"

"First of all, Mrs., they want to end the war. Then they want the government to own everything," the man said. "The government will be made up from the workers, peasants, soldiers and intellectuals. There will be no more aristocrats. The people will run the government for everybody."

"Ach, don't you believe it," a man behind us said. "They'll run the government for themselves. The Russians will never include the Jews."

And so it went on and off, back and forth, until we came to the end of our journey.

As the train slowed, everyone became quiet, gathered their belongings and stared out the windows.

We rolled into an old, shell-pocked station with people waiting by the tracks. Some stood with pushcarts, a few others with wagons pulled by broken-down horses, a mule, even a goat.

"Hey, Ma," Jerry called as we waited for the passengers in front of us to move. "I think I see Sam out there."

For an instant, a hopeful look crossed Ma's face. Then it vanished. "No, it can't be," she said. "Sam is in the army."

"No, Ma, I really think it's him. Look at that wagon over there."

We squeezed up to the window to see where Jerry was pointing. Rose saw him right away. "It is Sam!" she cried.

In a minute, Ma spotted him too. "Oy, it is Sam, thank God he's alive. But what is he doing here? And how did he know we were coming?"

"I don't know, Ma," I answered. "But I'm going to find out."

I pushed my way to the door with Jerry right behind me. We jumped down to the platform and ran toward Sam, yelling his name.

He turned, spotted us and jumped down from his wagon. We dropped our bundles and hugged him. In his usual quiet way, Sam said nothing, just smiled and hugged back. A few moments later, Ma and Rose were all over him.

After a while, we picked up the bags of beans and potatoes we had brought back with us and piled into the wagon. "So, Sam, tell us how you got here and what's been going on," Jerry said.

"And the family?" Ma asked. "Have you heard from anyone?"

"And Zayde?" I asked, looking up at Sam.

Sam looked down at me. "Zayde's gone, Beryl," he said softly.

My throat tightened with tears. Everyone was quiet for a few moments while I stared at the ground.

"The family is all home, though," Sam eventually continued. "After Zayde died, Brendel and the kids moved back in with her family about fifty miles from Horchov. But they moved back into Zayde's house when the soldiers left this spring, just about the time Moishe got home."

"And Ruchel and Ule and the children?" Ma asked.

"They got home two weeks ago. That's how I knew you were coming home, because Uncle Ule had a list from the burgomeister. But

Tante Ruchel and Uncle Ule are very unhappy right now, Ma. You'll have to talk to them."

"What's wrong?" Ma asked.

"I think Cousin Joe and Uncle Ule had a fight. I don't know exactly what happened, but Joe left home."

"No wonder they're upset," Ma said, shaking her head. "I'll talk with Ruchel. There must have been a good reason."

"And how did you get out of the army?" Rose asked Sam.

"Don't you know what's happening? There's a revolution going on," Sam said.

"We've heard some news, but not much," Jerry said.

"Well," Sam said, "when the officers ordered us to shoot the strikers in Petrograd, the soldiers refused. They wouldn't shoot their own people. Of course, we Jews couldn't say much or else we would be shot by the officers, but when the officers ran away, the sergeants let us go. Most of the men went home, but some of the soldiers are hanging around getting into trouble. Things are not so good here, but we can talk about all that later with the rest of the family."

Sam clucked to his horse and we headed east toward Horchov. I sat next to Ma on the hard wagon bench, laughing right along with everyone. I was happy to be back, but my heart hurt now that I knew Zayde wasn't at home waiting for us.

Ma knew what I was thinking. She put her arm around me. "Beryl, remember what I said before. Be glad God saw us through. Your Zayde lived a good, long life, and he would be happy to see that we stayed together and made it back safely."

I began to cheer up a little, and before I knew it we were home. Uncle Moishe, Tante Brendel, Tevia and all my little cousins welcomed us.

To my surprise, the littlest one remembered me — he took hold around my leg and wouldn't let go. And Tevia looked like he'd grown a foot. I wasn't the only one growing up.

When I asked Tevia how he got so tall, he kidded right back. "Oh, no, I'm not taller, it's just that my old pants have gotten shorter." It felt good to laugh together again.

It was good to be home.

We settled back into the house and Ma and Tante Brendel began to prepare a little supper. "Nu, Channah, so how was it with you?" Tante asked Ma as the two of them worked together once more in the old kitchen.

"I thought we had truly come to hell," Ma answered, shaking her head. "So many died on the train, frozen to death before we even came to Poland.

"Then, when they left us in that little village, in a tiny hut with no food and nothing to burn, I thought for certain we would die.

"But God was good, Brendel. He brought us among good people, Polish peasants who did their best to help us. And so you see, we survived."

"Well, thank God you're back safe and sound," I heard Tante say as I went off to find Tevia.

The next evening, Tante Ruchel and Uncle Ule came over. After all the hugging, we sat down to supper and compared stories.

Ma looked over at Ruchel. "So, Ruchel, what's this I hear about Joe leaving home. Where did he go? What happened?"

Ruchel didn't answer right away, but instead looked down and poked a little at her food. "Ask him," she finally said, nodding over at Uncle Ule.

"Ule, what's going on?" Ma asked.

Uncle Ule put down his glass of tea.

"Channah, we have nothing here and I'm getting too old to help all the children. Raising sixteen of them has not been easy. Not long before we were sent away to Poland, I told Joe it was time for him to leave and make his own way. It was the best thing I could do for him. But I'm afraid he holds it against me that I pushed him out."

Tears began rolling down Tante Ruchel's face. "We heard from an acquaintance that he has worked his way to America," she said, dabbing at her eyes. "But he hasn't written us, and we don't know where he is. I'm afraid we'll never see him again."

"Don't cry, Ruchel," Ma said, patting her on the back. "When things settle down and the mail starts getting through again, you'll hear. And if not, we'll ask Mordecai to look for him in America."

I almost said something about America being a big country and how it might be hard for Papa to find Cousin Joe. But I stopped myself, realizing it would only get Tante Ruchel more upset.

***

After supper, we all went to a meeting at the shul to find out what was happening.

Everything was different. Many people had died, Mr. Schwartz the tailor, Mr. and Mrs. Rabinowitz, the gabbai from the shul. All gone.

The shul had a big hole in one wall and part of the roof had fallen in. But we all piled in anyway and pulled up the few chairs and benches or sat on the floor.

"So, what's happening, Ule?" asked Mr. Miller the butcher. He and his family had also just returned.

"Things are pretty bad," Uncle Ule replied as everyone gathered around. "The entire country is in revolt. The peasants are marching around demanding land. The soldiers have no leaders and are running wild, looting and shooting people just for the fun of it. And the politicians can't get a hold on the government because they're too busy fighting with each other over what kind of government they should have."

Lev, the baker's son, spoke up. "The Germans left a lot of guns and rifles lying around. I think we should pick up what we can and bring them back to the shul. We may have to protect ourselves from all these hooligans."

"Shame on you, Lev," the old rebbe said. "We should put our trust in God and go back to studying his law. We have no business fighting with these people."

"No, rebbe, Lev is right," Uncle Moishe said. "We have to protect our families. I think we should organize our own militia to protect the community."

Everyone started talking at once. Finally, it was decided that Lev and Uncle Moishe would organize a militia made up of themselves and the other men who had been in the army. We kids would be sent out to pick up all the guns and ammunition we could find. The women would gather up what medicine they could and prepare bandages and a place to keep anyone who was wounded.

***

And then, talk about trouble. Everything just started up all over again. There was no work, there were no jobs. There was very little food.

Russia was without police, schools or newspapers. We didn't even have a government. The Kerensky group and the Bolsheviks struggled for power.

We hungered for news.

"Hear anything today?" Uncle Moishe asked Jerry as he joined us for a meager supper.

"Not much, Uncle."

Sam looked up. "The men at the market say Kerensky still is trying to restore the monarchy."

"Yes, but the Bolsheviks are fighting to take over," Jerry said. "They have people going around trying to convince everyone to join them."

"I know," Uncle Moishe said. "There was a group by the old market today talking to everyone going by."

"So, what do they say?" Ma asked.

"Well, Channah, they say they are for everybody — all people will be equal because the state will own everything. No one will be better off than the next person."

"They call it socialism," Jerry added.

"Ach, it can never be so," Ma scoffed. "How can aristocrats and peasants be the same? And where does a Jew fit into all of this socialism?"

No one had an answer. After a few moments, I spoke up.

"I don't know, Ma. But some of the men I talked with today are afraid. They say they don't know whether Kerensky or the Bolsheviks are right, but with so many peasants and soldiers running wild, and the Bolshevik Red Guards killing anybody who's against them, we'd all better watch out."

With that unnerving thought hanging in the air, we were all quiet for a while as we finished our soup. When the women rose to clear the table, Uncle Moishe broke the silence.

"Let's keep our eyes and ears open and stay close to home," he said. "Who knows what will happen with all of these different groups running around like meshuggeners."

***

Then everything became like a wilding. Ordinary people shooting one another. Peasants seeking land, shooting estate managers. Soldiers looting, raping and burning. Workers fighting in the streets over which party should lead the government.

One Shabbes, we heard horses pulling up outside the shul. Ten men with guns burst in.

"All right, Jews, give us your money!" the first man demanded.

The rebbe came down from the bima, the platform, and we all stood, hiding Lev as he crawled behind us and slipped out the back door.

The rebbe tried to calm the robbers as we took our time finding the few pennies we had in our pockets. Two of the intruders ran up onto the bima and took the Kiddush cup and Torah cover. Another took the brass samovar on the corner table.

A couple of the robbers ran down the rows collecting our money. "Hurry up, Jew, put your money in this bag, now!" one of them shouted, striking Yankel with the end of his gun.

The blood spurted from Yankel's face just as the doors burst open again. And there, in all its glory, was our little militia.

"Stop!" Lev commanded, pointing his gun at the leader of the gang. The robbers stopped dead in their tracks, stunned that Jews had guns and were fighting back. They dropped everything and raised their hands over their heads.

"Are you all right, Yankel?" Lev asked.

"I'm fine now," Yankel said, holding a hand to his face.

"We're taking you to jail until we can notify the authorities," Lev said firmly. With a no-nonsense expression on his face, he and the other militiamen marched the robbers out the door. Then, just as he left, Lev turned his head and gave us a quick little wink.

Everyone breathed a sigh of relief and began slapping each other on the back. It took quite a while before we could settle down and return to our Shabbes prayers, and that evening, the day's events were rehashed over and over. Everyone was very pleased.

"So, Moishe, what did the militia do with the hooligans?" Ma asked the next morning.

"We couldn't find any authorities to turn them over to, Channah, so we took their guns and horses, held them till they sobered up and let them go."

"You let them go?" I asked. "Uncle Moishe, won't they just come back?"

"I don't think so, Beryl. Not this group, anyway. I think we really surprised them."

Aside from Yankel's bloodied face, our little militia had passed its first test with flying colors. But I think everyone knew we might not always be so lucky.

***

So now some of the people in our town tried to start up in business again. The old tin man, Mr. Pinkus, pushed a cart with pieces of iron; another old man tried to sell a few vegetables he managed to dig from a field. A husband and wife took old uniforms and turned them into clothes.

Jerry and I got jobs helping to clean up a ranch where Papa had once worked. Rose remade old clothes at the tailor shop.

People worked at any little job they could find, just to get along and try to get their lives back together and clean up the town. But every time it got quiet for a while, something else happened to get things boiling again.

In November refugees from Petrograd told us of mass meetings staged by the Bolsheviks. By December we heard the Bolsheviks were in control of that city. But power struggles continued between various groups in Moscow, Kyiv and other faraway parts of the country.

We heard that people in some of those places were even trying to break away from Russia altogether and form independent states.

Although there were no newspapers, from time to time a notice would be posted on the door of the old burgomeister's office. We would also hear things from refugees or tradesmen traveling through.

Our Jewish people began meeting every Saturday evening after Shabbes at the big red shul. We would pass along any news we had heard the previous week and discuss how it might affect us.

We began to hear that the Bolsheviks were gaining more control. Private ownership of land was abolished, and banks, industries and the merchant marine were nationalized. Church lands were seized, religious teaching outlawed.

Class titles were abolished, and we were all supposed to call one another "comrade."

In the November 1917 elections, the peasants did not vote for the Bolsheviks because the Bolsheviks wanted to nationalize all land, while the peasants wanted the land divided up and given over to them. But even though the Bolsheviks failed to win control of the government in the election, they had the industrial workers and soldiers on their side and they soon ousted all the other convention delegates, including the peasant delegates.

Everyone braced for civil war.

As all of this went on, food and jobs became even more scarce as the winter became bitter cold. And even as the snow piled up, peasants and soldiers continued roaming the countryside making trouble.

The Bolsheviks knew the peasants wanted peace and believed they could win them over to the Bolshevik party if they could just stop the war. So in March 1918 at Brest-Litovsk — against the wishes of Russia's allies — the Bolsheviks made a separate peace treaty with Germany.

"Jerry!" I yelled, running as I spotted my brother down the street.

He stopped and turned, waiting for me to catch up. "Beryl, what's going on?"

"Yankel just told me the Bolsheviks have signed a treaty with Germany."

"Hey, that's great news!"

"I know. Yankel said we got word so fast because they signed the treaty right near here, at Brest-Litovsk. So, what do you think? Do you think things will get back to normal now?"

Jerry hesitated, his excitement cooling.

"I don't know, Beryl," he said. "The peasants are still very angry about the land, and you know the ex-soldiers and Reds are still making a lot of trouble. Let's go see what Uncle Moishe thinks."

We made our way to Uncle Moishe's old store, which was now a shop where people could bring things to trade for other items they needed.

"What do you think, Uncle?" Jerry asked after we had shared our news.

"I don't know, boys, this is an awfully big country. It's going to be hard for the Bolsheviks or anyone else to control things, at least for a while. Why, there are pockets of Austrian and German troops scattered all over. How are they going to pull out and get home without causing more trouble?

"And the peasants will fight for getting some of the land for themselves. They've had enough of being almost slaves to the landowners."

We all looked at each other and Uncle Moishe shook his head. "I'm afraid it's going to be a mess for a good while yet," he concluded.

Deflated, we left the store just as some stray horses galloped past. We jumped back into the doorway and watched as a couple of people who had been in the street ran for cover. The speeding animals kicked up a messy mix of snow and mud.

"You know," Jerry said, "there are horses running around all over the place. There must be something we could do with them."

We were willing to work hard and do just about anything we could to survive. But it wasn't Jerry or me who thought of a way to make money off the stray horses. It was Sam.

When Sam cornered us in the shul one evening that May, we were ready to listen.

"Yankel, Herschel and I just bought a few horses," Sam told us. "If you two can catch some strays to put together with ours, we'll have enough of a herd to sell."

"Who are we going to sell to, Sam?" I asked.

"If we can get across the lines, the Germans or Austrians will buy them. They lost a lot of horses this past winter."

Jerry was skeptical. "How are you going to get across the lines and find the Germans? And who's going to help you?"

"You are," Sam replied with a grin. "We've all worked with horses."

"Hey, that's right, Sam," I said. "We could handle them easy. When do we go?"

"Not so fast, Beryl," Sam said. "First see if you can catch us a few strays. We'll try to get a herd together by next month and leave right after your Bar Mitzva. Meanwhile, Yankel is going to see if he can find out where the nearest Germans are camped."

"We'll have to go at night, so we'll have a better chance of getting through," Jerry reasoned. "Have you got any idea which way we should go, which way would be the easiest?"

"Let's wait till we know where the nearest camp is," Sam answered. "Then we'll figure out which way to go."

I was really excited about the prospect of catching and selling a herd of horses. It would be a real adventure and maybe we could make some real money for a change.

***

Meanwhile, I was spending every spare minute studying with the rebbe. And on the Shabbes just after my thirteenth birthday, I had my Bar Mitzva.

The rebbe called me up to the bima and I read the portion of the Torah for that day. Afterwards we had a little drink of wine with our family and some of the other people at the shul.

From then on I could study with the other men and read from the Torah when called upon. I had the responsibilities of being a good Jew and observing the laws as God commanded.

And so I became a man.

***

It was pitch dark but clear on that late-spring night in 1918. Just a sliver of moon peeked between the trees. The night air was cool, but with all the excitement and my warm horse under me, I wasn't cold.

There had been no problem finding stray horses. In fact, there were so many wandering loose that we'd had our pick. We'd even sold a few to nearby farmers who were trying to get their farms back in order.

Now here we were. Jerry and I kept our horses close together under a few trees on the edge of town, waiting for Sam and his friends to bring the rest of the herd.

Jerry rubbed his hands together and blew on them. "Cold, huh?"

"Not me," I whispered. "I'm too excited. This is great."

"I think I hear them," Jerry said, standing in his stirrups and peering down the dark road. "Yes, it's Sam. Let's move out and join them. Slowly, though. We don't want to spook their horses."

We gently nudged our horses out onto the road. Sam motioned us over and quietly explained his plan to everyone.

"The Germans are northwest of here, near Pleve and Riga. We'll head that way until we find one of their camps. It could take us a good five or six weeks altogether, so we packed a couple of the horses with supplies. But keep your eyes open for places where we can pick up some food. What we have here won't last the whole trip.

"And don't rush. Just keep them moving at a steady pace. We'll travel at night, and in the morning we'll find a gully or some woods and get the horses under cover so they won't be spotted."

"All right already," Yankel whispered impatiently. "Let's go."

We dropped back and urged the herd forward, off the road and across open country.

Skirting the small towns and farmhouses, we moved across the fields, splashing through shallow streams and riding through meadows of sweet-smelling springtime grass. My excitement gradually wore off as I settled into the rhythm of my horse. But I kept a close eye on the herd. It was awfully dark, and I didn't want to lose a horse or have them startled by something unexpected.

We rode all night. The sky was just beginning to turn a pearly pink at the horizon when Sam led us toward a small group of trees.

It was just light enough to see. There were no houses nearby and the fields were unplowed, so we figured we were a good distance from any town.

We moved the horses under the trees and ran a rope around to pen them up. They seemed content to nibble at the dew-wet grass, and we were soon asleep, heads on our saddles. We had no blankets, but I was so tired the cold didn't bother me. Besides, I figured it would warm up during the day.

Next thing I knew, Jerry was nudging me.

"Have some hot tea, Beryl," he said, handing me a tin cup. "Sam's got some bread too."

I stretched my stiff muscles and took the cup. The tea tasted good, and I sipped as I walked over to get some bread. My bottom and my legs were really sore. I wasn't used to riding a horse all night.

The sun had already set, but twilight would last awhile. Everything was quiet except for the birds settling down for the night. We continued heading northwest, still wary but far more relaxed than when we had started our journey.

Most of the time during our trek the weather was good, though the countryside was still pretty wet from the melting snow and spring rains.

The farms were barren and still — either the men had not returned from the army or were afraid to plant this close to the fighting.

Every once in a while, one of us would head off to a farm or town to buy a few supplies. We didn't have to worry about water, there was plenty in the streams along the way.

We rode along night after night in an eerily peaceful existence. The rhythmic movement of the herd and the company of my brothers and friends was soothing after the turmoil of the last few years.

But in our second week, just as we were being lulled into thinking we would have an easy trip, we had a surprise.

We had just started moving the herd out for that night's ride. The sun had set, but it was still light and I noticed the horses seemed uneasy.

"What's bothering the horses?" I asked Sam.

"I don't know. But they sure seem nervous."

Just then Yankel, on the other side of the herd, started yelling and frantically waving his hat to get our attention. He pointed behind us, shouting something we couldn't hear.

Peering through the dust in the fading light, we saw a group of riders galloping straight for us.

"They've got a red flag, Sam! Bolsheviks! If they catch us, they'll take what they want and leave us for dead."

"Let's go!" Sam hollered, waving his hat at Yankel and Herschel and Jerry. "We're not far from the border. Follow me and let's hope we run into some German troops."

Off we flew, shouting at the horses, chasing them across the fields with the Reds chasing right after us.

Shots rang out.

"Beryl, stay low!" Sam yelled.

He didn't have to tell me. I was hanging on and riding for my life. But I could tell my horse was getting winded.

More shots, bullets pinging off nearby rocks. They were gaining on us.

I thought for sure they would catch us. Then, I saw campfires.

Sam saw them too and veered off in that direction, the herd following him.

The pounding hoofbeats behind us quieted. The Reds were falling back. They must have seen the fires too, because suddenly they gave up the chase and were gone.

As we slowed and regained control of the herd, Sam trotted back to us.

"Let's not go into the camp right now. We don't know for certain who they are. We'll stay up here on the hillside, on this side of the ridge so the sentries don't spot us. In the morning, we'll see what's what."

I was glad to stop for the night right where I was, and the horses seemed to feel the same, their sides heaving, their heads hanging down.

When I awoke the next day, Jerry told me Sam and Yankel had already gone down to the camp.

"I'm not sure when they'll be back, Beryl, so get something to eat and let's be ready for anything."

"Your brother is right," added Herschel. "For all we know, these soldiers may want to take instead of buy."

While keeping an eye out for any sign of Sam and Yankel, we prepared everything so we would be ready to run if we had to.

Finally, late in the morning, I jumped up. "There they are! They're not running, so maybe everything's all right."

As they drew near, we could see that Sam was grinning.

"They bought?" Herschel asked.

"Every last one!" Sam cried, jumping down from his horse and hugging him.

Sam told us the camp was made up of German soldiers plus a handful of local farmers about to start their spring planting. It took us no time to get the herd into camp, and several soldiers helped us get them into a pen. Then Sam and Yankel went to see the lieutenant to collect our fee.

We stayed in the camp that night, sitting around one of the fires with the men, talking about our trip and catching up on important news.

"We hear there's more fighting going on around Moscow and Kyiv than there is here," one soldier told us.

"Did you hear they killed the tsar?" another asked us.

"Killed the tsar?" Sam exclaimed, almost spitting out his tea in surprise. "Who killed the tsar?"

"The Reds, of course. His whole family, too. The Reds want to take over everything."

"His whole family?" Yankel asked, astounded.

"How could they get away with killing the tsar?" I asked.

"Those socialists are making trouble everywhere," the first soldier said. "In Germany and Austria, too," another added.

"What do you mean?" Jerry asked.

"They're trying to push socialism on the whole world," the second soldier answered. "People say the kaiser is furious. He thinks it's all those Jewish socialists making trouble again with the workers."

"Sure, it's the Jews. They're always making trouble," agreed the first soldier.

"But what makes the kaiser think it's the Jews?" I asked, as Sam nudged me to keep quiet.

"Everyone knows the socialists are Jews and they want to run the world," the first German replied, starting to sound a little hostile. "They already own all the banks and newspapers."

Yankel abruptly poured the remains of his tea on the ground. "Well, I guess we better get some sleep if we're going to get an early start tomorrow," he said.

"Thank you for your hospitality," Sam added as we rose and headed toward the nearby woods where our horses were tethered.

"Are all socialists really Jewish?" I whispered to Jerry as we walked away. "I never heard of Jews owning banks and newspapers."

"I don't know, Beryl. I guess maybe some banks and newspapers are owned by Jews, somewhere in the world. But you know how it is. If people are looking for someone to blame, they'll blame the Jews."

***

Without the horses to tend, our trip back was pretty quick, but it was already the first of August by the time we got home. Ma and the rest of the family were really glad to see us back.

"Any trouble, Sam?" Uncle Moishe asked, clapping him on the back.

"Not much trouble at all," Sam said with a smile.

"Oh, yeah, right," I said. "And those bullets the Reds were firing at us weren't real, were they?"

Everyone wanted to know all about what happened and began talking all at once, but Ma insisted on first things first.

"Not until they've had something to eat," she said above the clamor. "Come and sit, children. You too, Yankel. And Herschel, I can't send you home without some dinner. Sit. Eat."

Everyone found a place at the table and in between pieces of bread and mouthfuls of watery cabbage soup, we told of our adventure.

"We got a good price for the horses, too," Sam said, concluding the tale. "This money should see us through for a while."

"Things have been pretty bad around here," Moishe said. "Without a government, no supplies are moving, no mail is getting through, and I suppose you've heard about the tsar."

We nodded. "What happened?" Jerry asked.

"Who knows," Moishe shrugged. "The Reds have gone crazy, they're all meshugge. If they can slaughter the tsar, they can get away with anything."

***

And again, people were on the move. Refugees coming through town stopped at the shul or someone's home for a day or two before moving on. Their stories left no doubt that things had gone from bad to worse.

They were calling it "the Red Terror."

As if the world war hadn't been bad enough, now we were caught in the middle of a civil war, and the Reds were killing anyone they thought was against them. Bandits and hooligans took advantage of the chaos, using it as a convenient excuse to burn, rape and kill.

Farmers couldn't plant and few supplies made it through because the trains weren't running. So, wagon groups were formed to bring in food from other parts of the country. But most of the wagons never reached their destination because of the bandits.

People were starving, dropping dead in the streets.

***

The ark opened, and the Torah was taken out as we sang the song of praise on that Rosh Hashanah morning. It was a warm fall day, and the sun coming through the windows kept the shul hot and stuffy even with the doors propped open.

Several young people were standing just outside talking. This was one of the few opportunities for young people to meet and talk. In good times, there had been a dance after Yom Kippur, sometimes resulting in weddings the following spring.

After the Torah reading, Jerry and I had been planning to go outside too. But we never got the chance.

Several men rushed in, ran down the aisle and whispered something to the rebbe.

The rebbe turned to the congregation. "Friends, we are visited yet again by calamity," he announced. "Yodel here tells me a gang of armed peasants is marching on the town. Those of you in the militia, follow your conscience and go if you must. These are terrible times inflicted upon us. I pray God will understand."

Many of the men had risen as soon as Yodel and the others had rushed down the aisle. Now they hurried out. Sam gave me a pat on the back and handed me his tallis as he left with the others.

"I know our hearts and minds are with them," the rebbe continued after our militia had left. "But let us continue with our prayers and ask the Lord to watch over all of us for a good year to come."

He started reading the Torah portion again and I tried mightily to concentrate.

Later, around the dinner table, Sam told us what had happened.

After picking up their guns, our men had headed out to confront the gang marching up the road. A group of gentiles and policemen from the town joined us.

"We met them out by the dump," Sam said. "They were carrying guns and clubs and burning torches. It was a big, angry group, and they were shouting that they would burn us alive and make sure even our babies were dead.

"Some of our men hid behind the old barn that's out there. Then Lev yelled, 'Stop right there! We have guns and we mean to protect our families. Turn around and go home, while you still can!'

"That slowed them for a minute, but then they came running all at once. Lev turned to us and shouted, 'Hold on. I'm going to fire a warning shot.' The gun sounded like an explosion. They stopped and scattered into the ditches by the side of the road and behind some trees, then started firing at us.

"We fired back. Lev shouted, 'I got one,' and Yodel thought he also might have hit someone. Then the hooligans began to run away. We waited a few minutes, then looked around to see if anyone was hurt."

"Was everyone all right?" Ma asked.

"No. Yodel had been shot. But he wasn't hurt badly, just a small wound to his arm, and we took him to the first-aid building. And then, guess what? When we went to look around a little more, we found we had killed two men!"

"I didn't know you guys were such good shots," I said.

"Well, if nothing else, at least the army trained us to shoot straight," Sam replied. "Lev says the hooligans will think twice before coming after us now."

"Ach, but to kill people," Ma said, shaking her head. "How can we do this?"

"Ma, we have to," Jerry answered. "If we don't fight, they'll kill us."

"So now they'll just go someplace else to kill Jews."

"Maybe not, Ma," Sam said. "For one thing, we didn't recognize them. We don't think they were from around here. And maybe they'll think before they try again."

"A drunken hooligan doesn't think," Ma said firmly. "Take care and stay away from strangers."

***

Even though Russia had signed a peace treaty, the war was still going on between the Western allies and Germany and Austria. From time to time, we got a little news or heard rumors about what was happening.

In October 1918, there was a revolution in the German council chamber. Prince Max of Baden took over the government but the kaiser was still the figurehead.

We also heard that a Polish state had been declared in Warsaw. Then, at the end of October, Austria asked for a separate peace and Hungary declared itself independent and opened peace negotiations.

But for us, the winter of 1918-1919 passed in a fog. It was constant trouble with marauding peasants and ex-soldiers on one side and the Red hooligans on the other. It was a constant struggle to keep warm and find something to eat.

**

And then — influenza.

A great influenza epidemic struck the world. Later we learned that fifteen-hundred people died in Berlin in one month. Twenty-two-hundred died in London in one month and twenty-thousand American soldiers just brought over to Europe died in two months.

Our town was hit pretty hard. People who had to go outside wore masks over their faces. When we lost our doctor to the sickness, the barber had to help out.

When he died, Ma went out to help.

People thought that the "evil eye" was making them sick or that they somehow had evil humors or fluids inside their bodies. Those treating the sick would take little glass cups with wicks inside, light the wicks and hold the cup on the patient's back or chest near the lungs. When the flame went out, the oxygen was gone, creating a vacuum and the hot cup stuck on the sick person.

Eight or ten of these cups were applied, depending on the size of the patient. It was very painful, but people thought the hot vacuum cups would pull the inflammation out of the lungs.

People dropped like flies. Burial societies went down the streets daily, collecting the corpses in big carts.

Ma barely let us out the door. She made us wear masks all the time and we couldn't visit anyone or bring anyone home.

When Ma would come home from treating the sick, she would get into a tub of hot water and sit there with steam rising all around her. Tante Brendel or Rose would keep pouring in more hot water.

No one in our family got the influenza. We were very lucky.

***

Meanwhile, the people of the world were tired of war and sickness and death.

The Red Guards rampaged throughout Europe, trying to capitalize on everyone's dissatisfaction and gain control of other countries. Revolution was breaking out everywhere.

The city of Sarajevo declared itself part of the South Slavs, which would later become Yugoslavia. There was a Red revolution in Vienna and another in Budapest.

German troops began to mutiny and the socialist deputies in the Reichstag called for a general strike and demanded that the kaiser resign. Then Germany had a real revolution and the socialists took over.

**

The rebbe of the big red shul called the meeting to order. "People, Mr. Saltzman from the Hebrew Sheltering and Immigrant Aid Society, better known to all of us as the HIAS, has come all the way from London. He has some interesting news for us. So, please, let's all settle down and listen well."

Mr. Saltzman stood to speak. He looked like a pious man, in his dark suit and black hat, his beard neatly trimmed.

"Quiet, everyone, quiet," the rebbe called, banging his hand on the table.

"Friends," Mr. Saltzman began, "it is true that the war is still going on. But the good news is that Austria and Hungary are already negotiating for peace and the kaiser has abdicated."

A murmur passed through the audience. "Good riddance!" someone shouted, and others around us were quick to agree.

"What is he saying, Beryl?" Jerry asked. "I can't hear a thing."

"He said that there's no more kaiser in Germany."

Jerry nodded, then turned his attention back to Mr. Saltzman.

"So, who's running Germany now?" someone shouted.

"The new chancellor is a socialist by the name of Friedrich Ebert," Mr. Saltzman answered. "But the most important thing is that Germany has agreed to meet with the Allies in January for a peace conference."

"What about all these new countries?" a man near us called out.

"Yes, there are quite a few new ones," Mr. Saltzman replied. "Austria is by itself. Hungary is by itself. And the Serbs, Croats and Slovens are all in separate states."

"And what about us here?" someone asked. "Are we Russian or Polish or Ukrainian?"

"Don't you know?" someone else answered with a laugh. "It doesn't matter. We're Jews."

But it did matter. We had no Russian government. We had no German government.

We had nothing. And the people ran wild.

BULLETIN: June 28, 1919

PEACE! GERMANS SIGN
TREATY AT VERSAILLES

CHAPTER 13

Summer/Fall 1919

I t was a hot day at the beginning of July, and the door to Uncle Moishe's store stood open. I walked in and found him leaning over the counter, intently studying a piece of paper.

"What are you reading, Uncle Moishe?"

"Beryl," he said, startled. "I didn't hear you come in. They were handing out these papers in front of the old burgomeister's office. You know that peace conference that started in January? Well, the Germans have finally signed a treaty!"

I'd grown cautious about believing such developments would have much effect on us, but Uncle Moishe usually had a pretty good feel for these things and he was definitely excited. "This is going to change the whole world!" he shouted, rolling up the piece of paper and shaking it in front of my face.

Just then Jerry came in, and Tevia came out from the back of the store to see what all the excitement was about. Jerry and Tevia leaned on the counter expectantly and I hopped up on a barrel.

Uncle Moishe mopped his face with an old rag, put the paper back on the counter, flattened it out, and began telling us what it said.

"Now let's see here. The big Western countries are getting together in an organization they're calling the League of Nations, to try to control trade and keep countries from fighting one another. The bigger countries will each have a mandate over certain smaller countries and will watch out for them.

"France will get a mandate over Syria and Lebanon. Britain will get a mandate over Iraq and Palestine and German South Africa. Britain and France together will divide the responsibility for Cameroon and Togoland."

"Togoland," I laughed. "What a funny name."

"Quiet, Beryl," Jerry said. "What else, Uncle Moishe?"

"Japan is to get the Mariana, Caroline and Marshall islands in the Pacific."

"But what about here?" I asked.

"Yes," Jerry agreed. "Uncle Moishe, what does it say about here?"

Uncle Moishe used a finger to help keep his place as he scanned the rest of the paper for news about us.

"Ah, here we are. It says Poland is going to be a big country. She will get a part of Austria, all the land west to Germany proper and east through parts of the Ukraine."

We all looked at one another.

"I think we're Polish now!" Uncle Moishe declared with a laugh.

***

The treaty said the Poles had to treat all minorities in their area as equals to themselves, and their government did seem to make an effort to set things right. But the Bolsheviks wanted to spread socialism throughout all of Europe. They didn't want the Poles in charge of the Ukraine, so they attacked.

The Bolsheviks and Poland quickly were at war, and the Ukrainians didn't want either side in power so they were fighting everybody. It would have been laughable, except we Jews were caught in the middle, again. The minute someone thought we were siding with one group the other side came after us. I guess they thought we would use our small militia groups to fight against them. And, every time the Ukrainians won a battle against the Reds, they celebrated by attacking the Jews.

The pogroms in the Ukraine became terrible. More than forty-thousand people were tortured and killed in one year.

After a particularly bad pogrom completely destroyed the Jewish part of town in Brest-Litovsk, the ravagers came south and crossed the Boog River.

***

We were cleaning up the rubble around a group of bombed-out houses when the wind shifted and I thought I smelled smoke. So did the others.

We stopped working and lifted our heads to sniff at the wind. Then we saw the rising, dense black cloud. About a mile away, I judged.

"What's going on?" I asked one of the other men.

"Looks like trouble," he said. "Better we should stay here and just keep working. Don't go over there."

But I had to know.

"Herschel," I called to Sam's friend, who was working nearby. "Let's go take a look."

"All right," he said, putting down the bricks he was carrying.

We ran off toward the fire. As we got closer, I started to hear screaming and hollering, and the smoke got thick and stung my eyes and throat.

"It's bad," Herschel said, stopping. "I don't think we should go there."

"Well, you go back if you want and see if you can find some people to help. I'm going to see what's happening."

I watched Herschel run off, then turned and continued walking swiftly toward the smoke and noise. A minute or so later, I turned a corner, stopped dead in my tracks and quickly backed into a doorway.

About half a block away, some men were beating a Jewish couple. A few of the hooligans had set fire to the Jewish man's long beard and were laughing as he screamed. Another man ripped a baby from the woman's arms and flung it against a nearby wall like it was a rag doll. The woman screamed and one of the men ran a sword through her. She was dead in a second.

Another group chased a young woman down the street — they caught her and lined up to rape her, laughing and dancing as she begged for mercy. Homes and businesses were on fire.

I couldn't watch anymore. I ran back the way I had come, hoping to find Lev or Moishe or Sam, anyone from our militia. Tears streamed from my eyes — whether from the smoke or the crying or both, I didn't even know.

***

I never did find our soldiers, but Sam told me later that Lev and a few of the others had seen the smoke too and had come running to chase off the hooligans. But in that little Jewish neighborhood not far from our own, most of the homes and shops had been burned to the ground, and many people had been killed.

***

The new Polish government finally created an army that went into all parts of the Polish territory to restore peace and order. In each section, new town governments were established, with regular police departments and courts.

And finally there was a little peace.

Wagons and trains started coming through again with supplies. Farmers got in a late-summer planting that would be ready for harvest in late fall, ensuring that the winter of 1919-1920 would not be as desperate as the previous winter. By November, business was starting up again.

And the mail began to get through.

***

The back door slammed shut behind us as Tevia and I shook the snow off our coats and rubbed our cold hands together.

Everyone was sitting around the kitchen table watching Ma, who was reading a letter.

Ma had a strange look on her face but seemed very pleased. Tante Brendel looked sort of happy and sad at the same time.

Jerry was grinning from ear to ear.

"What's going on?" I asked. "You all look so funny."

"What's going on," Jerry crowed, "is that we just got the money and boat tickets from Papa.

"We're going to America!"

I was stunned. I almost had stopped hoping that we would ever be able to leave. I hadn't even thought about America in a long time.

Before I knew what I was doing, I turned around and walked back outside. I wanted to be by myself for a while. I had some thinking to do.

I wandered over to the little shul where Zayde used to teach and went back behind the stove where Tevia and I had once hidden after falling in the icy river.

America. What would it be like?

I had heard all sorts of things, how anyone could get an education, how everyone could vote for the government. It wasn't hard to have your own business, you could live anywhere you wanted.

I wondered how much of it was true. I wondered what it would mean for our family. I wondered what it would mean for me.

When I'd first heard talk of America, I'd been too young to really imagine what it might be like. Then we were in the middle of a war. We'd left Russia, gone to Poland, returned to Russia and now were part of Poland.

Through it all, it had started to seem like we would never really go to America. So I had just stopped thinking about it.

Now, crouched behind the stove, I thought.

What do I want from America? What do I want to do with my life?

I might have a chance now for an education. This was very important. Zayde had instilled in me a love of study and learning.

I would go to school for sure.

What kind of work I would do in my life would depend on my education. But I would get a job and help my parents have a little home.

Then, someday, I would marry and have a family and home of my own. And maybe then there would be time for a little music and laughter.

I sat there daydreaming for I don't know how long. Finally, I heard Jerry calling me.

I wiped away my tears, crawled from my hiding place, and ran to join Jerry in the street.

"Beryl, where did you run off to? We have a lot of planning to do and Ma wants you home."

"Just off by myself thinking," I replied. "I guess I never really thought we'd be able to go to America."

"Well, we're going all right. And we don't have much time. We're leaving next month, at the end of December."

"So soon? Can we get all the papers and make all the arrangements so soon?"

"Papa's taken care of almost everything through the HIAS and the landsmen's group in America. His letter tells us exactly what to do. We have to start soon, because with Europe still such a mess from the war, it's going to take a long time to get to the boat in Belgium."

"Belgium? We have to go to Belgium?"

"Yep. We leave from Antwerp. And the tickets are all paid for," Jerry said with a confident nod and a pat on my back.

Then the wind whipped up a new blast of snow. So we stuffed our hands in our pockets and walked back toward the old house.

***

The next few weeks passed quickly. We had so much to do.

Ma and Sam took care of the legal details with the new Polish authorities. We had to find some decent clothes for all of us, pants without holes, sturdy shoes for everyone, and supplies of beans, kasha and other staples to be packed and carried along.

One morning when I woke up, Ma was busily restuffing an old feather pillow.

"What are you doing, Ma?" I asked as I gave her a little hug. "We'll get new pillows in America."

"Oh, no, Beryl. We'll take my feather pillows and the feather comforter with us. You can't buy as good as this. It takes a long time and a lot of goose feathers to make enough for a family. My mother gave these to me when I married your Papa.

"Besides, this pillow will be special."

"What do you mean, Ma?"

"Did you forget about my brass candlesticks and silver salt dish?"

I had completely forgotten about the candlesticks and salt dish that Jerry and I had hidden down by the river on that summer day five-and-a-half years ago — the day we had first seen the Russian army units march down main street.

"Oh, Ma! Do you think they are still there?"

"I think you should go see," she replied, continuing to stuff the pillow. "If you and Jerry did a good job, they will be there. That's why I'm adding extra feathers. This pillow will be good and thick to hide a thing or two from the authorities. Things that are our past and our future. Things that will go with us to America."

"I'll go right now," I said, reaching for my coat and cap.

As I ran out the back door and headed for the river, I thought about what Ma had said. The authorities apparently were not allowing people to leave the country with anything of value, but Ma thought she had found a way. The candlesticks and salt dish meant a great deal to her, and she was determined to keep them in the family.

But as I neared the water's edge, I could see that the old rowboat was gone, washed away over the years like my hopes of ever really going to America. My heart sank. I thought of Ma, back in the house stuffing her pillow, and how disappointed she would be when I returned empty-handed. "No!" I shouted, angrily kicking at the ice near the base of the willow.

To my surprise, the early-winter ice at the river's edge wasn't as thick as I'd expected. It cracked. I kicked until I broke through, then plunged both hands into the icy water and desperately ran them through the rocks and silt around the willow's base. I was just about to give up when suddenly I touched metal. It was one of the oarlocks, which had caught in the tree's gnarled roots.

My fingers were numb by now, but I was pretty sure I felt something tied to the oarlock. I dug around some more and a moment later felt the bag.

And through the wet material, I could feel Ma's precious possessions still inside.

My heart leaped. I pulled the bag through the tangle of roots and out of the icy water, then ran back up to the house. I handed Ma the bag and watched her open it. She carefully washed everything in the pot on the stove and lovingly inspected each piece.

"Everything is still good, Beryl," she finally said, looking up with a smile.

That smile warmed my cold hands better than anything else could have. "Yes, Ma," I said. "We hid them well."

"Yes, you did," she declared. "Even the little salt spoon is here. I'm going to wrap them up and hide them again, in the middle of my pillow. And you'll help me make sure they get to America."

"I'll be with you every step of the way," I assured her with a laugh. "Is there anything they're actually letting us bring?"

"Besides our food, clothing and bedding, not much," she said. "The samovar they'll let us take, and a pot to cook. That's all."

"Well, we don't have much else anyway," I shrugged. "I think I'll go over and see if I can help Uncle Moishe in the store. Is there anything else you need, Ma?"

"No, Beryl, but Tante Ruchel and Uncle Ule are coming over for supper. Be home early so you can say goodbye."

***

That evening at supper, there was much excitement and also sadness.

We were so busy talking about our plans — what we were taking with us, where we were going to catch the boat, how we were going to get to Belgium — we barely had time to eat our soup.

"So, Channah, you're ready to go?" Uncle Ule asked.

"Yes. We've put together some clothes, my feather pillows and comforter, and as much food as we can carry. Even if we had anything else, they wouldn't let us take it out."

"Your candlesticks and salt dish?" Tante Ruchel asked.

"Hidden in the pillows," Ma replied.

"So, Moishe," Ule said. "It won't be long until you follow them to America, eh?"

Looking at Tante Brendel, Uncle Moishe sat back in his chair and placed his hands flat on the table.

"No, Ule. We won't be going to America. We've decided to go to Palestine."

Moishe gave a little grin, pleased with himself at the surprise he'd sprung. "Brendel, you said nothing," Ma said accusingly.

"We just found out, Channah," Brendel replied, taking Ma's hand in hers. "And you were so busy."

"We only heard this week we could get our entrance permits," Moishe said. "We'll be leaving in the spring."

Tevia was grinning at me from across the table. "See, you're not the only one going to a new country. And now you'll have family in Palestine when you come to visit."

"What will you do there?" Ule asked Moishe. "Have you any prospects? Where will you live?"

Moishe sat forward again. "I have it all worked out. The Jewish Committee places new immigrants in a camp until they get adjusted and learn Hebrew. Then they arrange for a place to live and help them find a job. They're pretty well-organized."

"But you'll be living among Arabs," Ruchel protested.

"Look, Ruchel, Palestine is our land," Moishe responded. "Now, with Great Britain in charge, I think it's a good time to go home and help build a new country. This is our chance, because they say Britain is going to put a limit on how many Jews can get in."

"Well, you're still a young man, Moishe," Ule said. "You have a life to live, a family to care for. God willing, it will all work out for you."

"What about you, Ule?" Moishe asked. "What are your plans? Now that Joe is in America, you'll also be going, yes?"

Ule sat quietly, looking down at his tea glass and turning it around and around in his hands. Tante Ruchel said nothing.

"Ruchel," Ma said. "We will see you in America, won't we?"

"No, Channah," Ruchel said softly.

"No? Are you going to Palestine too?"

"No, Channah," Ule replied. "We're staying here."

"Ule, why?" Moishe exclaimed. "With Joe and Mordecai and Channah in America, they could soon help you ..."

"No, Moishe," Ule interrupted. "I'm too old to start over. And Joe doesn't want anything to do with us now."

"Of course he does," Ma said. "Joe was hurt like a child when he left, but he's not a child anymore. I'm sure he understands now why you pushed him out and realizes it was for the best."

"The thing I want most in the life that's left to me, Channah, is to make up with my oldest son," Ule said. "But I don't even know where he is. He's never even written a letter."

"We'll find him, Uncle," I said. "When we get to America, I'll look for him."

With tears in her eyes, Tante Ruchel smiled at me. "You're a good boy, Beryl. But do you really think you can find him in such a big country?"

I knew America was a big country. But I couldn't stand to see Uncle Ule and Tante Ruchel so unhappy.

"Sure, Tante. You'll see. I'll find him for you."

***

The next morning, we bundled up in our heaviest clothing and walked to the cemetery at the edge of town to say goodbye to Zayde and the rest of our family laid to rest there.

A bitter wind blew bursts of snow that swirled across the open field and stung our faces.

I knew it was traditional to leave a stone or twig on the grave of a loved one, something to show the spirit of the dead that you care and have come to visit. But snow covered everything.

Then, on the old tree stretching its gnarled gray branches over our family's graves, I spotted a lone leaf, dried and curled but stubbornly clinging to a twig.

The twig with the leaf would be the one I would leave for Zayde.

After the traditional graveside prayer, I quietly added a few words of my own. "I promise, Zayde, I won't forget you and everything you taught me. I'll work hard in our new world and make you proud. My children and their children will know of you."

It saddened my heart to say goodbye, but I knew how happy Zayde would be for us. I put the twig with the leaf on top of the grave and turned to rejoin the others.

In silence, we headed back toward Zayde's old house for the last time.

CHAPTER 14

Winter/Spring 1919-1920

I awoke suddenly. It was still dark, and it took me a moment to remember why today was so different.

Then I heard Ma making breakfast. This was the day we were leaving!

I realized it would be the last time I would sleep atop the old brick stove. I lay there a moment and thought back about our life in Horchov.

The warm family, the Jewish community. The hate, the fear, the death. The love.

The others began to stir. "Children, Uncle Ule will be here soon," Ma called. "Dress, and come have some kasha."

We were really leaving.

***

Uncle Ule had borrowed a sled from a neighbor, and by the time we finished eating he was bursting through the door in his big hat and long, ragged coat.

"Anyone here going to America?" he called out jauntily, rubbing his hands together and taking a playful punch at Jerry, who ducked out of the way.

"Come in and have a glass of tea, Ule," Ma said.

"No, Channah. I had already, and it's getting late. You don't want to miss the train, do you?"

Brendel, Moishe, Tevia, Toby, Ruchel, Brendel's little ones, they were all there, and they helped load our few bundles onto the sled. We had Ma's pillows and comforter, the samovar and a pot, a change of clothes and a few sacks of food.

Ma and Rose wore long coats buttoned over their long skirts, woolen babushkas tied on their heads and shawls over their shoulders.

Sam wore his heavy army pants and coat. Jerry and I wore clean, mended old knickers, short jackets and caps that came down over our ears. And somehow, somewhere, Ma had found us all some decent used shoes.

The sled wasn't big enough for the whole family to come see us off at the station, so we said our goodbyes in the cold, gray dawn. "Take care. Write a letter. Let us know where you are." Hugs and kisses all around.

We climbed onto the sled. Snowflakes gently landed on our faces and mingled with our tears.

"Hup, hup," Uncle Ule called to the horses as he flicked the reins. And then we were looking back waving to them. The big flakes thickened and Zayde's old house faded from sight.

"Turn around, children," Ma said. "From now on, we only look forward."

I knew she was right. I sighed, then turned to look ahead.

***

We were to take the train to Warsaw, where the HIAS would put us with a wagon group going through the Radzivil area and across the Austrian border to Brody. This was the best way for us to go. People who lived farther north went through Danzig, and the route south to Odesa and over the Black Sea was too expensive.

Papa had warned Ma in his letter that we could trust only the HIAS people. There were many, gentile and Jew alike, who would try to take advantage of us. These people made a living stealing from refugees, especially those traveling without passports.

But Ma and Sam had taken care to get our papers in order. They had brought our passports first to the Polish authorities, then to the American consul, who had assured us we would get our visas from the American consul in Antwerp.

Now that we were on our way, it finally felt real, and I was looking forward to the trip almost as much as getting to America.

As the station appeared in the distance, it occurred to me how trains had played such an important part in our lives. People coming and going in happiness or fear.

Now a train would take us on our first step toward a new life. We couldn't know if that life would be good or bad, but we knew we could no longer have a life in Horchov.

We hugged Ule. I told him I wouldn't forget to look for Joe, and he smiled sadly.

We boarded the train, and I saw my uncle through the window as he turned and walked back toward the sled. For the first time he looked old to me, and I realized I might never see him again.

***

Except for being relocated during the war, we had never traveled before. And there was a feeling of anxiety; a fear of what was before us. How would we manage? What kinds of situations would we have to deal with?

Strange places, strange people.

We shared the train with hundreds of others, refugees, soldiers, peasants carrying crying babies and live chickens, salesmen carrying goods.

At first we talked excitedly about the trip ahead and our prospects and hopes in our new country. Then we gradually became quiet, staring out the windows and thinking our own thoughts about the past and the future.

We ate from the food we had brought and slept in our seats. We got to Warsaw the following day.

When we arrived, a man at the station was holding a HIAS sign. "Travelers to America, this way," he called.

That's what we are now, I thought. *Travelers to America!* I liked the sound of that.

The man with the sign gathered a large group and led us like schoolchildren to the HIAS office several blocks away.

We settled down in the courtyard of the building, among several-hundred other refugees and everyone's bags and parcels. After a while, another HIAS man came out.

"The next wagons to Brody will be leaving in about five or six weeks," he announced.

There was a huge collective groan.

"Don't worry," the man continued. "We have places for you to stay, either with other Jewish families in town or in a camp we have set up for travelers. Now, if you will kindly come up to my desk when your name is called, we will get all of you settled."

When we heard our name, we picked up our things and went inside the building, where we were directed to a small room just to the right of the entrance.

There the HIAS man sat, behind a desk completely covered by folders full of papers. In fact, as I looked around, I saw that the entire room was covered by folders — on the chairs, on the tables, on the floor, spilling out of file cabinets.

"Good afternoon," the man said. "Can I see your passports?"

Sam handed him our papers and he looked them over.

"These seem to be in order. Do you have people in America?"

"Yes," Sam answered. "My father and brother are there."

"Good. You have money?"

Sam nodded.

"Boat tickets?"

Sam nodded again.

"All right, then. Take care and don't throw away your money with people who tell you they can get you to America faster than we can. You shouldn't have any problem getting your visas. I see the Polish authorities and the American consul have signed your passports. That's good because otherwise the American consul in Antwerp would send you back for the signatures."

None of us said anything, and the man continued.

"They are going to ask you a lot of questions at the border and also give you a physical exam. Be sure to take care of yourselves. Don't get sick, keep yourselves clean, don't get upset. Cooperate with the authorities and you will be much better off.

"As for now, we have assigned you to live with the Roskov family. We are very crowded here in Warsaw and you will all have to be in one room, but they will try to make you comfortable. It's better for you, I think, than going to the camp."

The man said his assistant would give us directions to the Roskovs' apartment and tell us how much we should pay for our room. "Goodbye and good luck," the HIAS man concluded, handing Sam back our papers.

Sam lingered a moment as the assistant gave him directions. Then we were outside and on the streets of the big city of Warsaw.

Our little town seemed so small and backward compared to this huge city with its tall buildings and busy streets. Everywhere we looked, people scurried about. There were refugees with their bundles and babies, tradesmen with their tools, and businessmen hurrying down the street toward some important meeting. Ma was aghast as she watched a well-dressed man stuffing his face with food as he hurried past, running to catch a trolley.

The trolleys clanged along. Horse-drawn carriages rushed by seemingly without thought to pedestrians trying to cross the street. Jerry and I looked at each other. We were definitely going to do some exploring in Warsaw while we waited for our wagon.

The main streets were wide, with wagons and carriages able to pass each other. But after we left the center of town the side streets were narrow and dark, closed in by giant tenement buildings that shut out the sunlight.

Frozen wash hung from the windows and children played in the narrow sidewalks like they grew there. Mothers yelled down from above, while fathers in long black caftans and big black hats headed into the half-dozen little shuls we passed.

At last, we arrived at the right apartment building. It towered above us and had a big central courtyard bustling with tumult. Here and there, kids played kickball and men played cards. In one corner, three pious Jewish men argued over some text they had been reading. A group of women washed clothes at a big tub, the sloshing water turning their coats icy in the late-afternoon shadows.

Someone emptied a pan of water out a window. "Watch out, Ma!" Sam shouted as the water fell short of us and spilled down into the yard, adding to the sheet of ice already growing there.

People were selling things right in the courtyard, pieces of rag, iron rods, food. An old woman sold potato latkes. There was even a juggler entertaining and begging for pennies.

We found the right apartment number and entered a dark hallway that smelled like cooked cabbage. After dragging our things up three flights of rickety stairs, we knocked on the door. The baleboosteh, or housewife, who answered appeared harried, with a baby in her arms and two little ones clinging to her skirt while peeking out at us.

"Oh, welcome," she said. "Please, come right in. You must be the Aynbinders. I'm Mrs. Roskov."

Of course, we understood her, because we spoke both Russian and Polish, living so close to the border

Ma introduced herself and all of us, and we entered a dark room crowded with cots and a table in the middle. Drying diapers were strung across a line from one end of the room to the other and everything smelled damp.

"Come right this way," Mrs. Roskov said. "Your room is on the other side of the kitchen."

She opened the door and showed us a room with several cots. A basin of water sat on a movable cabinet. "I know it will be crowded," Mrs. Roskov said. "But I hope you will be happy with us. Let me know if you need anything. The bathtub is at the end of the hall, and as for water, we're very modern here. The city pumps water right into the houses. You can get it from the spigot in the hall. And when you're done, just throw the dirty water out the window," she proudly instructed.

Mrs. Roskov continued the orientation. "Supper will be at about six o'clock, when my husband gets home from evening services. Then you'll meet the rest of the family. I'm sure you young people will get along nicely with my children. There are eleven of us altogether."

Our house had always been full of people, so we were not surprised that a couple with nine children of their own was renting us part of their apartment. Money was dear since the war, especially with a large family to raise.

And so, Mrs. Roskov left us to settle in. Ma supervised as we put our things out of the way, under the cots and on a small shelf. Here we would stay until the HIAS contacted us about our transportation.

At dinner time, we all came into the big front room. The diapers had been taken down, and we sat at the table using the few chairs and the cots. Mr. Roskov made us feel welcome, and the kids, the oldest being about Jerry's age, had all kinds of questions.

While Ma and Rose helped Mrs. Roskov, we explained where we were from and where we were going.

"I haven't heard of Horchov," Mr. Roskov said. "Of course, I haven't heard of a lot of places. But it sounds like a nice town. We have a river here also, the Vistula. It too is a big river. You might want to take a walk down there and have a look."

"Is it safe to walk about?" Ma asked. "There is so much trouble at home."

"Oh, yes, Mrs. Aynbinder, it is safe here," Mr. Roskov replied. "Walk around and take a good look at the city. All the fighting is farther east, nearer to where you are from. No one will bother you here."

Although it was apparently safe to walk around, we learned from Mr. Roskov that Warsaw was not without its problems. "Unfortunately, many of our cotton mills and lace factories were destroyed by the war, so a lot of people are out of work. And if you do go around, be sure to stay away from any street with a sign posted for sickness. Those streets have been closed so the typhus doesn't spread."

Our meager meal that evening consisted of watery potato soup, one piece of bread for each adult, a half-slice for the small children, and hot tea. Mrs. Roskov was very apologetic.

"There's just so little food coming in that everything costs a fortune," she told us.

"Our shul has put together a group that travels once a month across the Austrian border to Brody, to get flour and other necessities," Mr. Roskov added. "There are many people starving in Warsaw."

"There are many starving in Horchov too," Ma said.

We spent the next couple of days exploring the city. Mr. Roskov took us to his shul and introduced us to some of his friends and the rebbe. They too made us welcome, and a couple of people asked us to come have Shabbes dinner with their families. We understood this traditional courtesy to strangers and thanked them for their invitations, but we declined since we knew they would have very little food to share with us.

***

We had thought the courtyard of the building in which we were staying was a busy, noisy place. But when Jerry, Sam and I finally ventured into the center of the city, we were overcome by the jam of people and the feverish activity.

This was a big city. So many big buildings, so many people.

We saw a few well-dressed people with fur coats and tall hats riding in beautiful carriages. But most of the people seemed very poor.

They were selling things or entertaining on the streets for their living. Refugees with bundles looked lost and scared. Crippled ex-soldiers in ragged uniforms begged on street corners.

But it was obvious this city was doing its best to recover from the terrible effects of the war. Groups of workers cleaned up rubble at burned-out buildings, boarded-up shop windows were being fitted for glass and government buildings were being repaired.

Everyone seemed determined to make do and pick up their lives again, despite the shortages, As we walked, we saw many big factories and houses that had been destroyed by fire. We noticed people living in every nook and cranny they could find, in tin or even cardboard huts squeezed between buildings, or in made-up shacks in the tenement courtyards.

Finally, after asking directions from several people, we found the river. The narrow, dark street we were directed to take wound its way downhill from the chaotic heart of the city. Suddenly we came out into sunlight. And there it was, the big, beautiful Vistula.

The Vistula was bigger than the Boog River behind our old home, which by this time of year was always frozen over. Here, ferries and barges steamed by even though it was the middle of winter, and people hurried past on foot, anxious to escape the cold wind along the quay. We walked down some steps and wandered along the riverbank, marveling at the variety of sights and sounds.

People fished for their dinner. Ferries loaded people. Small sailboats and rowboats crossed back and forth. Yet the big river seemed to move through the city calm and steady with a life of its own, unburdened by all the activity on its back.

At the apartment that night, we learned why there were so many small boats on the river. Mr. Roskov said that the Russian army, retreating from the advancing Germans, had blown up all the bridges. So people now used any kind of makeshift boat they could find to get across.

***

After we had regaled Ma and Rose with talk of the big river and our adventures in the big city, Jerry told them, "Tomorrow you're both coming with us. We're going to show you the town."

"Oh, no, Jerry," Ma said. "For Rose it's all right. But it's not for me to go."

"Oh, yes it is, Ma," Sam said. "You'll enjoy seeing the sights."

"I don't know, Sam. Do you really think so?"

"Yes," Sam replied without hesitation. "It's all settled. You're both coming with."

***

The next day was cold but sunny, so off we went, shepherding Ma and Rose around the city like we owned it. What a day we had. We took them to see the biggest shul any of us had ever seen, then walked along a street lined with all kinds of shops.

Many of the shops were empty, their windows still boarded up. But of the shops up and running, Rose managed to find one that especially interested her.

"Ma, will you look at the clothes in this window," she said. "The models are wearing such short dresses. Why, you can see above their ankles!"

"Too short," Ma said, shaking her head. "It isn't nice. But such beautiful material. I never saw such material."

"And the hair on the models, Ma. Look how short they are wearing their hair."

"A good Jewish woman doesn't show her hair," Ma said flatly, touching the wig under her babushka. Jewish women cut their long hair when they were married, and from then on wore a wig as an adornment. "Besides, such styles are only for the store dummies," Ma went on. "Real women don't look like this."

"Maybe not, Ma," Rose conceded. "But I wonder if the aristocrat women dress this way. I wonder if women in America look like this."

Just when it seemed we would never be able to drag the women away from the clothes store, Sam spied a street vendor. "Come on," he said. "Let's have some potato latkes."

We stood on the cold street, watching all the people and relishing the hot treats. Ma was clearly enjoying herself, although she made it a point to criticize the latkes. "Not as good as mine," she proclaimed. We all laughed and licked our fingers.

As we walked back to the tenement, rosy-cheeked and full of latkes, I nudged Sam. "Look at Ma," I said. "I haven't seen her so carefree in a long time. This was a good idea. It took her mind off all our past troubles and what might be ahead of us."

"You're right," Sam said. "We get so wrapped up in our own problems we forget how hard these past few years have been for her."

***

Jerry, Sam and I got a little work here and there during our stay thanks to Mr. Roskov, who introduced us around the community. The few pennies we earned clearing rubble and taking down boards from windows helped us pay for our room.

There were still not enough supplies coming in to take care of the needs of a whole city, so we spent a lot of time trying to find food and fuel to help the Roskovs.

Ma was determined to keep us healthy, so she and Rose kept busy washing our clothes and keeping our room sparkling clean, along with helping Mrs. Roskov with all the children.

***

Our six weeks in Warsaw went quickly. And before we knew it, a messenger was at the door telling us to be at the HIAS office the following Monday to depart for Brody.

When it came time to leave we thanked the Roskovs, and Sam paid Mr. Roskov for the final week of our room and board. Mrs. Roskov took Ma aside.

"My heart goes with you," she said. "Here, I've put together some cheese and bread for you. Please take it. It could be very hard to find food on your journey."

"Oh, thank you, Surah," Ma said, hugging her. "I know how much this food means to you."

When we got to the HIAS office, there again were hundreds of refugees waiting in the courtyard. "You are to wait here until you are called by the clerk," we were told.

Looking around, I saw lots of families but also many young people traveling alone. Some were even younger than me. Everyone was uneasy. A woman next to us was crying and her husband was trying to comfort her. Their children looked hungry and dirty.

"May I ask if I can be of help?" Ma softly inquired.

"Thank you, Mrs.," the man replied. "It is only that my wife is very afraid we won't be accepted at the border. And the children are hungry."

Ma pulled some scraps of bread out of her bundle and fed them to the children.

"Oh, thank you, Mrs.," the woman wept. "We simply cannot go back. The pogroms, every day, every night, the killing and burning. We must leave."

Ma talked with her quietly while we waited. After an hour or so, our name was called and we went into the office building. Another HIAS clerk looked over our papers.

"Is everyone well?" he asked.

"Of course," Ma replied. "Why do you ask such a question?"

"The inspectors at the Austrian border examine everyone very carefully, Mrs. They don't want anyone bringing sickness into their country."

"No one is sick," Ma said firmly.

The HIAS man looked us over slowly and carefully before signing a piece of paper on his desk. He pinned a tag on each of us with our name, hometown, where we were going and who was to meet us.

Then he handed the paper to Sam. "We have six wagons going to Brody. The drivers will leave you at the border and you will have to make your own way across and into the town. Be careful. There will be plenty of thieves near the border, hoping to make money off the refugees. Don't listen to anyone who says he has a better, faster way to get you to America. And when you get into Brody, go straight to the HIAS office."

"How far is Brody from the border?" Jerry asked.

"About eight miles. But you won't be alone. There will be plenty of people on the road with you. Brody is handling a huge number of refugees, but we are pretty well-organized there now. They have an embarkation camp where you can stay until they find you transportation for the rest of your journey."

"Good luck to you," the man concluded, already picking up the folder full of papers for his next case.

The clerk had written down the name of a wagon driver, and we went outside to look for him. We showed the driver our papers and he also looked us over carefully.

"All right," he said at last. "Not much baggage, I see. Some of you people want to bring along everything you've ever owned. Up you go. Find a seat. We're ready to leave."

As we squeezed in and introduced ourselves to our fellow travelers, the driver clucked to his horses and we were off, following five other wagons.

We wrapped our comforter around us and held our feather pillows close. Brody was more than a hundred miles from Warsaw, through cold, late-winter weather. The trip took us through the plains to the south.

In the evening, the drivers stopped wherever they found a little shelter, a barn they had used on other trips, an inn where you could get a hot meal if you had the money. Throughout the countryside we could see the ravages of war. Railroad tracks stopped in the middle of nowhere, blackened remains of barns and houses protruded from the white snow, straggling refugees begged for food along the roads.

Many times, we had to get out and push when the wagon got stuck in deep snow or mud. We slogged our way through the wintry wind, heads bent against the blinding snow, pushing until the road got better.

Finally, we came to the Austrian border. There was a gate in the road with guards standing ready.

Thousands of people were waiting to cross.

"Hurry up, this way," the guards yelled. "Get in line. Don't push. Wait your turn."

They looked at everyone's papers very carefully. Some people they let through the gate. Some they sent to the side. These people moaned and cried. They wouldn't be allowed in.

We spent most of the afternoon waiting in line. At last, it was our turn. The guards looked at our papers and matched our faces to the pictures on our passports.

"All right, go through to the barracks over there," one of them finally motioned. "The doctors will make sure you are not bringing any sickness into our country."

We approached the barracks.

"Men to the left. Women to the right," a clerk shouted.

Ma was upset. "Why? Where are they sending us?"

"Go quickly," a guard yelled at her. "You can't get into Austria unless the doctor says you're well."

"Go ahead, Ma," Jerry said, putting an arm around her shoulder. "It won't take long. We'll meet you after."

"Everything will be all right, Ma," Sam added. "We're not sick."

Ma took Rose by the arm and reluctantly went through the door on the right. Sam, Jerry and I went through the door on the left.

First they made us take off our clothes and doused us with some kind of powder they said was to kill lice. Then we took a shower.

I'd never had a shower before. I wished I had time to enjoy it.

Afterwards, we stood around with the other men, waiting for the doctor to get to us.

The doctor treated everyone the same. First he looked at our eyes, then inside our mouths and ears. Then he quickly listened to our chests and looked us over all around.

"Pass. Pass. Pass."

Sam, Jerry and I proceeded to a desk, where a clerk stamped a paper, handed it to us and gave us clean clothes. We each received underwear and a school-type uniform, with a jacket that buttoned up the front and had a high collar.

"Go through that door," the clerk instructed. "They'll give you a haircut. And keep those papers with you. The authorities in Brody will ask for them."

We put on our new clothes, bundled up our old ones and went into the next room. When the barber was finished with us, we looked like newly shorn sheep.

Outside, Ma and Rose were waiting. They had new clothes also, and they had a good laugh at our new haircuts. No more sidecurls for us; we were modern men.

"Are you all right, Ma?" I asked.

"Hmph," she sniffed. "They thought we would have lice. Never. Not in my house!"

We laughed, picked up our bundles and started down the muddy road toward Brody, following the trail made by thousands of refugees before us.

Late that evening we came into the town. We smelled it first. I'd never been in a town that smelled so bad. And the mud — we sank almost up to our knees in some places.

There was no need to ask directions. We just followed the trail of other people until we came to a fence. Inside was a big camp with barracks lined up along the muddy street.

Outside the gate, we collapsed on our bundles like everybody else, waiting our turn to get in. Inside we were split up again, the women in one group of barracks, men in the other.

"Take care," Ma called after us. "We'll meet out here in the yard in the morning."

We entered the barracks we had been assigned to and looked around. It was a long building with rows of two-tiered cots so close together you could barely squeeze between them. But the place was pretty clean.

Bundles were kept under the cots, and socks and rags were spread out to dry on the rail at the foot of many of the cots.

At the far end of the barracks was a water trough for washing up, and a back door that led out to the yard and the outhouse.

We found empty cots, put our things underneath and plopped ourselves down. We were very tired and glad to be inside, out of the rain.

The next day, after helping to clean the barracks, we met Ma and Rose in the yard and went to a big mess hall for breakfast. Some people at our table told us about Brody and the camp.

In the early 1800s Brody had been a growing center of business and Jewish culture. But as Austrian Galicia failed to industrialize, the town gradually went down.

Brody had a big Jewish population for its size, so it was natural during the heavy immigration period from 1880 to 1905 for Jewish refugees to pass through there. The Brody community had done its best, but they were some of the poorest Jews in the entire area. It was the HIAS that finally helped, setting up a camp and bringing in food and medicine bought with contributions from Jews around the world. Everything was free to the travelers.

After breakfast, we walked around looking at the camp. Everybody was busy. People washed clothes; men chopped wood for the stoves. And a long line of people waited in front of the administration building.

"Well, what do we do now?" Jerry asked a man waiting at the back of the line.

"If your papers are in order, you're lucky. The clerks inside will tell you how to get to Krakow. From there, who knows? You're going out from Antwerp?"

"Yes," Sam answered.

"The clerks will tell you. Best to talk to them when you get inside."

"What about you?" Jerry asked the man.

"Me, I'm not so lucky. I have to wait for my wife and children to catch up with me. I hope we can all get through soon before they close the immigration doors."

Sam, Jerry and I looked at one another. "What do you mean?" Jerry asked.

"Don't you know? The American Congress is having a big debate about limiting the number of immigrants they will let in."

This was a big surprise to us.

"But I thought America was made up of immigrants," I said.

"Sure, but now that they're in, they don't want anyone else to come."

As I left Sam and Jerry waiting at the administration building and went to find Ma and Rose, I thought about what the man in line had said. It hardly seemed fair that those who'd managed to get over to America ahead of us would now be able to keep us out. I wondered what we would do if we weren't allowed in.

I had known our journey to America would be long and difficult, but I hadn't thought for a minute about what would happen if we didn't make it.

Would we return to Horchov? Would we join Moishe and Brendel and Tevia in Palestine? Would we settle someplace else?

As I came upon Ma and Rose outside their barracks, I decided it would be best to keep such worries to myself for now.

***

It took Sam and Jerry most of the day waiting to talk to the clerks, but finally they joined us on the steps in front of the women's barracks.

"Nu?" Ma said. "So how do we go now?"

"There aren't any trains here, Ma," Jerry said. "The tracks were pulled up by the soldiers. So, we have to walk to the nearest depot. It's six or seven miles from here."

"And there are no regular trains," Sam added. "The Austrians are making up big freights to move all the refugees across the country."

I didn't have a good feeling about this, remembering the freight car that had taken us to Poland during the war. I could tell Ma was thinking the same thing.

***

We spent about three weeks in Brody. It was much smaller than Warsaw. But except for the mud and the smell, the town itself was clean and modern. There was more food and other necessities and comforts in the shops — the shortage of supplies wasn't as critical as in Warsaw and wasn't nearly as bad as back home.

The Jewish people we met were decent but very poor. They spoke Yiddish in a different, sing-song way, and there was a big difference between the older people in their long caftans and sidecurls and the more modern people who wore up-to-date clothes.

But the big difference in Brody, as far as we were concerned, was the feeling in the air. People felt free to stand and talk with one another. Free to go wherever they wanted. Free to just walk around in the park on Shabbes. That was the big difference we noticed between Austria and Russia.

It took some getting used to.

***

During our third week in Brody, a HIAS man came into our barracks and handed papers to Sam and the others on his list.

"The train to Krakow will be at the depot tomorrow," he said. "It will wait for one day. Those of you who have your papers and are ready to go should leave first thing in the morning. I'll give you a map that will show you how to get there.

"As for food, don't worry. The HIAS will give each family a small package, a little bread, a little cheese, to tide you over. It's not much, I know, but it will help."

After the HIAS man left, Sam, Jerry and I conferred next to Sam's cot. "We'd better go find Ma and Rose," Sam said.

We headed over to the women's barracks and spotted Ma, outside washing our clothes in the metal trough.

"Ma," Jerry called as we walked toward her. "We have to leave tomorrow to get the train."

"Good," Ma said, as she squeezed water out of a skirt and hung it on a line. "I'm ready to leave this smelly place. Thank God the rain has finally stopped."

***

The next morning, we packed up and left with a big group of people all traveling together to America. The weather was cool but sunny for late March, and most of the snow had melted. But it was still a long walk, six or seven miles along roads and fields that were nothing but muck.

As we slogged along, our shoes and clothes got heavier and heavier from the clinging mud. It was late that afternoon by the time we got to the station, and it wasn't much of a station either. But a clerk handed out cards, showing everyone which car to get on. That way, he said, one car wouldn't be more crowded than another.

That night we slept right where we were, on the ground near the station, leaning on our bundles. Everyone crowded together to keep warm.

The next day, guards checked everyone's papers again before allowing us to climb aboard. Several people were rudely pushed aside and not allowed to continue with us. We never found out why.

By late morning we were on our way.

We had feared that this freight ride would be like our last one, but it wasn't nearly as bad. This time there was enough room and benches to sit on. And, thank God, it wasn't the dead of winter.

As for food, though, we had only the package the HIAS had provided, and some people had none. Ma made sure all the children in our car at least had a crust of bread.

The train stopped at a few stations where hawkers tried to sell food or newspapers, whatever they could to make a living. Then, on the second day of our ride, we pulled into Krakow.

As the refugees piled off the train, waiting HIAS people handed out a list of hotels and rooming houses that would take us in. We took a copy of the list, which included a rough map, and started walking through the town.

It was a cold, rainy, miserable day that felt more like winter than spring, so we didn't stop to see the sights of the city. We barely even looked up to see where we were going. But at least it didn't smell bad like Brody.

Finally, we came to an old pensioners' hotel. People were standing around outside talking among themselves, and the small lobby was jammed with people, standing, sitting, strewn about on the furniture and floor. Everyone was talking, pointing and trying to make themselves understood in what sounded like a hundred different languages.

Sam finally found a clerk in the middle of a group of screaming, crying women and much to the man's relief, dragged him away.

We were not destitute. We still had a little of the money Pa had sent. After the man looked over our papers, he took us upstairs to a room.

The dark little room he gave us had one big bed, a cot, a table with two chairs and a small stove for heat. The room was so tiny we couldn't all stand in it at the same time — the furniture took up all the floor space, and you pretty much had to sit to even be in the room. On the table was a wash bowl, and the clerk told us we could get water from a spigot down the hall. The outhouse was in the back yard along with a tub for washing clothes.

We tried to make ourselves comfortable. We didn't know how long we would be here. It was April 1920, and we had already been traveling for more than three months.

We didn't know how long it would take us to reach Antwerp. There were so many refugees, and the war had left so many trains and wagons destroyed. Even horses were scarce.

Countries were trying to rebuild, but there was very little money available. The Allied governments were trying to organize a relief effort, bringing food and medical supplies to the worst areas. But the farmers were only now just starting to plant again, and we knew food would be very hard to come by for a while yet.

In the following days, we took turns going with Ma on trips to the HIAS office and the Jewish Committee, trying to make arrangements for the next leg of our journey. When we weren't waiting in line, we looked for any kind of odd job to make a few pennies.

I worked here and there, carrying messages, cleaning buildings and doing anything I could to find a few hours of work. But in between, I had plenty of time to wander around the town.

Krakow was a very old Polish city that had been given to the Austro-Hungary Empire in 1795 when Poland was partitioned. The people here spoke Polish, German, Hungarian and, of course, Yiddish, so I managed to get around pretty well.

It was a beautiful, civilized city. As I walked the cobbled squares, I stared up at buildings with spires reaching for the clouds and intricately carved gargoyles set on jutting cornices.

I discovered the great university in Jagiellonska, which a sign said had been founded in 1364. I strolled through the main market square with its open-air cafes and horse-drawn cabs, and the Cloth Hall, a huge covered market in the center of town.

Again, I was struck by how different things were from back home. I never would have wandered around a strange city in Russia.

Here the people seemed so relaxed. They shopped or just looked in the windows. They sat in the cafes with friends. They sat in the square and fed pigeons with bread scraps that people back home would have gladly gobbled down to stave off starvation. Parents took their children to the parks and walked little dogs on leashes. They seemed in control of their lives.

Jewish traders had settled in this crossroads city in about the twelfth century. But in 1494, because of conflicts with the gentiles over trade, the Jews were made to live in a separate district called Kazimierz. Before the 1795 partition, Krakow had a vital commercial and intellectual Jewish community and some of the most celebrated Jewish physicians and scholars. Now, about fifty-thousand Jews lived in the Kazimierz district.

It seemed like everybody was busy planning and talking and arguing. My favorite place was a little cafe near the hotel, where people sat at tables drinking tea or coffee. There were often heated discussions, and one day in particular I stopped to listen.

"I tell you, the Reds are right!" a man shouted, pounding his fist on the table. "You can't have capitalism with a bunch of peasants who have no education. The aristocrats would get right back in."

"And the Reds are any better?" the man across the table yelled right back. "They want to take over and make one giant government to control everything."

"That's right. And no one will have more than the next man. Only the state will own and have power. Everyone will be taken care of equally."

"Surely you don't believe that. Ach, you'll see. Sooner or later, some people will rise to the top and have more than the next person. It's human nature."

A man at a nearby table turned and joined in. "Meanwhile," he said, "we all starve. The Reds and Whites are still fighting each other, the Reds have attacked Poland and the Ukraine is having terrible pogroms. Every time the anti-Bolsheviks win, they go wild against the Jews. Everybody is suspicious of everybody else, and especially of the Jews."

"So, what's new about that?" the first man shrugged.

"I thought the treaty said the Poles were supposed to treat all their people equally."

"Yes, but they think the Jews are helping the Reds. Can you believe that? So, of course, the Reds and the Ukrainians think the Jews are helping the Poles."

"Ach," the first man said, waving the waiter over for more tea. "The papers say they completely destroyed Brest-Litovsk. Bialystok too."

The men were quiet a moment, looking down at their empty glasses.

"Do you have anyone left there?" the first man's companion asked softly.

"My old parents and a younger sister. As soon as I get settled in America, I'll bring them over. If they're still alive."

And so it went. Refugees traveling to America, hoping for a new life and a way to bring their loved ones after them. Everywhere I went, people discussed socialism, communism, workers' rights, owners' rights. Who was right? It was impossible to tell.

***

BULLETIN: May 10, 1920

AMERICAN SENATE TO DEBATE IMMIGRATION RESTRICTIONS; WILL THE DOORS CLOSE?

One day, I was sitting in the lobby of our hotel listening to the stories of our fellow travelers when Sam came dragging in.

"Sam," I called. "Over here. You look tired."

"I am tired, Beryl. But today I finally talked to the committee. We have to be there tomorrow to answer questions."

"What kinds of questions?"

"Have we ever been in jail? Do we have someone in America to vouch for us? Do we have money to get there? Are we healthy? What kind of work will we do in America? What kind of politics do we believe in?"

"Why are they asking us all these questions, Sam? Is it because America is trying to close its doors?"

"The other people in line were all talking about that. It seems that they are trying to weed out the people who won't be let in anyway when they get to America. That way there is more room for those who have a chance."

"Well, I guess that makes sense," I said, not completely convinced. "But who made them the ones to decide?"

"I guess since a lot of money for helping the refugees comes from American contributions to the HIAS and the Jewish Committee, they think they have the right, and also the responsibility."

"I guess so," I said, still skeptical. "What happens if we pass?"

"Then we get ready to go. There will be a train to Breslau next week. We should be able to get on that one. Come on, let's go tell Ma and Rose and Jerry."

We climbed the stairs, and back in our little room once again, Sam told us more about the questions the committee would ask.

"The people I talked to said to just tell the truth. It seems people who bought passports are getting in trouble. The original passport holder may have been a criminal or may be on the list of political troublemakers. Then the person holding the passport is caught between admitting that he has illegally bought a passport or being rejected because of the crimes of the original passport holder."

"But our passports are good," I said.

"Yes," Sam said. "So, we should be all right."

***

The next day we presented ourselves to the committee.

We came into a big room with a high ceiling and a couple of windows high up on one wall. Several serious men sat behind a long table with papers spread all over it. They were talking among themselves and smoking big black cigars. The air was thick with smoke.

They didn't pay any attention to us for a few minutes, while we just stood there waiting uncomfortably.

At last, one man started asking Sam a few simple questions. The others continued looking down at papers on the table or looked up and stared at us, eyes squinting through the cigar smoke.

Then they talked among themselves a little and after a couple of minutes seemed satisfied. They stamped our papers and handed them to Sam, along with train tickets.

In the few days we had before leaving Krakow, we washed our clothes, found a little food for our journey and said goodbye to some of the fellow travelers we had come to know. It wasn't far from Krakow to Breslau, but it took two days to get there because the tracks were so badly damaged from the war. The train stopped for hours at a time while crews made repairs.

This train had seats, but again it was overcrowded with all sorts of people. We squeezed together and made the best of it.

In Breslau, the HIAS sent us to a small inn they had an arrangement with. They gave us another tiny room, only this time we had to share it with another family.

The room was so packed we stayed out except to take turns sleeping.

We were in Breslau only a few days and didn't have to be approved by another committee since our tickets, it turned out, were good right on through to Antwerp. But we had to wait for the right train.

Breslau was in Austria, close to Germany, and the people spoke an Austrian-German dialect I could understand. This city too was trying to recover from the war. People everywhere were trying to put their lives back together again.

By the time we had learned our way around and bought more supplies, it was time to leave for Antwerp.

During the war, Antwerp had been occupied by the Germans, and we could tell there had been immense damage. But it was still such a pleasure to look at this city that we took our time.

CHAPTER 15

1919-1921

Antwerp, our first really Western city. The capital of Belgium. A port city on the Scheldt River leading out to the big Atlantic Ocean.

When we arrived, the familiar HIAS sign we had come to expect and respect was being held up by a man in a Western-style suit. He gave each family directions to their lodging, and we made our way through the city.

It was summer by this time, and we were plenty warm in our heavy clothes, carrying our bundles.

During the war, Antwerp had been occupied by the Germans, and we could tell there had been immense damage. But it was still such a pleasure to look at this city that we took our time.

Mixed in with attractive older buildings were big, empty areas where bombed-out structures had been cleared away. Now the city was being rebuilt in a more modern style. Construction was going on everywhere.

When we arrived at our hotel, we saw that it was the same type of place the HIAS had contracted with in the other towns we had passed through. Although this one was much bigger, refugees still clogged the lobby and pestered the frustrated manager at the front desk.

He looked up as we came in. After a few minutes he excused himself from the people trying to make themselves understood and asked if he could help us.

And soon he was showing us into a small room with a bed and two cots, a small table and a sink with running water. The toilet, he explained, was in a room down the hall and was shared by everyone on that floor of the hotel. Then he left us to go back to his crowded lobby.

We didn't know how long we would be in Antwerp. But the first thing we had to do was visit the HIAS office. Once again, a local committee was screening everyone going to America and helping those who passed to get their visas.

"Sam, tomorrow we will go to the committee," Ma said as we unpacked. "What is it called here?"

"Ezra. The committee here is called Ezra, Ma."

"Good. We will go to this Ezra and see what we have to do next. In the meantime, children, find a little work if you can. We have to watch our money but good until your Papa learns we are here and can send us some more."

While Ma and Sam waited to see Ezra, Jerry, Rose and I spent the next few days exploring the town.

Antwerp really opened our eyes. The hotel manager told us that the Socialist Party had been in power since the end of the war and had passed universal suffrage. Everyone could vote for the government and everyone had an equal chance for an education.

He suggested we walk down to the river and see the port.

"The Scheldt River has tunnels running under it from the main city on the right bank to the residential and business section on the left bank," he told us. "Go down and take a look."

We followed his directions to the river. It was easy to see why Antwerp had become an important port. We gazed at the many big, ocean-going steamships in the docks. Sailors were rushing around, big boxes were being lifted up onto the ships and little tugboats were importantly chugging around the big guys.

"Jerry, do you think we will be going to America on one of those huge ships?" Rose asked.

"I don't know, Rose," Jerry replied.

Rose pointed to an old derelict ship. "I sure hope we don't go on something like that."

"But there are people getting on that boat, Rose," I said. "It looks like it is taking on refugees."

"I know, Beryl. That's what I mean. I wouldn't want to be out on the ocean in that thing."

"Neither would I."

BULLETIN: August 16, 1920

REDS ATTEMPT TO STORM WARSAW

In the days that followed, I became quite friendly with the hotel manager. When I came down into the lobby in the morning, he would suggest places for us to see in Antwerp.

We felt safe walking around the city, so we visited the big university and the bridge where, legend had it, a giant once collected tolls until someone chopped off his hand.

One day as I came down the stairs from our room, I saw the manager trying to talk to some ladies who were very upset.

The manager called me over.

"Can you understand these ladies?" he asked. "I know they are upset, but I don't understand what they want."

I understood what they were saying because they were speaking a Polish dialect, and after spending a couple of minutes with them I was able to explain their problem to the manager.

"They are trying to tell you they have no money now, but money has been sent to them, via Ezra, and very soon they will be able to pay you for their rooms. They are begging you not to throw them out of the hotel."

"Ah," the manager said with a smile. "No wonder they're upset. I am so glad you understand them. Tell them I'll check with Ezra. No one is going to throw them out. They can rest assured I won't put them on the street."

I explained the manager's assurance to the ladies, and as they happily turned away from the front desk, one of them kissed me on the top of my head.

The sudden silence was a relief.

"Do you understand many of these languages?" the manager asked.

"Yes, I do," I replied. "When I come to a new country, it doesn't take me long at all to learn the language."

"You know, young man, you could be a great help to me. My name is Mr. B. What are you called?"

"My name is Yisroel. Yisroel Aynbinder. But my family calls me Beryl."

"Well, Yisroel, that won't do, and neither will Beryl. Not if you're going to America. You'll need a real American name."

"An American name? What kind of a name? I wouldn't have any idea what name to choose."

Mr. B. stroked his chin a moment. "I'll tell you what. I'll lend you my name. It's Bernard. Bernie for short."

"Bernard," I said proudly. "That's a fine name. Thank you very much, Mr. B. That's a beautiful American name."

"Now, Bernard," Mr. B. said. "It would make my job much easier if you were around to interpret. Everyone would be much happier. So I would like to hire you. You would work from eight o'clock in the morning until noon and then you would be free the rest of the day."

"You don't have to pay me for helping people," I said.

"All right, then. How about if I give you a little break on your room and board and teach you English while you are working for me. Then when you get to America you'll have a head start."

"It's a deal," I said, and we shook hands. I felt very proud to have such an important job and Ma was very happy for our lower rent.

From then on, I came down to the desk every day at eight o'clock. The refugees came in spurts. One morning there might be tumult for an hour or two, then it would be quiet again. The next morning it might be quiet the whole time, but the following morning might bring a full four hours of frantic travelers.

But in the quiet times Mr. B. taught me English, and I picked it up pretty quickly. Now, more than ever, I was looking forward to getting to America. But Ma and Sam were having no luck yet with Ezra.

We tried to be patient.

***

One afternoon, Mr. B. spotted me as I came through the lobby and waved me over to the desk.

"Bernie, have you ever been to a prize fight?" he asked.

"What's a prize fight?"

"It's a sport where two men get into a ring and fight each other. I have two tickets. How would you like to go with me?"

"That sounds great, Mr. B. When?"

"Tomorrow night. Meet me here at six o'clock. Don't worry about supper, I'll buy us a little something before the fight."

All that next day I was very excited. Six o'clock finally came. I met Mr. B. and we went to a small cafe and had dinner. Then, as we walked to the arena, Mr. B. tried to explain a little about what we would see.

But I still wasn't prepared.

The arena was filled with people, women as well as men. Everyone seemed to be smoking and it was very noisy. Men walked up and down the aisles taking bets on who would win the fight. Then the lights went out all around, except for the bright center ring where the smoke curled up and swirled around the lights. The ring, I realized, was really a square, raised platform. I don't know why they called it a ring.

In came the two fighters with their helpers. The spectators shouted for their favorite.

In the center of the ring, a referee talked to both fighters. Each man went to his corner. A bell rang. Out they came, circling one another carefully. Then the fists started flying.

So did mine. Up I jumped, punching my own fists in the air.

"Shlug him! Hit him!" I yelled, jumping up and down, throwing my fists left and right.

"You tell them, kid," a man next to me said, laughing. "Show them how it's done."

I looked down at Mr. B.

"It's all right, Bernie," he said, laughing and clapping me on the back. "Enjoy yourself! Everybody here gets into the act."

There were several fights with boxers of different weights. After the matches we walked home, busily discussing the merits of each fighter. Before I knew it, we were back in the hotel lobby.

"Thank you for taking me, Mr. B.," I said. "I have never seen such a thing in all my life. It was wonderful."

"Thank you for coming with me," Mr. B. laughed. "I enjoyed watching you almost as much as the fighters."

I went up to our room. It was pretty late, but everyone was awake having tea.

"Did you enjoy yourself, Beryl?" Ma asked.

"Was it bloody?" Jerry wanted to know.

I told them all about my evening.

"Grown men hitting each other," Ma said when I was through. "Like children."

"No, Ma," Jerry tried to explain. "It's a sport. They don't hate each other. They just want to show who is the strongest."

"Like children," Ma maintained.

"What are you all doing up, anyway?" I asked.

"We were talking about our visa problem," Jerry said.

"What visa problem?"

"Explain to him, Sam," Ma said.

"Beryl, after Pa got to America he changed his name from Mordecai to Max. But he signed our visa papers when he was still Mordecai. So now Ezra has to find him and get all new papers signed, with the name Max, before we can get our visas."

I sat on one of the cots, my excitement suddenly gone flat.

"What's going to happen now?" I asked wearily. "How long will it take? Will America close its doors before we get there?"

My questions went unanswered.

"Who knows?" Sam shrugged, frustration in his voice. "The Ezra people have written letters for us and told Pa what he has to do. But it is going to take some time."

"But it will get fixed, won't it? We can still go to America, can't we?" I felt bad, but I realized there was nothing to be done. We would just have to wait.

"They told me everything should work out fine," Sam said. "It's just a matter of getting all the papers signed."

We sat in silence for a few long moments, hoping Sam was right.

"So, children, we may be here awhile," Ma finally said. "We must be careful to make our money last. So now let us go to bed. Tomorrow we will start again."

***

I worked every day for Mr. B. and my English really improved. He took me to a couple more fights and a couple of shows at the Jewish theater. What fun that was. The plays were in Yiddish and the Vaudeville acts were too, and the costumes and stage sets were a wonder.

Mr. B. opened up a whole new world for me, teaching me and showing me things I never dreamed of back in Horchov.

Meanwhile, the weeks turned into months. But this time I never gave up hope, and since I was speaking English every day I couldn't forget about America even if I wanted to.

***

It was April 1921, more than sixteen months since we'd left Horchov. We'd been in Antwerp ten months.

I was at the front desk with Mr. B. when a messenger came in asking for the Aynbinders and several other families.

"I'm Bernard Aynbinder," I said. "What do you want with us?"

"I have a message for you from Ezra. They want you all to come to the committee tomorrow and sign for your visas."

"You mean they're here? Mr. B., our visas are here! I have to go. I have to go tell the family."

"Go ahead, go," Mr. B. said, waving me on. "I'll see you later."

I ran up the five flights of stairs that led to our room and burst through the door. Everyone was there.

"Ma. Everybody. We can go!"

I clung to the doorknob, out of breath. Everyone looked at me blankly.

"A messenger just came. We have to be at Ezra in the morning. Our visas are there."

Jerry jumped off the bed and grabbed me. "Are you certain? Beryl, are you sure?"

"Sure, I'm sure. And by the way, everybody, now you can start calling me by my new American name, Bernard."

"American name?" Jerry teased. "Where did you get an American name?"

"Mr. B. gave it to me. From now on, I'm Bernard Aynbinder. Bernie for short."

"Bernie. It's almost like Beryl," Ma said.

"That's right, Ma. And I asked Mr. B. what Channah would be in English. From now on, your name can be Anna."

"Anna? Oh, Ma, that's a pretty name," Rose said.

"Yes, almost like Channah," Ma said. "A new name for a new life. It is good."

***

We sat up for a long time that night, talking and planning. The next morning, we made our way to Ezra.

Again, there was a large group of people waiting in the courtyard. But those of us who had received messages were led inside to a big waiting room.

When our names were called, we went in to be examined by a doctor and were given shots in the arm.

When I finished and came out to wait for the rest of the family, another family was causing a stir. It seemed everyone had passed their physical exam except one daughter who had pinkeye. She would have to stay in Antwerp.

"What are we going to do?" the mother cried. "How can we leave her here by herself?"

"We can't lose the tickets," the father said. "We'll never be able to save enough for new tickets for the whole family. Stop crying, both of you. Shandel will just have to stay here until she is better. Once we get across, we can save enough for one new ticket and bring her later."

"No, no," the woman wailed.

"It has to be," the father said with finality. "She will stay at the hotel until she is well. Ezra will help us find someone to look after her."

After that, I was full of dread. As each member of our family came back into the room, I looked up in fear. "Are you all right?" I asked. "Did you pass?"

Sam, Jerry and Rose all had passed, and the four of us ended up waiting for Ma.

It was only when she finally came out and said she had passed that we took a deep breath and felt like we could breathe again.

When we showed the Ezra clerk our papers from the doctor, he gave us our visas and pinned new name tags to our jackets.

"Keep these name tags on until you are passed through the American immigration," he told us. "Tomorrow morning, go to the dock. Your boat is called 'The Lapland.' Make certain you have everything you need with you, your tickets, your papers, your money, everything. You won't have time to go back."

We tried to act casual as we walked away. But after we got through the courtyard and back onto the street, we stopped and looked at each other. We were all grinning from ear to ear.

"Come on," Jerry said as we hugged each other. "Let's go someplace and really celebrate. Let's stop at a cafe and have a coffee."

"A coffee?" Ma said. "Not tea?"

"No, Ma, a coffee," Jerry said, playfully putting his arm around her. "People drink coffee in America."

We walked down the street with light hearts, stopped at a cafe, and enjoyed our coffee sitting in the bright spring sunshine. We sipped and laughed. We talked about what it would feel like to be out on the great ocean, and what it would really be like to live in America.

"So, what do you think of the coffee, Ma?" Jerry asked with a wink at us.

"At least it's hot," she replied, and we all laughed.

The next morning, we said goodbye to our friends at the hotel and I spent a few minutes with Mr. B., thanking him for everything.

"I'll miss you, Bernie," he said as we hugged. "Have a good life."

Then we hefted our bundles and headed for the harbor.

***

At the dock, people crushed toward the narrow gangplank leading up to the boat deck, where a lone sailor stood checking tickets.

Women carried their bedding on their heads, babies in their arms. Men lugged large parcels on their backs and tied-up old cases in each hand. Little children clung to their mother's skirt or their father's trouser leg as best they could. Everyone pushed and shoved to get on first so they could get a good spot.

But Pa had spent enough money on our tickets so we didn't have to be in steerage, down in the hold of the ship. We were shown to a small room with two bunk beds, a sink, a toilet and a porthole we could open for air.

Ma and Rose would share the bottom level of one bunk bed, while Jerry and I were to squeeze in together above them. Sam would have the top level of the other bunk bed to himself, with a single man who was also assigned to our room underneath.

They gave us straw for the bunks and a metal dipper for taking our drinking water.

We introduced ourselves to our roommate. He was a tall, thin young man named Aaron, from Lemberg. His family had been killed in a pogrom, and now he was on his way to America by himself.

After we got our bundles stowed away, we went out together to explore the ship.

"Don't go far," Ma called after us. "And whatever you do, don't get off the boat."

"Don't worry, Ma," Sam answered. "We won't go far."

"Ma's a little nervous," Sam confided to Aaron as we wandered up to the deck and looked around.

A winding line of people still snaked across the dock and slowly made its way up the gangplank. Once aboard, most people were directed down into steerage.

The crew bustled about getting the ship ready, stepping over baggage and shouting at people to get out of the way.

By late afternoon, everyone was aboard. We sailed with the evening tide.

With nightfall approaching, nearly every passenger on the ship came out onto the deck, where we all quietly watched Europe slip away in the darkening eastern sky. Then, almost as one, we turned west, where a brilliant sunset beckoned us to a golden future.

***

Our first day was spent exploring the ship. We were outside on the deck most of the time. Even though the weather was good, some people had trouble adjusting and were seasick.

But we all were fine and having a good time meeting our fellow travelers.

"Bernie," Jerry called as I came up on deck. "Come on over."

"This is my brother, Bernie," he said, introducing me. "Bernie, this is Chaim, and his sisters, Surah and Leah. They come from Bialystok."

"Nice to meet you," I said. "Where in America will you be living?"

"We're going to be in New York," Chaim said. "My father is in the garment industry there. I understand you're going to Washington, D.C."

"Yes," I replied. "Our father is in produce."

As we talked on, comparing our pasts and discussing our plans, more and more people came up from steerage. I noticed when they got up on deck, they looked about, half-blinded by the bright sun, and took a deep breath of the clean, salty air.

People sat around or stood by the railing talking to one another. Pretty soon one fellow started playing a clarinet and we began to sing some Russian songs.

I kept looking over at Surah. She had bright red hair and seemed about my age. Jerry had his eye on Leah, the dark-haired sister.

We lazed around talking with our new friends. It was a perfectly beautiful day, so beautiful that we were completely unprepared for what followed.

Early the next morning I woke up when I was practically thrown from my bunk.

The ship tossed furiously. Everything that wasn't tied down had fallen to the floor and was sliding back and forth, banging against the walls. The lamp hanging from the ceiling was swinging violently.

Rose was sick, vomiting into a bowl. Ma was hanging onto the bunk trying to help her.

Sam, Jerry and I didn't feel all that well either and decided to go up on deck for some fresh air.

As we pushed open the door, the storm hit us full in the face.

For a moment it felt good. But screaming sheets of rain quickly soaked us.

Evil-looking black waves towered high above. Each one rose up like a giant fist, pounding down on the ship as if the mighty ocean had a will of its own and was determined to push us under. We cowered down by the stairwell.

The crew ran about in rain slickers coated in ice. There was no protection and we had to stay out of the way, so we scurried back down to the cabin.

Rose and our roommate Aaron were sprawled on their bunks groaning. Ma was busy wiping their faces and holding the bowl. The overhead lamp still swung crazily.

"Come on," Jerry said to Sam and me. "We'll play some cards."

We climbed onto one of the bunks and wiled away most of the day playing cards and trying to keep from being tossed onto the floor.

The storm lasted all day. The cabin was hot and stuffy with all of us packed in, and the stench of vomit didn't help. But every time we tried to open the porthole; water came pouring in.

"Chaim and his family must be having an awful time down in steerage," I said.

"I'd hate to be down there right now," Jerry agreed, throwing a card on the bed.

Sam picked up the card.

"I was down there," I told them as I looked at my cards. "Even before the storm it was bad. I almost threw up myself."

Sam put down a card. I picked it up.

"I win," I announced with a grin.

"Not again," Jerry moaned.

"Yep. You owe me three-hundred American dollars when we get there."

By the next morning, the storm had subsided and we all went out on deck. The air was fresh and salty damp, the ship washed clean.

Ma took a deep breath. "Ah, such a mechaieh, such a blessing. It smells so good."

"I think I'm hungry," Rose declared.

"I know I'm hungry," Jerry agreed. "Hey, there's Chaim."

"Hey, Chaim, how did you make out yesterday?" Jerry called.

Chaim walked over. "It was awful," he said. "We were all sick. I wasn't too bad at first so I tried to help the others. But just as I got out of bed, somebody leaned over and threw up all over me. By the time I washed up, I was too sick to help anyone."

"And your sisters?" I asked.

"They're still pretty bad."

"Can we help?" Jerry asked.

"Don't even try to go down there," Chaim warned. "You wouldn't believe how bad it is. The smell is terrible."

Rose, who looked much better today, took Ma by the arm.

"Come on, Ma," she said. "Let's take a walk around the deck."

"All right," Ma agreed. "We'll enjoy the air."

Most of the passengers spent the day on the deck enjoying the sunshine, relaxed and happy. They talked with one another about their experiences, the towns they came from and their prospects in America.

Dinner was served out of big buckets. We brought up our pails for our share. Ma wouldn't eat the meat because she was sure it wasn't kosher, even though the HIAS had assured her it would be.

Though she encouraged us to eat the meat, we filled up mostly on bread and kasha.

That evening several people brought their musical instruments on deck and started playing some lively tunes. We began to dance and shout, and the Norwegian and Italian refugees joined us in happiness and celebration.

When everyone was good and tired, the musicians played some sad old songs of Russia.

The fourth day was much the same as the third. We had made a number of friends by this time, but it was the little redhead, Surah, who

I asked to walk the deck with me. Later, Jerry teased me about having a date, but I told him he was just jealous.

Then toward evening a fog came down from the north and closed in all around the ship. We were startled when the foghorn bellowed its deep bass call.

The night was strange and eerie. When we could no longer see even two feet in front of us, we went back to our cabin. In between the blaring of the foghorn, we talked more of what to expect once we arrived.

"Chaim says they will give us another physical exam when we go ashore," Jerry said. "He says it will be even more strict than it was in Austria. If someone is a little sick, they'll put him in quarantine. Anyone who is very sick will be sent back."

"That's right," Aaron said. "The tailor's son in our town was sent back. They said he had tuberculosis."

"Wash good. Eat well. You won't get sick," Ma told us. "Now, tomorrow we will get ready for Passover. First, we'll clean up this cabin, then we'll wash ourselves."

"You mean we're going to have Passover right here on the ship?" I asked.

"Yes, indeed. I was talking with the old rebbe from Bialystok. The HIAS made arrangements with the steamship company and we will have all the matzo we need for the rest of the trip. Tomorrow night we will have a Seder."

The next day we cleaned our little area as best we could, washed ourselves good, then went up on deck. The women spread tablecloths and laid out matzo and eggs. There was even a little wine. Everyone gathered around.

The old rebbe began with the blessing, and the prayers floated out over the sea in the cool evening air.

And so once again, this time among strangers turned friends, we told the age-old story of the exodus from Egypt into freedom. As the setting sun disappeared on the horizon, I knew that just like me, everyone there was thinking of Seders past with loved ones now gone – and of Seders to come in the golden land.

PART IV
THE GOLDEN LAND

A T THE END of World War I, the Bolsheviks pursued world revolution but were beaten back by Poland in a decisive battle at Warsaw in 1920. At the same time, the United States Senate was rejecting the peace treaty, the Treaty of Versailles.

Meanwhile, the huge influx of immigrants coming into America as a result of the war and subsequent fighting was causing great consternation.

Americans feared that radical elements from eastern Europe were immigrating to the United States and would instigate revolution within its borders. America was undergoing a "Red Scare."

Italians and Jews were most suspect among the foreigners. And Jews from Bolshevik Russia were especially pursued by the U.S. Attorney General. Those thought to be radicals were sent to special detention camps and subjected to swift deportation hearings. Hundreds were deported during the months following rejection of the Treaty.

The special emphasis on deportation of Jews and vitriolic editorials appearing in certain newspapers sparked one of America's most disturbing anti-Semitic periods and precipitated a drive in Congress for some kind of drastic resolution to the perceived immigration problem.

To put some limit on immigration, Congress had already passed the literacy law of 1917 and tightened restrictions on political undesirables.

Now the House of Representatives passed a bill proposing a total ban on immigration for one year, to give Congress time to draft a more general law addressing the entire immigration issue. But Senate committee hearings beginning on January 3, 1921, concluded there was really no danger of a huge influx of radical immigrants in the near future and therefore no reason for emergency legislation.

However, the Senators were convinced that the "new type" of immigrant now coming from southern and eastern Europe in unprecedented numbers should be limited.

Under a bill presented in Congress in April 1921, in the upcoming fiscal year immigrants from any one nation would be limited to three percent of the number of people of that nationality residing in the U.S. as of the 1910 census.

The bill was passed by the Senate in May and took effect in June. As a result, immigration from eastern Europe was reduced to a little more than fifty thousand in fiscal year 1921-1922, down from one-hundred-twenty thousand the previous year.

Europe and Russia, reacting to the hardships of war and reconstruction, had resorted to that old scapegoat, anti-Semitism. Terrible pogroms were taking place in the Ukraine. Jewish communities in Brest-Litovsk, Bialystok and Kyiv were destroyed.

Remnants of these communities became refugees with nowhere to run. The golden land had closed its doors.

Meanwhile, the majority of Jewish refugees allowed to enter America after World War I made substantial progress during the boom period of the 1920s.

Through hard work and dogged persistence, they found employment, educated their children and strove to become part of their new country, while trying to maintain their Jewish identity and heritage.

The Jewish community developed its own religious education system; public school was augmented by Hebrew school. Their ideal was to see their children achieve a higher education, a better life, to become lawyers, doctors and scientists.

The arts had always been important to Jews wherever they found themselves. In America, the Yiddish theater prospered. Poetry and music became part of everyday life and great Jewish artists, actors, musicians and comics became part of the American scene.

The immigrants of that time, Jewish, Italian, Irish, Chinese, had come to this country with next to nothing. All they wanted was a chance. They were not afraid of hard work, and bosses found a new source of cheap labor. Mothers worked at home on piecework or in factories where government work rules were ignored. Underage children worked next to their mothers in the same factories, twelve to sixteen hours a day sewing or rag-picking, or at packaging and delivery.

Conditions in these sweatshops were abominable. There were no mandated break times. There were no fans and few had enough windows or doors for sufficient ventilation. Sanitation was minimal, fire protection nil.

Men also worked in the sweatshops, or as peddlers, selling anything they could, fruits and vegetables, ice for ice boxes, rags and pots and pans, or they worked in the mines or building railroads. If a man had been a tailor or a shoemaker in his old country he tried to save enough to open a similar shop in America. These were the lucky ones. As hard as they worked, it was for themselves instead of the slave drivers at the factories or mines.

The Jewish immigrants faced special hardships. Quotas limited the number of Jews allowed into the professional schools of the universities, quiet real estate understandings kept Jews from buying homes in certain neighborhoods, and anti-Semitic propaganda spread.

Then came the Great Depression. The economy collapsed in 1929.

It is said today that the primary cause of the stock market crash was the widespread practice of buying on margin. People borrowed money to invest, then used the stock they had bought as collateral for their loans. This was fine as long as the market kept rising. When the market began to go down, stock used as collateral lost its value and banks began calling in their loans.

Most investors had no real money to pay off these loans. They tried to borrow or put off paying or went bankrupt.

People stopped buying anything that wasn't absolutely necessary. Industry stopped manufacturing. Thousands of workers were let go. Factories closed. Banks closed. People had no money, no purchasing power, so more companies went under and more people lost their jobs.

It was a vicious circle that didn't end until 1942, when World War II put everyone back to work.

Still, despite the problems of adjusting to a new country and dealing with the devastating depression, the immigrants had faith. They believed that in America they had an opportunity they never would have had back home. If they worked hard enough, they could make something of themselves and make a future for their families.

Every refugee on the ship wanted to be up on deck for that first glimpse of America. We found a place along the railing and strained to see ahead in the early morning light. The sun wasn't even up yet and the wind-blown spray from the ocean was salty on our lips.

CHAPTER 16

Spring 1921

I was so excited I hardly slept, and everyone seemed to wake up at the same time that morning.

"Hurry up, everybody," I called. "Let's finish packing so we can get a good spot on the deck."

"Wait for the rest of us," Rose gasped, pulling on her shoes.

"All right, but hurry."

We finished quickly and scampered up the stairs. Even Ma was in a hurry today.

Every refugee on the ship wanted to be up on deck for that first glimpse of America. We found a place along the railing and strained to see ahead in the early morning light. The sun wasn't even up yet and the wind-blown spray from the ocean was salty on our lips.

We stared westward, an electric feeling of excitement running through the crowd.

"Mrs. Aynbinder, is someone meeting you?" one of Ma's new shipboard friends asked.

"Yes, my husband Mordecai and my oldest son, Morris. And you?"

"My husband Simon will be there to meet us."

My heart was pounding. "Do you see anything, Jerry? I don't see anything. What time did they say we're supposed to dock?"

"I don't know, Bernie. I don't see anything either. Let's ask one of the sailors."

We went over and asked a nearby sailor how long it would be before we could see land.

The sailor pointed toward the horizon. "You see that darker blue edge and what looks like a bank of clouds? Well, that's America."

Sure enough, when we looked really hard we could make out the land, under the bank of clouds.

Word passed quickly around the deck. See the dark blue, over there? That's America.

Excitement grew as the land became clear and before long we could see the skyline of New York. The tall buildings seemed arranged especially to welcome those coming in from the sea. They grew taller as we watched, the rising sun glinting off their windows. And before we knew it, we were entering the harbor.

"The lady! See her? There she is — Liberty!"

People cried and hugged and laughed and pointed as the ship slid by the beautiful Statue of Liberty.

"Thank you, God," Ma said, pulling us all close. Tears streamed down her face as she stared up at the statue.

"Ma, you should be happy," Jerry teased, noticing the tears.

"I am happy, Jerry. Never in my life have I been so happy."

"Come on," Sam said. "We'd better go down and get our bags."

"I want to watch the boat pull into the dock," Jerry protested.

"We'll be docking for a while and since everything is all packed, it will only take us a minute to bring our bags up on deck," Sam countered. "Come on. Rose, you stay here with Ma. We can handle everything."

Sam, Jerry and I ran downstairs and brought everything up on deck so we would be ready to go. Sam's reasoning made sense. I certainly didn't want to waste a minute more than I had to on the ship.

When we came back up on deck, we were still inching our way into the harbor. Little tugboats scurried around in the water like ants next to a giant, but they still managed to gradually push and pull the big ship into her berth.

Looking out over the dock, we saw several big red buildings. A sign on the first building proclaimed, "Ellis Island — United States Department of Immigration and Naturalization."

Again, word spread like wildfire, but this time a different feeling ran through the crowd. Fear. Anxiety.

Ma looked nervous. I felt it too, in the pit of my stomach.

Here was the big test. Now that we had come this far, would they let us in?

I looked around at our fellow passengers. Faces suddenly looked white and strained. Mothers clutched their children. With dread, people stared down at the buildings and the authorities lined up on the dock.

But amid the authorities, I spotted a couple of men holding up the familiar HIAS sign.

"Don't worry, Ma," I said, pointing down to the dock. "The HIAS is here to help us."

We learned later that the HIAS had people on hand to help those with special problems. They intervened and tried to help when there was a question of a waiting job or a need for money.

Ma said nothing, but she clutched her feather pillow tightly. She wasn't about to lose it now.

The gangplank was let down and a group of officials walked up onto the deck. They talked with the captain for a few minutes and some papers changed hands.

We stood with all the other refugees, watching and waiting. Then the group of Americans turned to the passengers.

Interpreters started shouting instructions at us in a dozen different languages. We were to line up. We were not to push.

They came up to the first few people and started pinning numbers and tags on their jackets. This immediately caused a panic. A woman screamed. A child ran off.

"It's all right," the interpreters shouted. "Don't worry. Remain calm, please. This is only to help you get through immigration."

The passengers calmed down a little and began to line up as instructed. "As your number is called, you may leave the ship. Go directly into the first big building you see on the wharf."

Everyone wanted to be the first one off, but we were lucky. They took the first-class passengers first, then it was our turn. The steerage passengers would be last.

We were all herded into the customs building. I never saw such a huge room; it ran the entire width of the building with a big, high ceiling. I felt like an ant waiting to be stepped on.

Again, the interpreters were shouting at us. Everyone was confused. Parents tried to keep families together. Lost children screamed and cried. People tripped over spilled baggage. And such noise. We could barely hear anything the interpreters were yelling.

Between all the shouting and pushing, we found ourselves divided into lines between metal railings. Ma clung tightly to Sam and Rose and kept looking over her shoulder to make sure Jerry and I were right behind.

As the line inched along, I saw we were moving past a doctor in a bright white coat. An interpreter and a nurse stood with him. The doctor seemed to be looking people over and making check marks on a piece of paper held by a clipboard. Most people were sent along to another line. You could tell because after each exam he would point and give the person a push in the right direction.

But as I got closer, I noticed that sometimes he used a piece of chalk to mark a big 'X' on someone's coat. Then he pushed that person toward a big cage in another part of the room. The unlucky person being pushed would cry and reach out to other family members still in line.

Fathers were separated from families, mothers from children. Families were confused and terrified at being split up. They didn't know what to do. But they were pushed on.

Finally, it was our turn. I watched as Sam, Ma, Rose and Jerry were pushed on through to the next line, away from the dreaded cage.

Then it was my turn. I was afraid.

The doctor looked me over carefully. He listened to my chest, looked in my mouth, inspected my head.

"Can you hear?" the interpreter asked. I nodded.

"Can you understand what I am saying?"

"Yes," I replied in English. "I understand."

"Good," the doctor said, making a check mark on his list. "You can move on down the line." He gave me a push like the others in the direction he wanted me to go.

I moved on. The line took a sharp right turn and there was a second doctor. The women were taken into one screened area, the men another.

An interpreter said the doctor was inspecting us for contagious diseases. When it came my turn, I had to undress and this doctor looked me over but good, up and down and all around, and asked me what seemed like a million questions while making check marks on his list.

"Have you ever had measles? Have you ever had cholera? Have you ever had any sexual diseases?"

I answered all his questions. He seemed glad I had been given a typhus shot in Russia. I was told to dress and move on.

Then came the third doctor. After all the first two had done, I wondered what the third could possibly do. But before I could wonder very long, he took my face in one hand and stared hard right at me. I stared back and before I knew what was happening, he took his free hand, flipped up my eyelids with a little piece of paper and peered into my eyes. He made a check mark on his list, while a nurse gave me a clean cloth to wipe my running eyes and pushed me on.

I dabbed at my eyes. I was beginning to get a little farblondjet, a little mixed up, from all this pushing and poking. I wondered how many more doctors I would have to see.

"What is your nationality?" someone shouted at me as if I was hard of hearing.

"Russian," I said.

"Then go to that line over there. The second one from the right."

Now it seemed we were being directed into new lines based on nationality. If you were Russian go to this line, if you were Italian go to that line.

At the front of each line was a long row of desks with an inspector sitting behind each one.

Again, I waited for my turn. When it finally came, the inspector spoke to me in Russian.

He asked me if I'd ever broken the law, if I'd ever been in jail, if I was a Bolshevik. I answered no and he made check marks on his list.

They sure make a lot of check marks around here, I thought.

Then he asked if I had family in America.

"Yes. My father and oldest brother."

"And they paid for your passage?"

"Yes."

"Are they meeting you here?"

"Yes. I hope so. They are supposed to meet us," I said nervously. Check. Check.

"Can you read and write Russian?"

"Yes," I said. Then, in English, I added, "And English too."

For the first time the inspector looked up directly at me. "All right," he said in English. "And what will you do to earn a living in America?"

"I'm going to work with my father selling produce and I'm going to go to school and get an education," I said proudly, in English.

He smiled. Check. Check.

"You can move along to the luggage inspector," he said.

As I waited for the rest of the family near the luggage inspection line, I looked back over the vast room. Swarms of people were being processed through the various lines. The doctors and inspectors did their work quickly and pushed people along. They were hurried and harried, all business, no fooling around. Sometimes they got aggravated and shouted at people who didn't understand, but they didn't go out of their way to be nasty or mean.

I thought about how different it would have been in Russia. There would have been suspicion and accusations. We would have been expected to bribe one of the clerks to get through such an interrogation.

Jerry came up behind me and we compared experiences.

"It wasn't so bad," I said.

"No, but I was scared they would find something wrong," Jerry said. "I sure hope Ma gets through."

Sam and Rose joined us, and after another minute or two, so did Ma. There were no chalk marks on any of us.

"What now?" Rose asked.

"So far, so good, I think," Sam replied. "At least none of us were sent to the cages."

We turned to look at the two cages filled with scared, weeping refugees. "What's going to happen to them?" I asked.

"One of the interpreters told me the doctors found something physically wrong with the ones in that cage," Jerry said, pointing at the cage to our right. "Some will be sent back and some will be put in quarantine. The ones in the other cage are politically unacceptable. They will be sent back."

"What is politically unacceptable?" Rose asked.

"Either the officials think they're Bolsheviks or they might have been in jail for something," Jerry answered.

"Step up here. Move along," the baggage inspector shouted, startling us. "You're holding up the line. Put your bags up here on the table. Quickly."

We hurriedly placed our things on the table and the inspector looked through everything but good.

He opened our boxes and bundles and felt all around the edges and through our clothes. Then he made us open our rolled-up bedding and felt the comforter carefully. And suddenly I remembered why I'd been dreading the baggage inspector.

The feather pillow.

Would he find Ma's dear possessions?

I looked at Ma. She was watching tensely.

The inspector picked up the pillow and fluffed both ends.

Then he let it go.

Ma and I both started to breathe again and looked at one another through the sides of our eyes.

"All right," the inspector said. "Move along. Through those doors you'll find the ferry to the mainland. Welcome to America."

Welcome to America!

We looked at each other in disbelief.

"Are we done?" I asked the interpreter. "Have they let us into America?"

"Yes. You are finished here." The interpreter smiled as he handed us our passports and some papers. "Keep these papers handy. You're going to need them to get work. Good luck."

CHAPTER 17

1921

The doors to America flew open and we walked through into the most beautiful day we had ever seen. Bright sunshine, blue skies, fluffy white clouds and the deep blue ocean flowing in to meet the great city.

We gazed across the bay at the strange new skyline of New York City. "Are we really here?" Rose asked in wonderment.

"I know what you mean, Rose," I said. "I can't believe it either."

None of us could believe it. We felt so good. So free. This time Ma wasn't crying. She had a beautiful smile on her face.

"We made it!" Jerry shouted, throwing his cap in the air. He grabbed our hands and we danced a little jig around Ma, laughing till we were dizzy and breathless.

A smiling immigration person directed us to the ferry boat.

"Oh, no, not another boat," Rose said. "I've had enough of boats for a while."

"This won't be a long ride," Sam told her. "We're just going a short way."

We boarded the ferry, found a place at the railing and dropped our bundles. Then we watched as other immigrants, beaming with happiness, boarded behind us.

Finally, with a whistle and a toot, we headed across the bay. Someone said we were going to the Battery, though no one knew what that meant.

Later I learned that the Battery had been built in 1811 as a place to put big guns to protect New York from the British. Years later it became a park for entertainment and was called Castle Garden. During the big immigration period of the late 1800s and early 1900s, Castle Garden was the port where immigrants landed. But it was too small even then to handle all the refugees, so New York decided to make Ellis Island the immigration port.

As the ferry drew near the dock, we looked out over the milling crowd, trying to spot Pa.

"There he is," Sam said, pointing over to our right. "And Morris is with him."

"Where?" Ma asked. "Where do you see them, Sam?"

Sam turned Ma in the right direction and pointed. The rest of us spotted them too.

"Oh, it is Pa!" Rose cried. "Pa. Over here. Here we are," she called, waving to get his attention.

Now Pa I recognized, but Morris I'd never really known because I was just a baby when he'd left Russia. So, I was interested to see what he looked like. He was short like the rest of us with a narrow face like Pa's. They were both well dressed in dark suits and black hats and looked well fed.

When the boat docked they came to meet us at the foot of the gangplank. Ma and Pa looked at each other a long time and then embraced.

The rest of us bombarded Morris with questions. What was he doing for a living? Where was Pa working? How would we get to Washington? And Rose wanted to know if he was married yet.

Morris tried his best to answer.

"Pa has a produce stand in the market where he sells lemons, and I have a little grocery store. And yes, Rose, I'm married. My wife's name is Sophie. I think you'll like her, but you'll have to learn English. She doesn't understand much Yiddish."

Then he took each one of us and hugged us. When he got to me he laughed. "So, this is my baby brother, Beryl," he said. "A grown man now."

"You'd better call him Bernie, his new American name, or he won't answer you," Jerry teased. And we all laughed.

"Even Pa's got an American name now," I said. "You changed your name to Max, didn't you, Pa?"

Pa nodded and smiled at me. "Nu, Bernie, you're a man now, yes?"

"Yes, Pa," I answered.

"Well, speaking of names, now that everyone is here, we're going to change our last name too," Morris announced.

"Why?" Sam asked.

"Our mail has been getting mixed up with another Aynbinder, so we've decided to shorten our name to Binder."

"Well, I guess if Zayde could change his name from Miller to Aynbinder when he came to Horchov, we can shorten our name to Binder now that we've come to America," I said.

"That's right," Morris said. "Oh, and by the way, Ma, we're going to spend the night in New York with your friends the Preiponts. They were very happy to know you were coming."

"Oh, it will be so good to see Rivke again," Ma said. "We'll get to talk over old times and hear all about their new life. Is she well?"

"Yes indeed, Ma, but you'll soon see for yourself," Morris answered as he led us toward the trolley.

We were all talking at once and looking around at everything at the same time. Pa and Morris spoke to each other in Yiddish, mixed with some English. "Morris, how come even though Pa's been here seven years he doesn't speak English very well?" I asked.

"He speaks a little," Morris said. "Enough to do a little business. But English is hard to learn."

"Well, you can speak to me in English," I said. "I learned in Antwerp."

Morris laughed and slapped me on the back. "Pa," he said, still laughing, "the greenhorn here says he speaks better English than you."

Pa put an arm around me and pulled me over with a hug. "That is good," he said with a big smile. "That is as it should be."

***

The trolley let us off in the middle of an area bustling with activity that seemed to shout out a single word — freedom! We looked around in awe.

Here, people crowded the sidewalks. Pushcarts, trolleys, trucks and automobiles filled the streets. Shops bulged with goods for sale, with signs in Yiddish, Russian, Polish and English.

Children ran or skated up and down the sidewalk, or rode scooters by pushing off with one foot. Girls jumped rope or hopped over lines of chalk in some kind of sidewalk game. Wash flew from clotheslines extending from window to window, and people sat on their front stoops enjoying the evening air and calling back and forth to their neighbors whenever they pleased.

We couldn't believe our eyes. No fear. No keeping to the house. Even talking to police officers who touched their caps in hello as they walked along. In Russia, everyone would go inside and hide if a policeman was coming.

Amazing.

"This is Hester Street," Morris said. "We're in the middle of the Jewish community now."

"Is it like this in Washington?" I asked. "Is everyone so free to walk around, to play outside, to open a business?"

"Not just in New York or Washington," Morris answered. "You can go anywhere in America. You don't even need a passport to go from one state to another. As for opening a business, well, you do have to pay for a license. But they can't deny you one because you're a Jew."

"Don't tell me everything is perfect here," Jerry said skeptically. "There must be some problems."

"No matter where you go in the world, you'll find problems," Morris said. "But the problems here are nothing compared to Russia. Here, at least, the government is supposed to be for everybody. Here we can choose the government we want by voting. Even the Jews can vote."

Just then Morris stopped at an apartment building. "Here we are," he announced. "This is where the Preiponts live."

We looked up at a five-story tenement building. Women were leaning out of windows, calling to their children. People sitting on the steps made way for us to go past.

"Greenhorns," someone said. "Welcome to America."

"What's a greenhorn?" Rose asked.

"People who are new to America. They are like young, green saplings that don't know anything," Morris answered.

We dragged our things up the stairs. The door flew open, and what a reception we had! Rivke had been Ma's best friend in Russia and I had been friends with her son, Louie, who was my age. And of course, Ma had practically raised Rivke's baby, Leah, after Rivke had gone to work in the pottery factory. Now Leah was a walking, talking, cute little eleven-year-old.

And did we talk. Louie wanted to hear all about our trip from Russia and I wanted to hear everything I could about America. Our folks reminisced about Horchov and all their old friends. Ma was happy to hear so many had made it to America.

"We have an Horchov Society right here in New York," Rivke told Ma.

"There is an Horchov Society in Baltimore too," Morris said. "It's not far from Washington, so we'll be able to visit once in a while."

"And we have an Horchov shul here and another in Boston," Rivke continued.

"So many shuls," Ma said.

"Boston is not so near here," Rivke said. "It's not as if you can walk there on Shabbes. Pretty soon we'll have two Horchov shuls here in New York."

"Why two?" Ma asked.

"Oh, you know what they say, Channah," Rivke said with a laugh. "Whenever you get three Jews together, they each want their own synagogue."

After spending half the night talking we got a little sleep, and in the morning we said goodbye to our friends, promising to visit each other often.

Then we took a trolley to the station and boarded the train for Washington, D.C. This train was nice and clean, I noticed. No live chickens here. But just after we boarded, I took Morris by the arm.

"Is that a Negro man?" I asked quietly, pointing out the window at a porter who was helping a lady with her luggage.

"Yes," Morris answered. "A lot of Black men have jobs as train porters. Haven't you ever seen a Negro?"

I had heard of Black people, but this was the first time I'd ever seen one. This porter seemed like a regular person to me. and very helpful to the passengers, so as we settled in for the ride, I thought no more about it. He was, after all, a man like any other, only with darker skin.

***

When we came out of the train station in Washington, Morris pointed to a big building a couple of blocks away.

"That's the Capitol of the United States of America," he told us proudly. "That's where the government meets to make the laws."

"Do you vote for the government, Morris?" I asked.

"No, Bernie. For some reason people who live in Washington can't vote. But every other citizen in the country has the right to vote if they are at least twenty-one years old."

"I guess I'll have to live in a different state when I turn twenty-one," I said, "because I'm going to vote."

***

The trolley we caught took us right by the Capitol and then turned and went down the hill.

"See that very tall spire way down at the end of the park?" Morris said. "That's the monument named for George Washington, the first president of the United States."

There was a big, open park between the Capitol and the monument with a small stream running down the middle. Even this early in the spring it smelled bad. Morris said people threw their garbage in it.

"What's that square building on the other side of the monument?" Jerry asked.

"That's the memorial to Abraham Lincoln," Morris answered. "He was the president who freed the slaves."

"And the slaves were the Black people, right?"

"Yes, that's right."

"Look at those beautiful pink trees," Rose said, pointing out through the window. "I've never seen anything like them."

"Those are the cherry trees Japan gave America, for friendship," Morris explained.

"They are beautiful," Ma agreed.

The trolley turned west and we left the center of the city behind us, heading toward an area of apartment buildings and row houses. We piled out of the trolley and after a short walk we were at Pa's apartment on Second and E streets.

The apartment was in a small three-story building above a shoemaker's shop. We walked up the steps and Pa opened the door. As we dropped our bundles and wandered about, I felt like I had dropped a load of trouble and worry.

Ma kept turning around and around in the middle of the kitchen. "Look, Rose, what a nice stove. And a box with ice to keep the food."

"And water coming right into the sink, Ma," Rose said, pushing the pump handle and letting the water run. "No more carrying water for everything."

The apartment had one large room that served as a kitchen and sitting room. There was also one bedroom and a closed-in porch. The outhouse was in the back yard. On the enclosed porch behind the kitchen, Pa had set up three cots for Sam, Jerry and me. Rose would sleep on a cot in the kitchen.

As we settled down around the table, Pa put on some water for tea. That's when I knew for sure we were finally home.

CHAPTER 18

1921-1925

For a few days we rested up and tried to get our bearings. Now that we didn't have to worry about where to sleep, or where to get food, or how to get to America, we didn't know where to go or what to do.

We had time to look around. But everything seemed strange. We had to learn different ways. Here everybody lived by the alarm clock. Get up when it rings and go to work. Eat at noon. Set the alarm clock when you go to bed.

We had to learn to find our way around, but I was better off than Ma, Sam, Jerry and Rose because I could read and speak a little English. So for a while, I was the interpreter, errand boy and general helper for the family.

Pa didn't have much in the cupboard or the ice box when we came because he had only himself to worry about. But now there were six of us to feed. So, one day during our first week in America, we went to the market where Pa had his lemon stand to buy food.

Ma insisted we all come with her and we didn't mind because we wanted to see more of the town anyway. Pa gave us directions before he left for work, and later that morning we took the trolley to the market.

The market was on Main Street, at the wharfs on the Potomac River. It was a huge shed of a building with all kinds of stalls. Merchants sold everything from fresh produce to live chickens to shoes.

Large overhead doors opened to the outside, where even more vendors had stands. Some stands, like the fish market and poultry market, spilled from their inside spaces to the outside dock that wrapped around the building.

It reminded me in many ways of the market square in Horchov and other towns we had seen on our way to America. But this was a very big market, the main wholesale market for the entire city of Washington and the surrounding area. And not only was it all under one roof, but it was open every day, instead of taking over the center of town on market day once a week.

The smell of sawdust, used to keep the floor dry, hung in the air and mixed with the smells of fresh produce, live chickens and dead fish – all those old, familiar smells. As we walked around, we just couldn't get over how much food and other goods there were in this one place. We had never seen such a plentiful stock of everything. In Russia, even before the war, we had stored things in the cool root cellar because you could never count on a regular flow of supplies.

But here the ships came right up the Chesapeake Bay and the Potomac River to deliver their supplies. The Potomac wasn't as big or fast as the Boog, but it gave us a good feeling to be living by a river again.

We stopped first at Pa's stand, which faced out toward the river. We were so proud of the huge stack of lemons waiting to be bought. Then we went off to buy what we needed.

Pretty soon we saw why Ma had insisted we all come with. We thought she was going to buy out the whole place. We stocked up on enough food to last a month, then had to carry it all back to the apartment in big boxes and bags.

We were so loaded down with packages we joked that we could have used an entire trolley just for us.

That evening, when Pa saw how much we had bought, he laughed and laughed. Then he explained to Ma that there was so much food in America — and it was so easy to get — that you could go to the corner store every day if you wanted and get fresh milk or anything you needed just for that day.

It took Ma a long time to get used to that idea. She felt more comfortable keeping a good stock of food in the house.

***

Sam, Jerry and I explored the city. We learned how to get around on the trolley and buses. We were amazed that we could go right into the big government buildings. No soldiers tried to stop us when we went into the Capitol and walked all the way up the steps in the George Washington Monument. The Potomac River made us feel at home and pretty soon we were having picnics along its banks at Hains Point Park.

Then, after a while, Sam and Jerry went looking for work and I started helping Pa at his lemon stand in the market.

After my first day on the job, I told Pa, "Now I know why you smell so good. You work with the lemons all day and then you stroke your beard with your hands. I'll probably smell like lemons too."

Pa laughed. "I didn't know I smelled so good."

While I was helping Pa, I got up at three o'clock in the morning and picked up the fresh produce at the freight station. Then I brought it to the market, unpacked it and spent the entire day on my feet selling it.

When I got home from work, I cleaned myself up and went to night school. The school started at seven each evening and was held in a regular schoolhouse after the children's classes were finished. Jerry and Sam met me there and we studied English.

Our class was full of refugees from all over the world. Everyone wanted to learn enough to get their citizenship papers, and you couldn't go to citizenship classes until you knew how to read and write English and could pass a test about the way the government was organized.

I loved going to school, but I was so tired after working all day that a couple of times I fell asleep right in the middle of class. One night as class was ending, the teacher asked me to stay.

"Mr. Binder aren't you interested in my class?" she asked. "Why do you fall asleep?"

"I am very sorry," I told her. "I am very interested in getting an education, but I have to work for a living. I get up at three in the morning and by seven in the evening I am very tired. I want to keep learning though and I'll work very hard, I promise you."

"Oh, you are doing fine," she said. "I just didn't understand why you were falling asleep. Perhaps you could find a different job where you didn't have to start quite as early."

"I'll think about it," I said.

But when I got home that night, all hell had broken loose.

Even outside, as I came around the corner, I knew something was wrong. There was no light coming from the windows. When I came in, there was no smell of supper cooking.

"Is anybody home?" I called out from the hall.

"In here," Jerry called from the kitchen.

I found Jerry and Rose sitting in the dark. The only light in the room came from the streetlamp outside. Rose sat on the sofa, crying softly. Jerry sat in the rocking chair, head in his hands.

"What's the matter?" I asked. "Why are you sitting in the dark? Where are the folks?"

"Oh, Bernie," Rose blurted. Then she began crying even harder. Jerry looked up, and I could see he had been crying too. "Bernie, Ma's in the hospital."

"The hospital? What happened?"

"You know how she's not used to everything here yet," Jerry said, holding himself and rocking back and forth. "So when she lit the lamps this evening, I guess she didn't notice when the flame blew out. The gas almost killed her. When we got home, she was unconscious. We had to call for an ambulance."

"An ambulance! My God, is she all right? I want to see her."

"Come on, we'll take you," Jerry said, getting up from the rocker. "Sam and Pa are with her. Rose and I came back to get you."

We rushed out into the dark, unfriendly night and caught a trolley. It seemed so slow, stopping at every corner. We didn't talk. We just sat there. I urged the trolley forward with my thoughts, my body tense as if I was pushing it along to get us there faster. Finally, after what seemed an eternity, we came to the hospital.

A nurse directed us to the right floor. There was Ma.

She looked so small lying there in that big, white bed in the middle of a big, white hospital ward.

The place smelled of sickness and lost hope. There were fifteen or twenty other beds in the same room, all filled with sick people, families standing around trying to help. We couldn't afford a more private room. Only rich people had private rooms.

Pa sat on a corner of the bed and Sam sat on the floor facing him. They looked exhausted.

"Is she all right?" I whispered.

"She'll be all right, Beryl," Sam said softly, using my old familiar name.

"When can she come home?"

"She's plenty sick yet," Sam said. "The doctor said she'll have to stay a few days until they're sure her lungs are clear."

"Oh, God," Rose said, her voice choking as she tried mightily to fight back tears. "Why now? Why now that we finally made it here?"

We said nothing. What could we say? We were all thinking the same thing.

***

For the next several days, I went around like I was in a fog. I worked, went to school and visited Ma in the hospital. Nothing felt right.

Ma came home about a week after her accident. But she was very weak and couldn't do much around the house. Rose had to take over most of the cleaning and cooking.

Rose was a young girl yet, but I was starting to worry that my sister really had no life for herself. She'd never had a chance to learn to read or write, but she was plenty smart. And sometimes, when I thought I was just too tired to go to school at night, it was Rose who pushed me out the door.

"You're going to get an education," she would tell me. "You're going to make something of yourself."

We all had to work even harder now because there were a lot of hospital and doctor bills to pay. I got a better job at the wholesale market, and Sam and Jerry also got jobs there. Gradually, we managed to pay off the bills.

But Ma was never really the same.

***

I was still going to night school but wanted very badly to go full-time during the day. I didn't even think about going to college. That was for rich people. I had to earn a living. So, I thought about what I could do, and one Sunday morning I cleaned myself up and went to see Morris.

He was working in his store but was pleased to see me and asked me to stay for dinner. At noon he closed the store and washed up, and we went into the apartment in the back.

My brother's wife, Sophie, was pleased to see me too. She liked when I visited because I could speak English. She didn't understand Yiddish.

After dinner, Sophie went off to put their two little ones to bed. Morris and I sat together, and I told him what was on my mind.

"You know, Morris, I would like to get a good education. I had some training in Russia and I'm young yet. With a good education I could do well in this country and help the entire family."

"Yes, that's true, Bernie. What is it you want of me?"

"I know you need help in your store. If you could help me a little so that I could go to school during the day, I would come here after school and on weekends and work for you for nothing."

Morris sipped his tea and thought for a few moments. He looked so much like Pa.

"Bernie," he finally said, "what you are saying is a good idea. But let me tell you something. When I came here I had nothing either, and I also wanted to go to school. But I had to eat. I found a job in a mattress factory in New York where they cut cloth. My job was to go around picking up the scraps. Day after day, week after week, I picked up the scraps. I was lucky I made enough to eat. I slept in a corner of a rooming house because I couldn't even pay to share a room with somebody.

"Then I found Ma's alter shvester, her older sister, along with her brother-in-law here in Washington. I came to work in their store and learned how to manage a grocery. But even here, they had no place for me in their little apartment, so I slept on a counter right in the store.

When I finally saved up enough money, I was so happy. I went out and bought my little business here.

"Bernie, I would like to help you, but you can see Sophie and I have a family now. And the store barely supports us."

"I understand, Morris," I said. "At least I can go to school at night. It's more than I ever could have hoped for in Russia."

I held no grudge against my brother. He was a hard-working man with a family to care for. He didn't need me as an extra burden.

So, I quit my job and went looking for a better one. I found a new job in the market with an Italian man by the name of Mr. Lagattuta, who treated me well. His stand was outside, with a canopy overhead to protect the food. We stood outside all day, winter and summer, in all kinds of weather.

Later that summer, I suggested that we could make a little more money if I walked up and down the alleyways and sold produce from a cart. Mr. L. thought this was a grand idea. He built us a nifty cart that worked like a wheelbarrow on one wheel while I held it by its two handles. The inside of the cart was divided into sections to hold the different kinds of fruit and vegetables.

Early each morning before the market opened, I took the cart on a round of alleyways calling out to the housewives.

"Fruits and vegetables, fresh fruits and vegetables." The ladies would come outside and choose what they needed without having to go to the market.

There was Mrs. Blum. She usually bought fresh carrots, beets and parsley if I had it, for her soup. Mrs. Contini liked tomatoes for her homemade spaghetti sauce. And old Mr. Brown liked the fruit.

"What do you have that's good today, Bernie?" he would ask.

"The peaches and plums are at their best right now, Mr. Brown. Better get them while you can." Then we heard the junk man's wagon turn into the alley and moved to the side so he could get by.

"Junk, old junk and new junk — buying and selling," he cried. "You got anything for me today, Mr. Brown? Or maybe you need a pot to put that fruit in?"

"Not today, Louie," Mr. Brown answered as he turned to go back into his house. "You fellas have a good day."

The junk man and I moved on down the alley calling out our wares and making our sales.

The Washington winter was plenty cold and damp, but it wasn't nearly as bad as in Russia. Here we didn't have winters with day after day of twenty below zero and snow five feet high. But here, summer was so hot and humid you could hardly breathe.

At least now, though, between the cart and the market jobs I was making some money, and I was still going to school at night.

***

After we paid off all Ma's hospital and doctor bills, we saved up until we had enough to help the folks buy a house. It was a little row house on M Street Southwest just up the hill from the market and the river.

Ma was very happy. The house had a nice little front parlor with a big, brown horsehair sofa and a rocking chair. In the bay window she put a tall, green rubber tree.

A pair of heavy wooden doors opened from the parlor into the dining room. And there on the small table next to the fireplace rested the old samovar. The brass candlesticks and silver salt dish occupied a place of honor on a bureau next to the dining room table.

The kitchen behind the dining room had a white enamel sink and a pot-bellied stove with a flue that went up through the ceiling. Upstairs were bedrooms and a bathroom.

Out in the back yard Pa raised chickens and grew blackberries, and there was also an outhouse — just in case. Ma made great blackberry jam and Pa made some terrific blackberry wine.

It was a nice house with room for all of us, and we rented the extra bedroom upstairs to a boarder.

***

About five blocks away from the house was a meeting hall. On a Saturday night after Shabbes, or sometimes on a Sunday, the young people in the neighborhood would come together there to meet socially. We found a lot of people our age and began to go out together.

Rose usually came with us boys, but with Ma still sick off and on, Pa expected Rose to do most of the work around the house. Pa even came down to the social hall one time to take Rose home because he found Ma trying to wash the dishes after supper.

But it was at the social hall that Rose met her beau.

"Bernie," Jerry said, coming over after spotting me in the crowd. "The last few weeks, Rose has sure been seeing a lot of that guy over there." Pointing over his shoulder with his thumb, he asked, "Do you know him?"

"Yes, Rose introduced us," I answered. "His name is Harry Gordon."

"Who is he? Where's he from?"

"He told me he's from Palestine — born in Jaffa, I think. He's working in a garage as a mechanic."

"Rose sure seems to like him," Jerry said.

"I think he's sweet on her too."

Just then, our conversation about Rose and Harry was interrupted by a friend. "Hey, Jerry and Bernie," our friend Jack Ohler called, winding his way toward us. "You want to go to Glen Echo next Sunday?"

"What's Glen Echo?" Jerry asked.

"It's an amusement park with fun rides and carnival games. Ben and Louis and Morrey are going."

"How do we get there?" I asked

"We'll take the trolley. There's one that goes right by the park. Meet us at the trolley stop on Pennsylvania and Seventh about one o'clock. OK?"

"Are any girls coming?" Jerry asked Jack. "Should we ask Rose?"

"Nah, only guys this time. We don't want to have to worry about girls."

"OK," Jerry said. "One o'clock Sunday. How about it, Bernie? I'll tell Sam too."

"Sure," I said. "It sounds like fun."

That next Sunday we met as planned, then talked and joked all the way to the park. And when the trolley finally came to the Glen Echo stop, I couldn't believe my eyes.

A giant wheel reached high into the sky, with seats filled with laughing people. A snake-like train zipped up and down and around on a wildly twisting track while the people screamed in delight.

More people, in toy cars, were doing their best to bump into each other on a big round platform.

This park was for families too. Little children sat on wooden animals that went around and around in gentle circles to the merry music of a calliope, their mothers and fathers holding them or snapping pictures from the side.

To me, this place was the eighth wonder of the world.

We dove right into the fun. Our first ride was on the snake-like train that people called a roller coaster. It took my breath away and I quickly understood what all the screaming was about as we rose higher and higher, then went over the top and plunged straight down. My stomach felt like it had dropped right down to my feet.

Dizzy and laughing, we stumbled away from the roller coaster, then stopped to watch some people throwing balls at wooden pins set up at the back of a little booth. If they knocked over enough pins they were rewarded with a stuffed animal. Jerry tried but couldn't do it. Sam was better. He took home a stuffed bear for Rose.

"How about a candy apple?" Jack said, turning to the candy stand next to the pin booth.

Biting through the sweet taffy into the tart apple was like tasting the forbidden fruit.

What a time we had. We got home laughing and tired and feeling wonderful.

Of course, we didn't always go around just with the guys. There were quite a few lively girls who came to the social hall and I knew Jerry had his eye on one in particular, a girl named Rose Love.

As for me, I didn't have anyone special. Between work and school, I didn't have much time, but I went out with our group of friends and palled around with some of the guys when I had the chance.

And then I bought myself a motorcycle!

Oh, she was a pretty little thing – silver and blue. One of the suppliers owned her and saw me looking every time he came to the market.

"You want to buy her?" he asked one day. "I just got a truck and don't need the bike anymore."

"How much?"

"I'll make you a good deal."

And so, a deal was made, and that evening I drove her home. First thing when I opened the door, I shouted, "Who wants a ride on my new motorcycle?" Everyone came rushing out of the kitchen.

"What motorcycle?" Jerry asked.

"Come out and look. I just got her today."

The family, including Ma and Pa, came outside and stood around the machine.

"It's very pretty," Rose said. "How does another person ride on it?"

I got on the bike and said, "Just sit behind me, Rose, and I'll take you for a spin." She took a minute to get on and I told her to hold on around my waist. Then we were off!

"Bernie, not so fast! We'll fall! Let me off!" she screamed.

Laughing with her, I drove back to the front yard and took first Sam and then Jerry around the block. Ma and Pa were very definite about not wanting a ride.

"Not for me," Ma said.

"A meshuggeneh machine," Pa added.

From then on I was able to get around much easier and it was a lot of fun riding around with my friends on the back.

***

Pretty soon Harry Gordon became part of the family and it was arranged that Rose and Harry would be married. Ma took Rose to some landsmen friends in Baltimore who were tailors to have a wedding dress made, and for a while, whenever I came into the kitchen the two of them would have their heads together making all kinds of plans.

Rose and Harry were married on August 17, 1924. It was a nice wedding with all our family and friends there, and Rose looked beautiful in her new-style, shorter wedding dress. As a matter of fact, we all looked great in new clothes we had bought for the occasion.

A couple months later, Pa took me aside for a talk.

"Bernie," he said, "your sister is married to a good man, but Harry doesn't have anything. A mechanic doesn't make much money. What can they do on thirteen dollars a week? We have to help them."

"What do you want me to do, Pa? I haven't got much myself. What can I do?"

"I had a talk with Harry, and he's interested in opening a little grocery store but doesn't have the money. I'm going to lend him what I can. Your sister has always been good to you. Help her. Lend them some money."

"You're right, Pa. I don't have much, but I'll match whatever you give."

"All right," Pa said. "I'm going to give them eighteen-hundred dollars."

"Eighteen-hundred dollars! That's every penny I have!"

"But you're young yet, Bernie. You can make it up. They'll pay you back."

"What about Sam and Jerry?"

"Your brothers are going to put a deposit on a store. So they have no money to lend. And Morris and Sophie are expecting another child. They need everything they have just to live. You're the only one with no responsibilities right now."

So, we loaned Rose and Harry some money to open their store and they lived with us in the house on M Street.

***

The next year I graduated high school, but I had no time or money to continue my education. Harry wasn't doing well with his store, so I didn't expect to be paid back the money I had lent him. Meanwhile, I was working hard for Mr. Lagattuta and pushing the fruit and vegetable cart up and down the alleys on Sundays and in the evenings and trying to save up enough to buy my own business.

On June 10, 1925 — my twentieth birthday — Rose and Harry had a beautiful baby girl they named Doris. Ma was happy and busy with her new granddaughter, but she was feeling poorly again. Between the two, I didn't think she had even noticed I'd graduated.

But one Shabbes I came home, washed up for dinner, and came into the kitchen to wait for the rest of the family. Ma was sitting by the stove rocking Doris while Rose prepared her food.

"Oh, Bernie, you're home," Ma said. "Come over here and take a good look at your niece. Isn't she beautiful?"

"Of course, she's beautiful, Ma. She takes after you and Rose."

"You have done well, Bernie. You are a good boy."

"What do you mean, Ma?"

"You think I don't know how hard you have been working? And you still managed to get an education and help your sister."

She reached under her apron and drew out a small box wrapped in pretty paper.

"This is for your birthday and for finishing school," she said.

"You bought me a present? When did you do that? How did you manage it?"

"Never mind how," she said.

"Open it, Bernie," Rose said, turning from the stove to watch, a big smile on her face.

Ma handed me the package and I carefully unwrapped it. I didn't remember when I had last been given a present.

"Oh, Ma, it's beautiful. A wristwatch. It's the most beautiful thing I've ever had. How did you know I wanted one?" I rushed over and hugged her, baby and all.

I put on the watch and held up my arm for Ma and Rose to see how it looked. It was a silver color with a black band, made by the Hamilton Company.

"It's wonderful, Bernie," Rose said, coming over to give me a hug. "I'm so glad you finished school."

"I wish you could have gone too, Rose. You're smarter than me."

Rose lovingly stroked the baby's tiny head. "Don't worry about me, Bernie. I have what I want."

"Thank you, Ma," I said. "How did you know what to get me?"

"The man at the store said every educated man should have a wristwatch," Ma answered. "Wear it in good health."

That night we celebrated Shabbes, my new niece and my graduation.

CHAPTER 19

1926-1928

Ma was in the hospital again the next year. When she came home, Rose went with her to Baltimore several times to visit a specialist named Doctor Barry. We didn't know what was wrong, but we thought it had something to do with the gassing a couple years earlier when she had tried to light the gas lamps.

We had more doctor bills to pay, but I managed to save up again and finally bought my own produce stand. Now I worked twice as hard, but at least whatever I made was mine.

Meanwhile, I still had in mind the promise I'd made to Tante Ruchel and Uncle Ule, the promise to find their son. Since arriving in America, we had corresponded on and off with them back in Horchov. The mail back there was pretty reliable now, so we'd been able to keep in touch a little bit.

So, one holiday weekend I made plans to go up to New York and see my friend Louie Preipont and see if I could find Cousin Joe.

Louie was happy I had come, and his mother, Ma's old friend Rivke, took me in like one of her own. The minute I came in the door, she made me sit and eat. Meanwhile, Louie could hardly wait to show me all around town.

First thing the following morning, he took me by the arm. "Bernie, I'm going to show you the greatest city in the world. Come on."

Louie still lived on a block of five- to six-story walk-up tenement buildings. Children were all over the place. You couldn't move without tripping over them. And as I looked around and into doors and windows I saw people everywhere, working. Every building was filled with little shops of shoemakers, tailors, metal workers and more. People pushed carts and hollered about what they had to sell or what service they could provide. There was the knife and scissor sharpener, the ice man, the strawberry man – everything a person could want.

We turned the corner onto Hester Street, where the trolley had dropped us that first evening in America. It was still the same riot of color, noise and smell it had been on that beautiful April night five years earlier.

There was such a jam of people we could hardly get through. Housewives busily haggled over prices with the pushcart peddlers. Men and boys shouted shrilly about the great merchandise in their shops as they tried to lure us inside. And we had to dodge automobiles, trucks and trolleys as we made our way down the street.

At one corner a bunch of men milled around.

"They're greenhorns," Louie said. "They come to this corner looking for work and the bosses come looking for cheap labor. They make a deal for a day's work."

The sound of a piano spilled from a doorway. "They sell sheet music in there," Louie said. "So, the boss hires someone to play the newest tunes to attract customers."

Louie took me to the corner of Mill Lane and South William Street. "What do you see?" he asked.

"Nothing in particular," I answered, looking all around.

"Read this plaque," he said, pointing to a tablet on the corner. "This is where the first synagogue in America was built, by Dutch Jews in 1730."

"I didn't even know Jews were in this country that far back."

"Oh, we were here even earlier than that," Louie said. "The first Jewish community was established in 1654. Now, come on, we'll go over to East Broadway and see the *Jewish Daily Forward* building."

"Do they print the paper right there?"

"Yes, I'll show you," Louie replied. "And I also want to introduce you to some friends at the Workman's Circle. They have their offices in the same building."

"What's the Workman's Circle?"

"It's a society for the workers," Louie answered. "They try to get better working conditions in the factories."

Watching the paper being put out was very interesting. Almost everybody I knew read the *Forward* because it was printed in Yiddish. Most Jewish refugees didn't understand enough English to feel comfortable reading a regular American paper.

There weren't many people in the Workman's Circle office when we came in, but Louie introduced me around and asked when the next meeting would be. Continuing our walk, we passed a vacant site at Washington Place and Greene Street, and Louie told me about the terrible fire that had consumed the Triangle factory building. "A lot of Jews were killed in that fire, Italians and Irish too," Louie said.

"Conditions in that old firetrap were just horrible. That's why I belong to the Workman's Circle."

We walked some more. "Come on," he said. "We'll stop by a couple of shuls and I'll take you to a couple of the landsmen societies. Maybe they can help find your cousin."

I had told Louie all about my Cousin Joe, about how he had made it to America but had never written a letter to Tante Ruchel and Uncle Ule. Louie took me around to the various places he had in mind, but no one seemed to know the right Joe Katz. By then it was late in the afternoon, so we headed back to the apartment. That evening we went to see a show at one of the Yiddish theaters on Second Avenue where we laughed till our sides hurt at a very funny comic named Jack Benny.

The next day, Louie took me on another sightseeing tour. As we walked down East Forty-Seventh Street late in the afternoon, enjoying the sights and sounds, a small sign on a store caught my eye. It read, "Joe Katz — Knee Pants Maker."

I stopped dead in my tracks and pointed to the sign. "Louie, that's him. That's my Cousin Joe."

"Bernie, you're crazy. There must be a million people in New York named Joe Katz. What makes you think this one is your cousin?"

"My Uncle Ule made knee pants. I just know this is the right Joe Katz. Come on, let's go in and see."

We entered the store and right away I knew the man behind the counter was my Cousin Joe. He looked just like my Uncle Ule.

But I didn't say anything yet. We introduced ourselves as landsmen, and Joe was happy to see us and asked us to stay for dinner.

We waited in the store while he closed up. Then he brought us upstairs to his apartment and introduced us to his family. While Joe washed up, I talked with his wife. "Can you keep a secret?" I asked quietly. "I'm Joe's cousin from Horchov. Don't say anything yet."

"Oh, I won't," she said. "He'll be so happy."

I waited until we were having dinner. Finally, I looked at him and said, "Don't I look familiar to you, Joe?"

"Yes," he answered. "But I can't quite place where I might know you from."

"That's because I was a small boy when you left Russia. I'm your cousin, Beryl Aynbinder."

He was shocked but tickled to see me and he jumped up and took me in a big bear hug. When he finally let me go I continued with my story.

"Joe, before my family came to America, I made your mother and father a promise. I promised them I would find you. They never heard from you after you left Russia. Why didn't you write?"

The excitement went out of his face. First he looked angry, then just sad. He stared down at his plate for a long time.

"My father pushed me away," he said when he looked up again. "He pushed me out of his house. He didn't care at all what became of me. Why would I care about him?"

"Oh, but he did care," I replied. "Joe, he pushed you out because he loved you and wanted you to have a better life than you could have in Russia. He had nothing to give you. He could barely even feed you, what with all the other children. His only hope was that you could make it to America."

Joe put his face in his hands and began to cry.

I got up and walked over to him. I put my arm around him and pulled from my pocket a letter from Uncle Ule. "Your father loves you, Joe. He's old now, too old to leave Russia. His only wish is to find you and make up. He sent this letter with me in case I found you. Why don't you send him a letter and a picture of your family?"

"You really think he's interested after all this time?" Joe asked through his tears.

"I know he is. He asked me to find you and now I have. We can be a family again."

Joe took the letter and read it, and then was quiet for a while. "Cousin, I can't tell you what a burden you have taken off me," he finally said. He went off for a minute to dry his face and then we all quietly finished dinner.

"And my mother?" Joe asked as his wife cleared the table. "How is my mother?"

"Getting older, Joe," I said. "But she was fine when we left and their letters say they're both well. So, you'll write to them?"

"Yes. And I'll take a special picture of my family to send along with the letter."

"Good," I said, sitting back content.

"But tell me something. How did you find me?"

I laughed and winked at Louie. And, when I told Joe how we found him, he could hardly believe it.

"So you see, Joe, it was meant for me to find you so you could make up with your father before it's too late."

"I will write," he said. "I promise you."

As we sipped our tea, Joe asked how long I would be in New York.

"I have to go back tomorrow," I said. "I have a produce business to run."

As Louie and I left, Joe thanked me again. We hugged and made plans for him to come to Washington with his family for a visit.

I got home the next day but didn't say anything until we were all together at dinner. "So, Bernie, how is Rivke?" Ma asked.

"She's fine, Ma. She wants me to be sure to bring you with the next time I visit."

"God willing," she said, poking at her food. She wasn't eating much these days.

"So, big shot," Jerry teased. "Did you have any luck finding Cousin Joe in the big city?"

"Oh, leave him alone, Jerry," Rose said. "You tease him too much."

"As a matter of fact, Jerry," I said calmly, "I did find Cousin Joe in the big city."

You could have heard a pin drop. Everyone stared at me.

"Bernie!" Jerry shouted. "You found him?"

I laughed, then told the whole story.

"It was truly God's wish," Ma said.

***

The following year, it was Jerry and Sam's turn to spring a surprise.

One Shabbes, just as we had sat down for dinner, Jerry turned to Pa.

"Pa, Sam and I have saved up a little money and want to buy a grocery store."

"So where is this store?" Pa asked.

"It's in Southeast, at 1200 Potomac Avenue," Jerry answered, "and it has a nice apartment upstairs."

"Do you think you'll have enough business for two families?" Pa asked.

"We'll work hard," Jerry replied.

"Are you going to live there?" Ma asked.

"Ma," Jerry said, turning to her. "You know I've been seeing Rose Love."

"Yes, a good family, a nice girl," Ma answered approvingly.

"I've asked Rose to marry me."

Ma looked very pleased and there was a sparkle in her eyes that I hadn't seen in a long time. Pa asked when the wedding would be.

"We'll have the wedding in the fall, after Yom Kippur," Jerry said. "We want to get the store started first and buy a few things for the apartment."

"You're awfully quiet, Sam," Rose said with a knowing look. "Haven't I seen you going out with Rose Love's young aunt?"

Ma looked up in surprise. "You also, Sam?"

Sam nodded and smiled sheepishly. "Yes, Ma. I think Miriam and I will be married not long after Jerry."

"Is the apartment big enough for all of you?" Ma asked.

"It will do," Jerry said. "There's a nice big kitchen downstairs behind the store."

"And what about you, Bernie?" Rose asked, laughing. "Do you have a surprise for us too?"

"Not that kind of surprise," I said. "But I do have a surprise."

Everyone looked at me. "Well, what?" Rose asked.

"I've bought an automobile."

"Oy, vey!" Ma cried. Jerry's jaw dropped. Sam and Rose just laughed.

"Well, I don't have to worry about a girl or a store," I reasoned. "So I might as well have some fun."

"I thought you had enough fun with that motorcycle of yours," Rose said.

I hadn't wanted to say too much about what had happened with the motorcycle, for fear of upsetting Ma. But now that I had an automobile instead, I figured there was no harm. "When I ran into a rut and fell on my head, that was the end of my motorcycle days," I confessed.

Pa burst out laughing, and Sam and Jerry teased me but good. Ma just looked worried and shook her head.

With all the news and plans to discuss, it took quite a while to finish eating. But after dinner all of us went outside and piled into my new car. Jerry and Sam and Rose got into the rumble seat in the back,

Ma and Pa got in up front with me. We went twice around the block and then back to the house — with Ma holding on for dear life and screaming "Oy, vey!" the whole way.

So, Jerry and Rose Love got engaged and so did Sam and Miriam. Jerry and Rose were married on November 13, 1927, and Sam and Miriam soon followed. In addition to being Rose Love's aunt, Miriam also became her sister-in-law, and they all lived in back of and above their grocery store.

Meanwhile, I had my first automobile – a nice little Ford, all gray with a rumble seat. She was the newest model and didn't need an outside crank to start. You just turned the key and pushed a button inside.

***

Nowadays when I wasn't working, I traveled around with my friends in my new car. We were real Americans now with our cars and straw boater hats and sporty clothes. We had some good times.

We motored to Baltimore or New York on long, unpaved stretches of road. Sometimes we stopped at the beach in Atlantic City. And sometimes Sam and Jerry and their wives came with me to North Beach on the Chesapeake Bay, where we would meet up with friends for a day of sun.

Often we got together at a friend's house to play cards. Or if some girls joined us we listened to the victrola, or someone in the crowd would play the piano and we would sing and dance.

Sometimes we met at the ice cream soda fountain at the drug store or joined friends or family at Hofberg's delicatessen. The deli and soda fountain became places to gather on hot summer evenings.

Rock Creek Park, Hains Point Park and Great Falls were favorite places for families to go to escape their apartments on hot summer days.

We couldn't go too far from civilization because there were very few good roads and even fewer gas stations. But times were good. People were trading their horses and buggies for automobiles and trucks, and the trolley went all around the city.

We all worked hard, but we really were making some progress in America.

Ma was tickled to have more grandchildren around, but she was very sick. She was in and out of the hospital all that year, and they finally operated to find out what was wrong.

CHAPTER 20

1929-1930

Then came 1929.

The year actually started out well. Business was booming. Even poor immigrants were investing in the stock market.

Jerry and my sister-in-law Rose had a son in May and named him Jack William after our Zayde, Yankel Wolfe. Six months later, Sam and Miriam had a son and named him Albert.

Ma was tickled to have more grandchildren around, but she was very sick. She was in and out of the hospital all that year, and they finally operated to find out what was wrong. After the operation, Doctor Barry told us she had cancer of the pancreas and wouldn't ever get well.

It was a terrible blow.

Again, there were hospital bills, and my brothers couldn't help much. Sam and Jerry were tied up but good with their new store and new families, and Morris now had three boys, Meyer, William Jack and Ben. And, though they helped as much as they could, it was up to me to do something to help pay for Ma's medical care.

So, when I was approached by Morris Ravitz, an older acquaintance from the market, about a business he wanted me to go into with him, I was ready to listen.

"Bernie," Ravitz said, "there's a little Jewish bakery over on E Street Southeast that I'm thinking of buying. But I need a partner."

"What do you know about the bakery business?" I asked

"Listen, it's a business like any business. We wouldn't have to do the baking. They have two bakers."

Ravitz could see I wasn't convinced, but he was persistent. "I'll tell you what I'm thinking," he said. "I'll do the buying and the inside work, and you'll do the deliveries and the outside work."

"Who would we sell to?" I asked.

"The same customers they sell to now. Only I'm sure we could build up the business once we owned it."

I didn't say anything.

"They make rye and pumpernickel bread, bagels and rolls, and a few sweets — apple turnovers and cakes on order. They sell to the Jewish grocers and delicatessens. It's a good business. We'll both invest a little and make a good profit. It will be a good future for you."

"Let me think about it," I finally told him.

That night I went home and talked to Pa about the bakery, and during the week I talked with my brothers. They all asked the same question I had asked Ravitz: "What do you know about running a bakery?"

"I can learn," I told them.

They encouraged me to try if I had the money to invest. And it seemed like a good opportunity. So, after a couple of weeks, I went to see Ravitz and told him I was interested.

"Let's go take a look at the place," he said.

I first saw the bakery through the big garage door that opened from the alley. Even though there was a regular shop up front, most people came to the back door to buy their bread.

When we came to look the place over, the first person we met was a customer. He was a thin, elderly Black man who walked with a cane, and he introduced himself as Mr. Brown.

With a big smile, Mr. Brown informed us he was a regular customer for his morning bagels since retiring from his job with the government. He was to become a good friend.

The bakery smelled delicious as the owner showed us around. There was a big open room with two big tables and a large brick oven. A big mixing machine churned away in the corner.

The bakers wore white shirts and white aprons, and white caps covered their hair. In fact, I noticed everything in the place, including the bakers, was covered with a thin layer of white flour dust.

One baker was arranging trays of finished bread on metal racks and packing loaves in paper bags. The other baker was busy making bagels. He shaped a long roll of dough, chopped a piece with his left hand and with a swift, rolling motion of his right hand, he had a bagel ready for the boiling pot.

His hands moved so fast I was practically hypnotized watching him. Chop, roll, chop, roll ...

Finally, his pot was full and he switched to pulling bagels out of another pot and putting them on a tray, then into the oven with a push from a long wooden paddle.

We pulled ourselves away from the baking and went to look at the tiny office, the storeroom and the front shop. Everything looked pretty good to me — and tasted good too. I couldn't help but try one of those fresh bagels right out of the oven. I think that's when I really made up my mind to buy the business.

Ravitz and I sat right down with the owner and made a deal.

***

Now I had to get up at three in the morning again, to pick up the fresh bread and deliver it to our customers before they opened their stores.

After my deliveries I would come home, have something to eat and take a little nap. About three in the afternoon, I was back out delivering for the evening restaurant trade, and I'd get home again around six or seven o'clock.

***

We had a long, hot summer that year. Ravitz and I worked hard and business was good. Then one afternoon, not long after Yom Kippur, I came home at noon to find the house a mess.

All the doors and windows were open to the cool autumn air. Pa and Rose were washing the walls and Ma was trying her best to wipe up the kitchen.

A light-colored dog calmly sat in a pail of water in the middle of the kitchen floor.

"What happened?" I asked.

Pa grinned and chuckled. Rose stopped washing, put her hands on her hips and looked at me with a grim expression. Then she shook her head.

"Well, is someone going to tell me what's going on?"

"Pupik saved us," Rose said.

"Saved you? Saved you from what? Will someone tell me what happened here? Hey, wait a second, I never knew Pupik was white."

Pa started laughing, Ma and Rose too. It was contagious and I started laughing, although I wasn't sure why.

Rose finally got control of herself. "The flue on the stove must have gotten stuffed up, because after you left this morning, the whole house filled with smoke."

"Pupik tried to wake me," Pa said, wiping his eyes. "He pulled and pulled at me until I gave him such a k'nock I almost killed him."

"Pupik barked and barked and finally managed to get Pa to realize something was wrong," Rose continued. "And Pa got us all up and out of the house, then went back to see what the problem was. What a mess."

"So that's why all the windows are open," I said. "But what happened to Pupik? He was always dark gray."

"To thank him for his help, we decided to give him a bath," Rose said, beginning to sputter with laughter again. "And would you just look at how white he is. Can you believe? I guess sleeping in the coal bin must have been what made him so dark!"

And we all started up again. Pa was doubled over, tears streaming down his face, and Ma had to sit down to catch her breath. Rose hung onto me and we laughed so hard we fell to the floor.

Pupik just sat in his tub watching us like we were meshugge.

***

Black Thursday.

On Thursday, October 24, 1929, the stock market crashed. At first people didn't understand what was happening, but by the following Monday and Tuesday the extent of the disaster started to become apparent.

In America, lots of people bought stock. The market was not just something for the rich. Some people took out loans to buy stock and some even used their rent money. And then there were those men who used money they had been entrusted with by their companies.

People bought stock because they were sure it would go up in value, and when it did, they would pay back their bank, landlord or company and keep the profit.

But now the market went down and it went down fast. The lucky ones were able to borrow from relatives or friends to pay the landlord or pay back their banks and companies. But there were plenty of people who lost everything.

Fortunately, our family wasn't involved in the market. Our money was invested in our businesses and we had very little in the bank.

But when we all came together at the house the following Sunday, the stock market was the first thing we discussed.

"What is this crash everybody is talking about?" Pa asked.

After Jerry explained what had happened, Pa asked, "So, does anyone in our family have stock in any of these companies?"

We looked at each other and shook our heads. "No, Pa," Jerry answered. "None of us has any money to fool around with."

"So then why should it affect us?" Pa asked. "We work hard. We are honorable people; we are not gamblers on the stock market. Why should we worry? How can this crash hurt us?"

"I don't know, Pa, maybe it's nothing," Jerry said. "But some of the people I know are scared. My friend Louie Cohen asked me to lend him some money so he could pay off his broker."

"And you lent him?" Pa asked.

"I told him I didn't have anything to lend. All my money went into the store."

We didn't say much more about it that evening. But from then on, the state of the economy was a topic of conversation whenever we got together.

***

Our bakery was doing well. But it was tough work and we had our share of problems.

First of all, the roads were very poor. The minute we had any bad weather I could count on getting stuck somewhere along my route. And the truck was always breaking down and it was hard to get parts.

Since our business depended on delivering the bread on time, if the truck broke down I had to fix it myself right there and then. In rain and snow, usually before dawn, I'd find myself fixing a tire or pushing the truck out of a muddy rut.

Inside we started having trouble too. The bakers belonged to a union so we had to honor their contract no matter what, and all of a sudden, things started going haywire. Businesses were letting people go and it was hard to find new jobs. People who had no jobs had no money to spend, so they couldn't buy bagels or cakes or go to restaurants.

Our business began to go down.

Then companies started to go bankrupt and close up altogether. More people were out of work. Banks began to call in their loans because the stock they held as collateral was worthless. They needed real money and only the very rich had any real money. Everyone else had paper promises.

Early in 1930 we watched as all kinds of companies went under. People were scared and didn't buy anything they didn't have to buy. That gave big companies in the automobile industry and steel industry too much inventory, so they laid off more workers, who then didn't have any money to buy anything.

"Have you been listening to the reports on the radio?" I asked Jerry before dinner one Sunday in May. "They're having a drought in

Oklahoma and Kansas. If it keeps up, it will push up the cost of wheat and we'll be hit pretty hard."

"I heard some of the little country banks are closing because they aren't getting their farm loans paid," Jerry said. "The report I heard said it was especially bad because the little banks wouldn't be able to pay back the big-city banks they had borrowed from to lend to the farmers."

"And people are taking any savings they have left out of the banks," Sam added.

"What about that German bank that failed?" Morris asked. "Germany says it's going to keep its gold at home."

"I'm not even sure what that means," I replied. "But Jack Ohler was saying that putting higher taxes on goods imported from other countries will only make them stop buying from us."

"It's got to get better soon," Jerry said. "People need things. At least they need to eat. They're going to have to start buying again. You'll see."

"If a person doesn't have money, a person shouldn't buy," Ma said flatly.

That shut us up and put a damper on the little bit of optimism Jerry was trying to generate because we realized she was right. Most people had no money and wouldn't be buying anything anytime soon.

***

There wasn't much more to say about the terrible troubles with the economy, so everyone's attention during dinner that night turned to my little nieces and nephews. But Ma, who usually took great pleasure in her grandchildren, seemed especially quiet.

Toward the end of the meal, I saw she had kind of a faraway look in her eyes. It seemed like everyone else noticed it at the same time, because we all became quiet and looked at her. Then she spoke.

"Children, last night your Zayde came to me. Do you remember, Bernie, when Zayde talked to you about the war coming and how there would be more wars after that one? Well, last night he told me there are more hard times ahead. There will be hunger and misery in the golden land. Then there will be another war. Take care of yourselves, my children. You are strong and have lived through terrible times before. If you help each other, you can do it again."

Ma got up from the table and slowly shuffled toward her room.

We sat in stunned silence.

Jerry looked over at me after Ma had left. "What was that all about?"

I shrugged as if I didn't know.

But we all knew.

We looked back down at our plates and finished our meal in silence, each thinking our own thoughts.

***

The call from Jerry came a couple of weeks later.

"Bernie, Ma's in the hospital again. It's real bad. You'd better come quick."

I went to the hospital. The whole family was there.

"What does the doctor say?" I asked Jerry.

"She doesn't have long, Bernie."

My heart turned over inside me. I knew she was very sick, but when Jerry said it was the end it hit me hard, like a fist in the middle of the stomach.

We brought her home and she lay in bed for a couple of days. Her friends and ladies from the shul took turns helping Rose care for her. But there was nothing we could do but sit there and watch her die.

She was only fifty-eight years old.

The night of June 11, 1930, she quietly passed. The shul's Chevra Kadisha, the Holy Society, washed and dressed her and laid her out in the living room. They placed a candle at each end of the plain wooden box, with fresh straw all around the floor.

My little niece Doris was frightened when she came downstairs the next morning and saw her Bubbe lying there. She ran to us in the kitchen, where we were sitting around the table, and we had to explain that Bubbe had gone to heaven and we would be putting her body in the cemetery where we could visit her.

The next day we buried Ma in the little Jewish cemetery on Fable Avenue in Capitol Heights, Maryland. It was a beautiful spring day, the kind of day that usually makes your heart want to sing.

My heart felt like a lead weight inside me.

The big old tree above the grave was in full bloom. I looked up through its branches and stared at the pale blue sky as the rebbe chanted the psalm about a woman of courage.

I thought about the train ride in the frozen boxcar when Ma had kept us huddled together and wouldn't let us go to sleep. I remembered the first night in the little Polish village, when she'd wrapped us in blankets and rags, praying to God and singing to us as snow swirled through the open windows. I thought about her helping the sick during the flu epidemic when people dropped like flies.

Courage?

If only you knew, rebbe. If only you knew.

CHAPTER 21

1930-1932

I felt so empty after Ma died. Sure, Rose kept the house and made our meals, and I was busy with work. But I walked around with a hollow feeling in my stomach, the feeling I remembered having as a child whenever I was worried or afraid.

The rest of 1930 passed in a fog.

In the meantime, the country was in real trouble. Banks closed left and right. People lost all their savings, and when the banks foreclosed on their mortgages, they lost their homes. People started wandering from place to place looking for work all around the country.

We still gathered at Pa's house on Sundays. It was the only time we had a chance to get together and we needed to keep feeling like a family.

***

Little Doris jumped up to hug me as I came through the door. "Uncle Bernie, you're late," she scolded, leading me by the hand into the dining room. "Everyone else is already here."

"Bernie, did you hear about Louie Cohen?" Jerry asked.

"No, what happened?"

"He lost everything. The bank called in his loan on the business and he couldn't pay. They had to move out of their house."

"Where did they go? They have two kids."

"They're living with his folks, all of them in a little two-room apartment."

"What do you think of all these bigwigs jumping off the buildings?" Harry asked.

"They're taking the easy way out," said Sam, "instead of working to pay back all those people they stole from."

"Look, Uncle Bernie," little Doris called from across the table. "I got a whole chicken wing."

"You sure do," I said. "And you better eat it before it flies away."

She giggled as I turned back to Jerry and Sam. "How are things at the store?"

"We have to cut prices and buy cheaper," Jerry said.

"I know what you mean," I said. "I'm going to try picking up some supplies down in Frederick. I heard it's cheaper there. Do you want me to pick up an order for you?"

Sam nodded. "I'll make up a list," Jerry said.

"How about you, Harry?" I asked. "Can I pick up anything for you?"

Harry hesitated and looked down at his plate. "I'm going to close up the store," he said. "We're barely taking in anything."

"What will you do?" Pa asked him.

"I've got a job delivering bread for one of the big bakeries."

Sam, Jerry and I looked at each other. We knew Harry wasn't making it with the store. This was probably for the best, and we were relieved to hear he had a job because there were more and more people out of work. They gathered on the street trying to keep warm around a trash fire or they begged at back doors to work for a meal.

***

About nine months after Ma's funeral, I came home at noon and was puzzled to see another woman's apron hanging on the back of the kitchen door. I asked Rose about it but she just turned away. So I went looking for Pa.

He was outside with the chickens. When I asked him about the apron, he told me he was going to get married again to a widow woman from our shul.

For a moment, I was stunned. Then I felt my anger rising.

"How can you do that?" I stormed. "Do you know what we went through with Ma in Russia after you took off and left us? Have you any idea what Ma had to go through to get us here?"

Pa stopped what he was doing and looked up at me, but said nothing.

"Don't you have any feeling for her memory? We haven't even put up a stone on her grave yet. It isn't even a year since she died."

"Bernie," Pa said softly. "A man can't live alone. And it's not fair to your sister. Rose should have a home of her own now."

"Well, I can't live in this house with another woman taking Ma's place." I stalked off across the yard and slammed the back door behind me.

When I calmed down, I realized I didn't have anything against the woman. I knew her — she was a nice old lady named Rivke. But I just couldn't stand the thought of her taking Ma's place.

I asked my brother Morris if I could stay with him and his family and told him I would pay my share. He and Sophie made me comfortable and I lived with them and their three boys.

We children were very upset, but we were not on the outs with our father. We all still went to visit him on Sundays and were pleasant to his new wife. I just couldn't stay there.

And so I lived like that for a while. I was busy with work and I traveled around with my friends.

But the hollow feeling wouldn't go away. I felt like there was no purpose to my life. And I was almost twenty-six years old.

***

There she is again, I thought. That pretty girl, sitting on her front stoop. I had noticed her many times before while driving the truck up E Street to the bakery each afternoon.

She must be the daughter of the man who owns the grocery on the corner, I thought as I continued on to the bakery.

Now each day, as I turned onto E Street, I found myself looking to see if she was there. If she wasn't, I was disappointed.

A few weeks later at the social hall, I was talking with Jack Ohler when I looked up and saw her talking with my friend Naomi and a group of other young women.

With her long coal-black hair and dark eyes, I already thought she was beautiful.

But when she smiled, everyone and everything around her melted away.

Later I took Naomi aside and asked her for an introduction. She took me by the hand and led me across the room.

"Jean Cutler," Naomi said, "I would like you to meet Bernie Binder. His older brother, Jerry, is married to my cousin Rose Love."

"Don't you drive for the bakery on E Street?" Jean asked. "I see your red truck drive by our store every afternoon."

"Yes. I own the bakery, and I've seen you sitting on your front stairs in the afternoon."

"It's the only time I have a few minutes to myself," Jean said. "I'm usually busy with my two little sisters while my mother helps in the store. But my sisters take a rest around that time of the day and I like to sit outside if the weather is nice."

"Do you think you would care to join my brothers and me at the beach next Sunday?"

"If it's all right with my folks, I'd love to."

***

From then on, Jean was the girl for me. We went to the beach with Sam and Jerry and their wives and met all our friends there. And we all went on picnics near the tidal basin when the cherry blossoms bloomed.

I was too much in love to think about what was happening outside my own life. But things became very hard for everyone that spring of 1931, and there was no way to keep the troubles of the world from intruding on our happiness.

As I delivered bread around to the stores, how could I miss the hungry children looking for food in the trash cans by the back door?

They would wait for me, and I would give them any unsold bread my customers had returned.

How could I miss the people who came to the shop begging for a day's work so they could feed their families?

When I went to the train station to pick up supplies, I couldn't miss seeing the men trying to catch a freight car without getting caught by the railroad cops. They hoped to find work in another part of the country but had no money for a train ticket. So, they hitchhiked or hopped a freight. They lived from one train yard to another, from one day's work to no work.

These men carried their few belongings in a bundle at the end of a long stick held over their shoulder, and people called them bindlestiffs or hobos.

The news now was all about the drought and blowing dirt in the middle of the country. The farms were blowing away – the farm families were moving in with relatives if they were lucky. If not, they traveled the roads.

We all gathered around the radio on Sunday evenings to hear Mr. Roosevelt's fireside chats. He told us what was happening and what the government was doing to help. They were starting new programs to put people to work. And they passed a law that had workers put part of their salary into a fund that would provide a "social security" pension for later when they retired.

Our family cut back to bare bones. We helped each other, as Ma had urged. We held on the best we could.

But through it all Jean and I began to get serious, and I knew it was time to introduce her to the family. So, one Sunday I brought her to Pa's for dinner.

She had already met my sister and brothers, but now she had a chance to meet everybody together, including all the children.

"Welcome to the family, Jean," Jerry yelled above the tumult of shouting kids and crying babies.

Jean laughed and took a seat at the table next to Miriam as two of Morris' boys came running through the dining room at full speed, Pupik in hot pursuit.

Pa came over, put his arm around me and led me into the kitchen. "Why do you bring me a child, Bernie? She is so young."

"I know, Pa, but she's used to working hard. She has taken care of her two sisters since they were born so her mother can help in their store."

"She's a good girl?"

"Yes, Pa. She's a good girl."

"It's not such a good time to take on a wife and family."

"I know, Pa. But I'm already almost twenty-six years old, and I want to settle down. You know I'm not afraid of hard work."

Pa nodded. "All right, Bernie, so be it. I wish you well. Your mother, may she rest in peace, I think she would have liked this girl."

"I think so too, Pa. And if we have a daughter, I'm going to name her after Ma."

***

Jean and I became engaged and she asked me to come to her family's Passover Seder.

By now I had met Harry and Esther, Jean's parents. And I knew her brothers, Henry and Irvin, and her little sisters, Evelyn and Doris. But when I arrived at their house, I quickly learned there was a lot more family to meet.

There was Harry's sister, Tante Becky, and her husband and children. And there was a beautiful lady from Worcester, Massachusetts, who turned out to be Esther's young Tante Chava with her son and daughter-in-law.

The Seder table stretched from the kitchen in the back of the house clear through to the store in front.

All the women were busy talking and helping in the kitchen. Kids ran around everywhere. The men poured wine and prepared Haggadahs, the Seder prayer books.

Then Harry asked me to sit next to him and help with the prayers. "Bernie," he said to me as we took our seats, "Esther and I will also be your parents now. I want you to call me Pa."

***

Esther lit the candles and Harry said the blessing. The Seder began, and once more we were reciting the age-old tale of our flight to freedom.

My thoughts drifted.

I remembered the Seders in Horchov, Ma working in the kitchen with Tante Brendel and Tante Ruchel, Zayde leading the prayers from the big armchair padded with pillows. I remembered the little Seder on the ship as we crossed the mighty ocean, with the promise of future Passovers in the golden land.

I thought of Ma, the delight she took in surprising us with the news that we would have a Seder at sea.

How I missed her. I still carried that hurt, hollow feeling.

But then I became aware of the familiar prayers floating through the room, the delicious smell of Passover dinner coming from the stove behind me.

From generation to generation, I thought.

I'm home again.

I looked up and saw Jean. She looked back at me and smiled.

And with that, the hollow feeling melted away.

***

Jean and I were married on August 21, 1932, in the middle of the Great Depression. My life finally became good and whole.

The hollow feeling never returned.

EPILOGUE

America, 1982

IN THE DEPRESSION YEARS that followed, the family struggled and grew.

Sam and Miriam had no other children after Albert.

Jerry and my sister-in-law Rose had another son after Jack William. He was born two years to the day after my mother died and they named him Arnold after her.

Morris and Sophie's three sons, Meyer, William Jack, and Ben, all grew up and went to school.

Rose and Harry had my niece Doris, of course, and just as they were beginning to think she would be an only child, they were blessed with their son Fred, just in time for my wedding to Jean.

As for Jean and me, we had two beautiful girls. The first we named Ann after my mother. Our second daughter we named Zelda after Jean's grandmother.

My father lived to a ripe old age and when he passed away, we children drew lots for Ma's few precious possessions.

Sam's family has the samovar, Jerry's family has the brass candlesticks.

And you, my grandchildren, now have the little silver salt dish and the watch my mother gave me.

341

Now dear children, as my Zayde would have said, "This life that God has given us is a terrible and wonderful thing. Love your family, give honor to the Torah and praise God for the gift of life."

And so, my children, I leave you this trust. Continue the story.

— Yisroel Dov "Beryl/Bernard/Bernie" Binder

1905-1983

AFTERWORD

America – August 21, 1994

I want to close this book with the death of my husband, Bernie, on September 3, 1983.

We would have been married sixty-two years today. We had a good life together, raised two lovely daughters and had five grandchildren. We retired to Florida along with the rest of my family.

Bernie died two weeks after our fifty-first wedding anniversary. He is buried along with his mother and father and brothers and sister at the National Capitol Hebrew Cemetery, on Fable Avenue in Capitol Heights, Maryland.

The big old tree watches over them all like a blessing.

— Jean Cutler Binder

1913-1994

THE GOLDEN LAND

ABOUT THE AUTHORS

Ann Binder Anovitz (1935-2019) was a skillful writer, caring community volunteer and successful commercial real estate executive. In addition to the novel *Charlie's Tale*, she authored "Grandma Annie's Stories From the Garden," an innovative series of children's books offering a unique educational reading experience for both English and Spanish speaking children.

Ms. Anovitz had always thought her father's life story would make a fascinating book that would serve as a tribute to him, a gift to her family and an inspirational tale relevant to all immigrants. In 1982, Ms. Anovitz initiated a series of recording sessions with her then-76-year-old father.

Beryl Bernie Binder passed away the following year, but not before his stories had filled a couple handfuls of cassette tapes. Preserving her father's own words where possible and conducting extensive research to fill in the gaps between his stories, Ms. Anovitz began forming a manuscript that would eventually become *The Golden Land*.

Ms. Anovitz and her late husband Robert were residents of Highland Park, IL and Tucson, AZ, and had three children. Their daughter Stacey is married to Keith Kramer, co-author of *The Golden Land*.

ABOUT THE AUTHORS

Keith Kramer is a professional writer and editor with vast experience in journalism, publishing, marketing and technical communication. He resides in Steamboat Springs, Colorado and was founding editor of the town's first and only daily newspaper, the *Steamboat Today*. He has authored articles for numerous publications over the years, ranging from *The New York Times* to *Ski Magazine*.

Mr. Kramer and his wife, Stacey Kramer, were married in 1984 and have two children. Ms. Kramer is the daughter of the late Ann Binder Anovitz, co-author of *The Golden Land*.

Mr. Kramer's collaboration with Ms. Anovitz on *The Golden Land* dates back to the mid-1990s.

FAMILY PHOTOGRAPHS AND MEMORIES

Yisroel Beryl Binder passport

Beryl Bernie Binder (foreground)
with parents Mordecai Max Binder
and Channa Anna Binder

Mordecai Max Binder

Jean and Bernie Binder in
Washington, D.C.

Bernie Binder at Hains Point Park

Jean Binder at Hains Point Park

Jean and Bernie Binder on their
wedding day, Aug. 21, 1932

Jean and Bernie Binder on their wedding day, Aug. 21, 1932

Bernie Binder at Rock Creek Park

Bernie Binder with baby daughter Ann

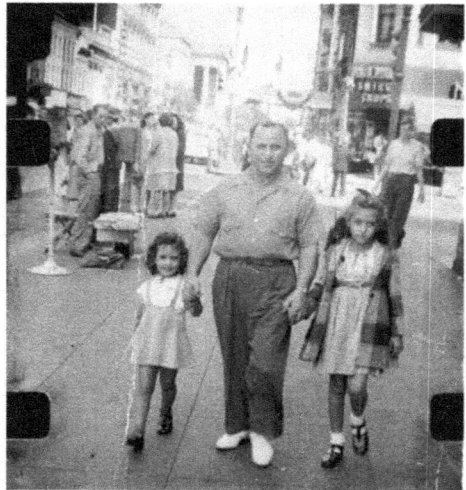

Bernie Binder with daughters Zelda (left) and Ann

Bernie and Jean Binder

Bernie Binder with daughter Ann

Jean Binder dressed up among
the blooming cherry blossoms

Bernie frolicking in the water
with daughter Ann and others

Jean Binder behind the wheel

Jean and Bernie Binder with daughters Ann (left) and Zelda, in front of their house on S Street in Washington, D.C.

Bernie bringing daughter Ann downstairs on the occasion of
Ann's surprise engagement party

Top row, from left: Rose Love Binder, Jerry Binder, Ben Binder,
Morris Binder, Harry Gordon, Rose Binder Gordon, Yetta Binder,
Miriam Binder, Sam Binder. Middle: Jean and Bernie Binder. Bottom:
Ruth and Meyer Binder

The journey to America from the
Ukraine area of Russia required
sixteen months of grueling travel.
The following pages map the route
from East to West.

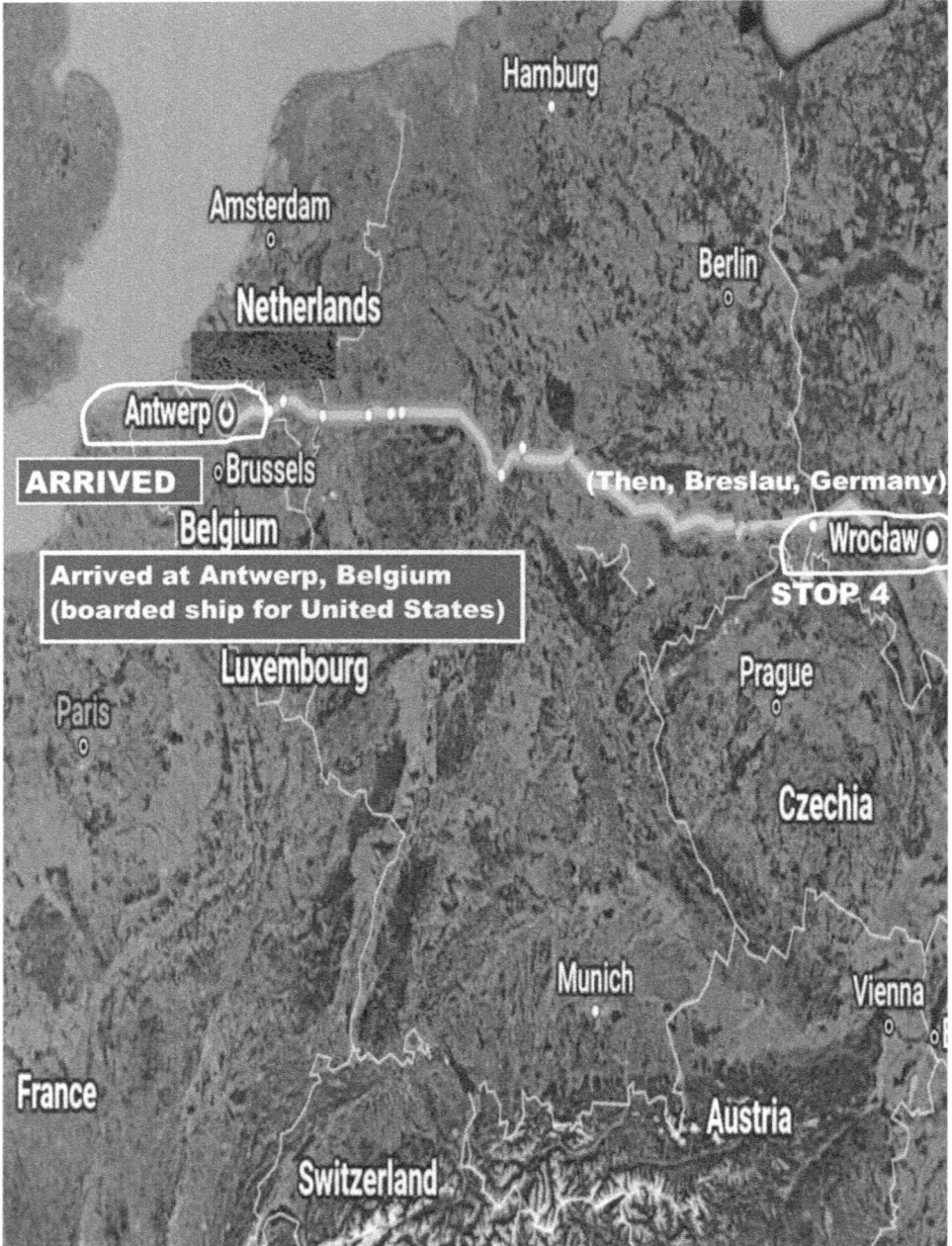

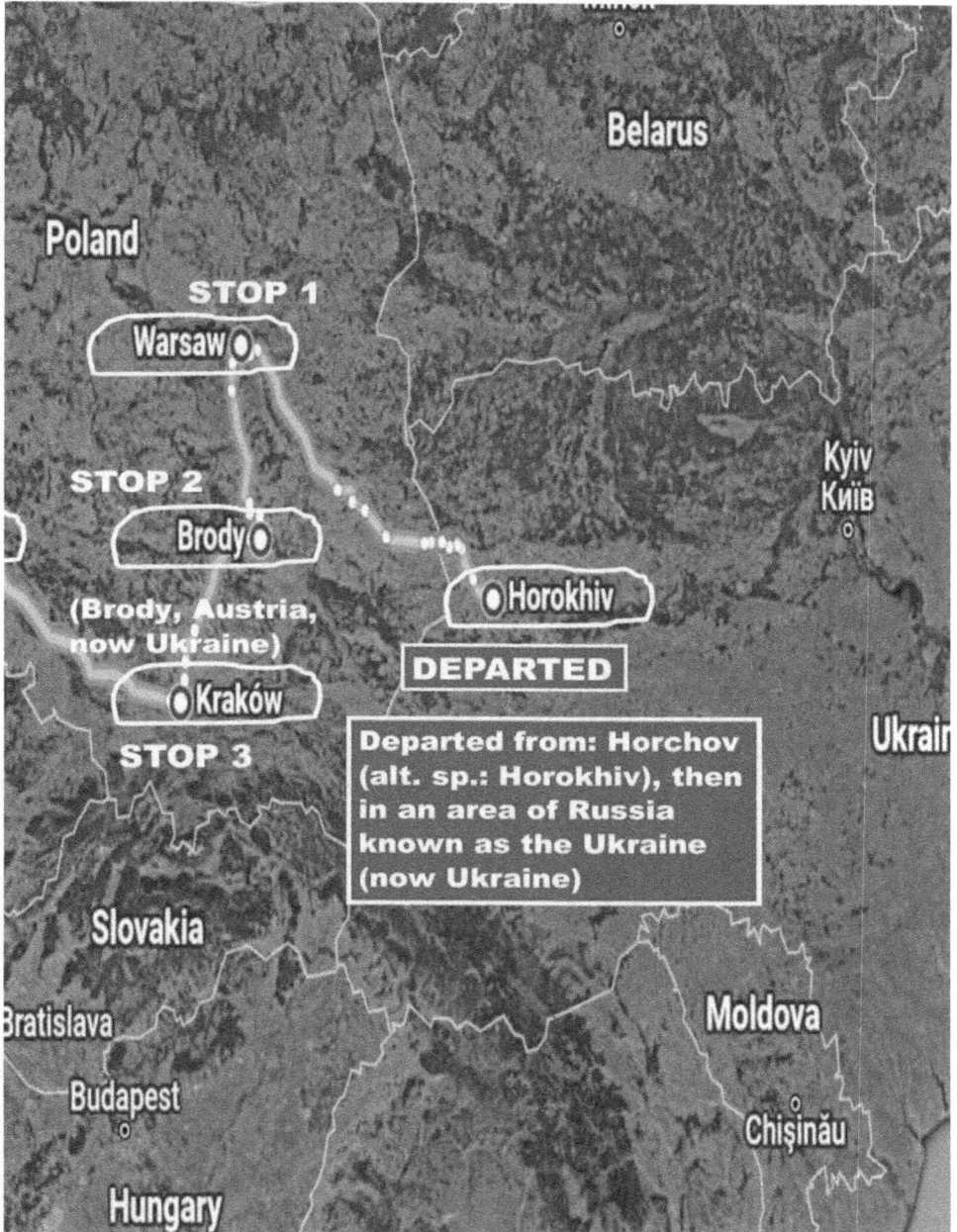

BELARUS

THE GOLDEN LAND

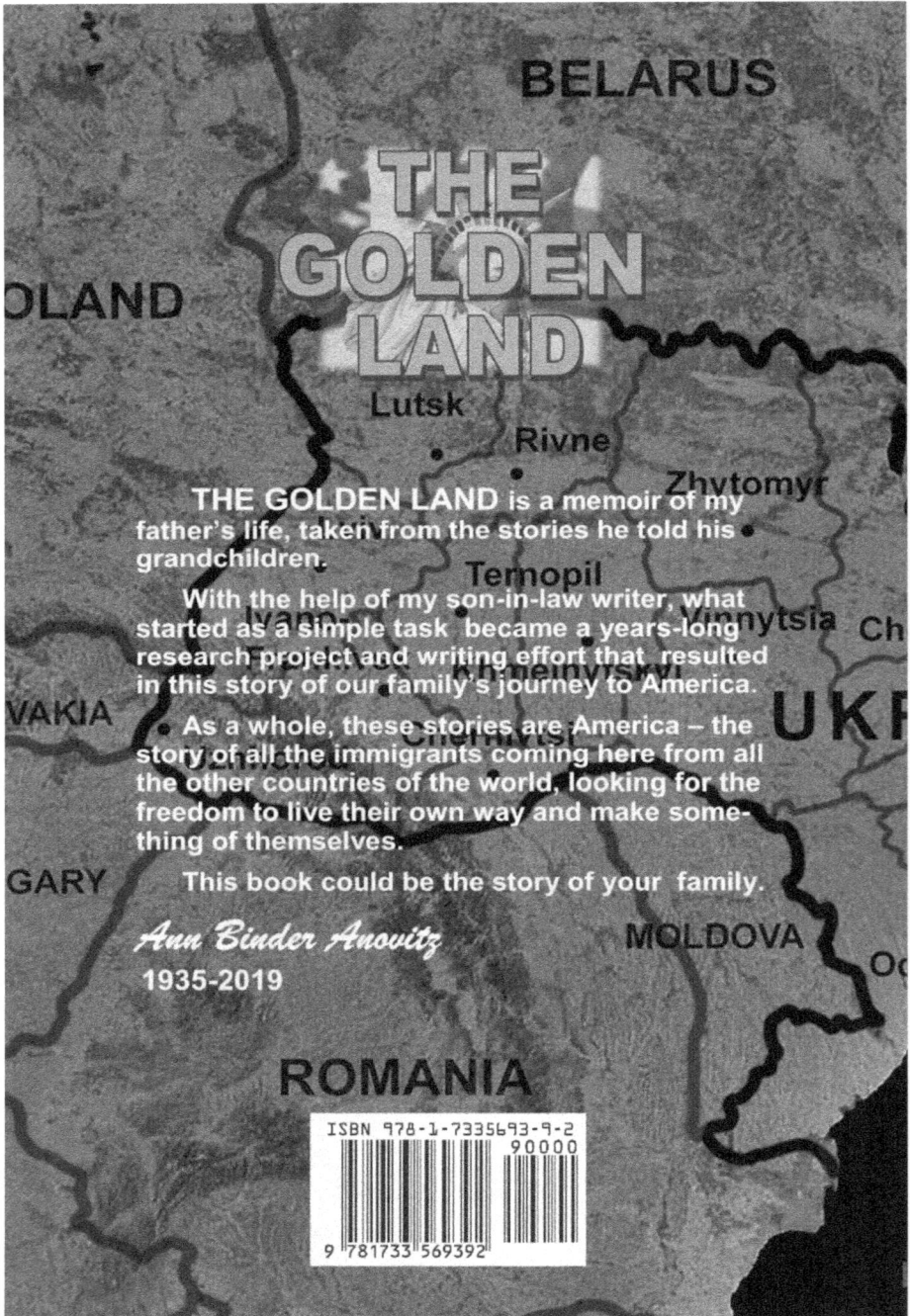

Lutsk

Rivne

Zhytomyr

THE GOLDEN LAND is a memoir of my father's life, taken from the stories he told his grandchildren.

Ternopil

With the help of my son-in-law writer, what started as a simple task became a years-long research project and writing effort that resulted in this story of our family's journey to America.

Vinnytsia

Khmelnytskyi

As a whole, these stories are America – the story of all the immigrants coming here from all the other countries of the world, looking for the freedom to live their own way and make something of themselves.

This book could be the story of your family.

Ann Binder Anovitz
1935-2019

MOLDOVA

ROMANIA

ISBN 978-1-7335693-9-2
90000
9 781733 569392

www.ingramcontent.com/pod-product-compliance
Lightning Source LLC
Chambersburg PA
CBHW021214090426
42740CB00006B/226